Lonely Planet

BEST BIKE RIDES
CANADA

BEST DAY TRIPS ON TWO WHEELS

ROBERT ISENBERG, JEFF BARTLETT, TAMARA ELLIOT,
MARY FITZPATRICK, ASHLYN GEORGE, AMY MCPHERSON,
DARCY RHYNO

Contents

PLAN YOUR TRIP
Welcome to Canada.............................4
My Perfect Ride...................................6
Our Picks..8
When to Go..16
Get Prepared for Canada 18

BY REGION

ONTARIO 23
Ottawa's Waterways 26
Niagara Trail......................................32
Lower Don River Loop....................38
Also Try..44

QUÉBEC 47
Eastern Townships 50
Mont-Tremblant................................54
Old Québec 58
Lachine Canal...................................64
Also Try..70

NOVA SCOTIA............................73
Salt Marsh to Atlantic Trail.............76
Bay to Bay Trail................................80
Landscapes of Grand Pré 84
Also Try..88

NEW BRUNSWICK....................91
Fundy Trail Parkway 94
Moncton's Riverfront Trail..............98
Fredericton Two Rivers Ride.......102
Also Try..108

PRINCE EDWARD ISLAND.................................111
Gulf Shore Parkway (West)..........114
St Peter's Bay to Lighthouse.......118
Three Rivers Trail...........................122
Bikepack the Confederation Trail..........................126

NEWFOUNDLAND & LABRADOR 129
Bonavista Peninsula Ride.............132
Bell Island Loop..............................136
Also Try..140

MANITOBA 143
Winnipeg..146
Lakeshore Trail...............................150
Also Try..154

SASKATCHEWAN 157
Meewasin Valley.............................160
Prince Albert National Park 166
Also Try..170

ALBERTA.............................173
Drumheller Dinosaurs 176
Calgary's Bow River Pathway.....180
Rocky Mountain Legacy Trail 184
Also Try..188

BRITISH COLUMBIA 191
Myra Canyon 194
Penticton to Little Tunnel.............198
NorthStar Rails to Trails 202
Vancouver Seawall 206
Also Try..212

YUKON & THE NORTH-WEST TERRITORIES..........215
Yellowknife & the Ingraham Trail.................................218
Whitehorse, Miles Canyon & Mt Sima..222
Also Try..226

TOOLKIT
Arriving...228
Getting Around...............................229
Accommodations..........................230
Bikes...231
Health & Safe Travel....................232
Responsible Travel.......................233
Nuts & Bolts...................................234

Land Acknowledgement
Lonely Planet respectfully acknowledges that Canada is the traditional territory of more than 630 First Nations communities as well as Inuit and Métis communities. We offer gratitude to the Indigenous Peoples for their care for, and teachings about, this land.

Welcome to Canada

Across Canada, flags bear the image of a red maple leaf, and no national symbol better represents a land and people. Canada is as strong as that silver trunk, as welcoming as a bottle of maple syrup and as beautiful as blazing foliage in fall. The maple tree is practical and dependable – a pillar of North American life.

One of the best ways to observe these qualities is by bicycle. Canadians have invested heavily in their cycling infrastructure, such as multi-use paths, separated bike lanes and trail systems that span entire provinces. These routes are designed to show you the full breadth of Canadian life, from vibrant urban neighborhoods to alpine valleys. Trails cut through Indigenous territories and immigrant communities, showcasing the diversity of Canada's people. Follow in the footsteps – and tire tracks – of so many travelers before you as you explore one of the world's largest nations.

Waskesiu Lake (p167), Prince Albert National Park
ASHLYN GEORGE/LONELY PLANET

My Perfect Bike Ride

Robert Isenberg

LACHINE CANAL

P64

I love a jaunt through Montréal in the middle of summer. Cyclists flood the city's bike lanes, pedaling the gamut of machines: cruisers, racers, folders, tandems, mountain bikes and e-bikes of every weight and wattage. First I'm coasting past skyscrapers, then I lose myself in a verdant public park. On a warm day, I feel like I'm a member of a vast, fast-moving club, as scores of passersby call out, 'Bonjour!'

Jeff Bartlett

YELLOW- KNIFE & THE INGRAHAM TRAIL

P218

The Ingraham Trail from Yellowknife is my favorite ride in this guide. It's just long enough to feel like a real challenge, yet it's achievable in a single day. The Canadian Shield never fails to surprise me with its beauty. It's a rugged landscape of rock, boreal forest and endless lakes. Riding here feels like a true adventure, yet it doesn't venture too far from Yellowknife.

Lachine Canal (p64)

Tamara Elliott

NORTH- STAR RAILS TO TRAILS

P202

This ride in BC's Kootenay Rockies region is my top pick. It delivers big views, an interesting history and diverse scenery. The NorthStar is quiet, car-free and easy to navigate, and long enough to get a good workout in without any intense climbs to make it feel too strenuous. The trail never gets busy, and everyone on it seems to be having a genuinely good time, which means a lot of smiles and a quick 'hello!' while passing other cyclists.

Top 5 Scenic Bike Rides

1. Niagara Trail — There are many ways to see this wonder of the world; cycling down its source river is tops.

2. Whitehorse River — Follow the river to where calm reservoirs and white water collide at Miles Canyon.

3. Mont Tremblant — Ride paved trails around this beloved ski area in the summer, then split off for some singletrack.

4. Drumheller Dinosaurs — Explore Alberta's badlands – and learn about its wealth of dinosaur remains.

5. Bonavista Peninsula Ride — Coastal scenery, with a historic lighthouse, puffins and dramatic rock formations.

Mary Fitzpatrick

KANAN-
ASKIS
RIBBON
CREEK
TRAIL
LOOP

P189

Everywhere is better when experienced from the saddle of a bike. My favorite rides for this book were in and around Alberta's Kananaskis Country, with its shady, just-rough-enough paths, glacial-fed streams, mountain views, solitude, wilderness vibes and occasional sightings of elk and bighorn sheep. The stillness of the forest, with birdsong as a backdrop, was so peaceful, putting life into perspective.

Ashlyn George

SQUIRREL
HILLS
TRAIL PARK

P155

This park near Minnedosa, Manitoba, is a small-town standout. From the spacious timber-frame pavilion to the decorated warm-up cabin and matching orange outhouse, every detail shows community effort and pride. Riding through the forest, the trails climb and curve with a flow that keeps it fun and engaging for riders of all levels. It's clear the community has worked hard to create something special for everyone to enjoy.

Top 5 Family Bike Rides

1 Vancouver Seawall
The Seawall's paved, flat trail is accessible for all, with family-friendly stops like beaches, parks and food stands.

2 Calgary's Bow River Pathway
Take in historic sites, skyline views, cafes and urban parks on this fun, flat family ride.

3 Lachine Canal
Ride the length of Montréal along its cycling superhighway. Continue along the St Lawrence and watch river surfers.

4 Fredericton Two Rivers Ride
The capital of New Brunswick is a charming riverside town with easy riding and plenty of sweet treats.

5 Lakeview Trail
Rent novelty bikes on a paved forest trail linking lakes, beaches, and picnic spots in Manitoba.

Amy McPherson

SALT
MARSH TO
ATLANTIC
TRAIL

P76

Nova Scotia's many rail trails gave me plenty of joy along traffic-free routes, and I fell in love cycling the causeways of the Salt Marsh Trail with its landscape and diverse wildlife.

Darcy Rhyno

FREDERIC-
TON TWO
RIVERS
RIDE

P102

This ride perfectly pairs urban and green-space cycling in historical and contemporary settings. On one side of the St John River, I'm peddling easily along a paved route past heritage buildings, historical museums and modern art galleries. Across a railway trestle retrofitted as a walking/cycling bridge, I'm drifting beside a tributary beneath a canopy of trees that filters dappled light onto the woodsy trail. Cafes and taprooms alike make perfect stops.

Our Picks

BEST COASTAL ROUTES

Canada has the longest coastline in the world, spanning about 243,000km, and these shores come in many forms – placid beaches, vertical cliffs and evergreen-covered mountains, to name a few. Bike routes parallel sections of both the Atlantic and Pacific Coasts, and some circumscribe whole islands. Explore the continent's watery edges up close, along with their photogenic boats, piers and lighthouses.

TOP TIP

Newfoundland's coast is famous for its passing icebergs, skyscraper-sized ice chunks that float by in spring and summer.

Gulf Shore Parkway (West)

Follow the undulating shores of Prince Edward Island on this fresh new path.

P114

Bell Island Loop

Ride along the rugged grasslands and primal cliffs on this tiny island off Newfoundland.

P136

Vancouver Seawall

Skirt cliffs and take in the glittering skyline right on the edge of Vancouver Harbour.

P206

Saysutshun (Newcastle Island Marine) Park

Just off Vancouver Island, this car-free land mass offers dirt paths and secluded woods.

P213

Fundy Trail Parkway

Witness cliffs, waterfalls and the highest tides in the world on the Bay of Fundy.

P94

TOP TIP
Note that the city of Vancouver lies across the bay from Vancouver Island, home of Victoria, BC's provincial capital.

Above: Stanley Park (p207), Vancouver; Right: Bell Island (p136)

TOP TIP
You can bike to many of Canada's inhabited islands over bridges, and ferries on both coasts accept bicycles.

TOP TIP

The bistros and brasseries of eastern Canada prepare some of the best French cuisine outside of France.

Our Picks

BEST FOODIE ROUTES

Canada is known around the world for its poutine, maple syrup and peameal bacon, but these are only the tip of the culinary iceberg. Each region has its specialties, such as Montréal-style bagels and Nova Scotian lobster rolls, and cities are wellsprings of international flavors. The best way to earn those calories: bike around for a few hours first. In Canada, you're never far from a hearty meal.

TOP TIP

Maple products keep well and make great gifts. True maple syrup gives cyclists a sugar boost – and antioxidants.

1 Penticon to Little Tunnel
Roll through British Columbia's wine country and choose from 40-plus tasting rooms.
P198

2 Calgary's Bow River Pathway
Explore Alberta's largest city via its expansive trail system, and sample diverse eateries along the way.
P180

3 Lachine Canal
Cavort with other riders in Montréal and stop for gourmet snacks at Marché Atwater.
P64

4 Fredericton Two Rivers Ride
Follow up waterfront parks and historic bridges with restaurants and taprooms in small-town New Brunswick.
P102

5 Rocky Mountain Legacy Trail
Finish your tour of snow-topped mountains with a heaping meal in Banff, Alberta.
P184

Left: Banff (p184); Above: Vineyards, Kettle Valley (p198)

Our Picks

BEST WILDLIFE ROUTES

Trust us: you'll spot wildlife. Canada has vast amounts of open country, where packs, herds and flocks roam free. 'Protected areas' – basically, wilderness – make up about 12 percent of Canada's land mass, and once-endangered species like the swift fox and whooping crane are making a comeback, thanks to conservation efforts. Cyclists in rural Canada can enjoy animal encounters without much effort, from white-tailed deer to circling eagles.

TOP TIP

Bears live in every province in Canada except Prince Edward Island. They're generally shy and fun to spot, but food vaults and bear spray are good ideas in the backcountry.

Wakamow Valley Trails
Bring your binoculars to spot any of 190 bird species around Moose Jaw, Saskatchewan.
P170

Bonavista Peninsula Ride
Come for the rocky coastal scenery; stay for the puffins and whale-spotting.
P132

Mont Tremblant
There are hordes of deer in the Laurentian Mountains. Keep your eyes peeled for moose and fox.
P54

Yellowknife & the Ingraham Trail
The Northwest Territories are home to wolves, bears and wood bison, among many other species.
P218

Prince Albert National Park
Cormorants and white pelicans congregate around Waskesiu Lake, and elk sometimes appear.
P166

Above: Puffins, Bonavista (p132); Right: Elk, Prince Albert National Park (p166)

TOP TIP
You're likely to spot deer in Canadian woods, but you may luck out with a moose sighting.

Our Picks

BEST HISTORIC ROUTES

Humans arrived in these lands as long as 20,000 years ago, and waves of immigrants have settled in Canada (formerly New France) since the 1500s. Trappers, pioneers and factory workers have all left their marks on the land, and cycling down rail trails is a powerful way to explore their legacies. Pass through train tunnels, soar over ravines and spot age-old ruins along the way.

TOP TIP

Many bike paths lead through First Nation communities, such as Wandake in Québec and Squamish in British Columbia.

Old Quebec

This magnificent stone-laid city seems perfectly preserved since the 1700s. Forts, churches and more.

P58

Drumheller Dinosaurs

Excavate Alberta's badlands for fossils, dinosaur relics and a primeval landscape.

P176

Myra Canyon

Railroad fans can cross 18 historic trestle bridges through the mountains of British Columbia.

P194

KVR: Chute Lake to Adra Tunnel

Venture into the 483m-long Adra Tunnel, a century-old railroad corridor in British Columbia on the Kettle Valley Rail Trail.

P212

NorthStar Rails to Trails

Follow in the footsteps of miners and railroaders on this former Rocky Mountain train route.

P202

TOP TIP

Train lines across Canada have risen and fallen since 1836. Thousands of kilometers of converted rail trails honor this legacy.

Trestle Bridge, Myra Canyon (p194)

Our Picks

BEST ART & CULTURE ROUTES

Creativity flourishes across Canada, from the art galleries and public sculptures of big cities to the totem poles of the Pacific Coast. Rural monuments and natural wonders also speak to Canada's hardy heritage. A cyclist moves at the perfect pace to spot cultural artifacts – such as a building-sized mural of Leonard Cohen in Montréal, or the Gothic towers on Ottawa's Parliament Hill – and consider their significance to Canada's national character.

TOP TIP

It's easy to buy local here: more than 200,000 Canadians work as professional artists, creating across all media.

Rideau Canal (p26), Ottawa

1 Niagara Trail

Trace the Niagara River to the most famous waterfalls in North America.

P32

2 Ottawa's Waterways

Admire Canada's capital and Ottawa Canal on well-trafficked bike paths through the city.

P26

3 Whitehorse, Miles Canyon & Mt Sima

Get a taste of the Yukon Territory by way of its capital and wild outskirts.

P222

4 Pinawa to Seven Sisters

Gaze in wonder at the Seven Sisters Generating Station, along with the backwoods beauty of Manitoba.

P154

5 Eastern Townships

Browse scores of sculptures along the EstriadeRail Trail through Québec's Eastern Townships.

P50

TOP TIP

In many cities, guides lead groups to the major sights by bicycle – a great way to learn the area.

BEST BIKE RIDES: CANADA   15

When to Go

> **I LIVE HERE**
>
> **CYCLING IN MONTRÉAL**
>
> **Mathieu Murphy-Perron is a Montréal-based bike commuter.**
>
> Canada may not be the first place that comes to mind when thinking about cycling. More often, people picture frigid winters, hockey fights and majestic wildlife. For many, winter and cycling seem incompatible. Yet anyone who has pedaled over a fresh coat of crisp snow knows that's far from the truth. Canadian cities, whether Montréal or Edmonton, are steadily adapting their cycling networks for winter. This shift doesn't just make commuting possible year-round; it opens up a whole new way of experiencing the country, where cycling becomes a celebration of resilience, beauty and the joy of movement in every season.

Canada is colossal, stretching from the continental climates of the south – where most people live – to the permafrosted Arctic Circle. Still, cyclists can follow a general rule of thumb: summers are warm and buggy, while spring and fall are cool and moist. Most will want to hit Canadian roads in June, July or August, when temperatures are pleasant and seasonal businesses are bustling. Canadians know how to take advantage of their warmest months: towns are busy with festivals and waterways are full of boats. Summer is Canada at its liveliest.

That said, locals aren't afraid of a little nip in the air. You'll spot bike commuters pedaling through cities all winter, and fat-tire cycling in the snow is a popular alternative to skiing and snowshoeing. Lycra-clad athletes are already hitting cleared roads in February, demonstrating that, with the right clothes, there's no such thing as bad weather.

Fat bike, Ontario (p23)

Weather Watch

JANUARY	FEBRUARY	MARCH	APRIL	MAY	JUNE
Average daytime max: **-16C°**. Days of rainfall: **8**	Average daytime max: **-15C°**. Days of rainfall: **6**	Average daytime max: **-10C°**. Days of rainfall: **7**	Average daytime max: **-2C°**. Days of rainfall: **7**	Average daytime max: **5C°**. Days of rainfall: **8**	Average daytime max: **12C°**. Days of rainfall: **6**

Vancouver Dragon Boat Festival

> **BUSY SKIES**
> Rainstorms are common, and weather can change on a dime. Parts of Alberta are known as 'Hailstorm Alley,' thanks to dramatic ice storms, even in summer. Both coasts are famous for their fog; pack headlights and flashers.

Accommodations

Canada's cities are full of modern hotels, and the trendier neighborhoods have hostels and boutique accommodations as well. Sizable towns have chain hotels and local inns, with diminishing options as you enter the vast countryside. In the summer high season, prices are generally high across the country. Tent camping is popular – a boon for bikepackers.

> **CONSTRUCTION SEASON**
> Each spring, frost heaves rip apart pavement, leaving spoke-snapping potholes in their wake. Expect lots of construction through summer, as motorways are resurfaced and bridges are repaired. Be patient with workers; they're maintaining more than a million kilometers of public roads across the country.

> **THE BUZZ ON BUGS**
> Mosquitoes are no joke here. They swarm around wetlands, and their presence is so stressful that moose have been known to lose body mass. Bring repellent for mosquitoes and their welt-raising brethren, the black flies.

POPULAR FESTIVALS

Canadian National Exhibition This colossal fair in Toronto started in 1879. Exhibits, a food-truck rally and an air show. **August/September**

Sunfest Ontario Artists and musicians take over London, Ontario. **July**

Montréal International Jazz Festival Love a jazz performance? How about 3000 of them, all across Montréal? **June/July**

Québec Summer Festival (FEQ) Québec City throbs with world music for more than a week. **July**

OFFBEAT FESTIVALS

Montréal Complèmente Cirque This 11-day showcase of acrobats and clowns takes place in the streets. **July**

Vancouver Dragon Boat Festival Athletes paddle their colorful boats across the bay. Coupled with pan-Asian arts and food. **June**

Calgary Stampede This massive event ain't Alberta's first rodeo, but it sure is its biggest. **July**

Winnipeg Folk Festival Join thousands of fans for world-class folk concerts. **July**

JULY	AUGUST	SEPTEMBER	OCTOBER	NOVEMBER	DECEMBER
Average daytime max: **15C°**. Days of rainfall: **8**	Average daytime max: **14C°**. Days of rainfall: **9**	Average daytime max: **13C°**. Days of rainfall: **12**	Average daytime max: **1.5C°**. Days of rainfall: **8**	Average daytime max: **-6C°**. Days of rainfall: **8**	Average daytime max: **-13C°**. Days of rainfall: **8**

Get Prepared for Canada

Useful things to load in your bag, your ears and your brain

Clothing

From fur caps to lumberjack flannel, Canadian fashion is well known throughout the world – and no nation is more familiar with the concept of layers. Prepare for humid summers, bone-chilling winters and plenty of showers in between.

Cycling jersey and padded shorts Some of these rides will take you a full day, and the saddle-sore struggle is real.

T-shirts and shorts Canadians are generally laid-back about fashion, so wear the clothes that feel comfortable (and breathe well).

Gloves and sunglasses Padded gloves protect your palms from long hours leaning into your handlebars.

Canada has lots of overcast days, but when the northern sun comes out, it shines bright.

Closed-toe footwear Diehard cyclists may opt for clip-in shoes, but any athletic footwear should do the trick.

Wool or fleece Shoulder-season temperatures can drop low in the mornings and evenings. Lightweight wool sweaters and fleece vests are ideal for spring and fall.

Shell No matter when or where you pedal in Canada, you're likely to face off with rain and wind. A waterproof jacket can be a lifesaver.

Swimsuit Canada is riddled with swimmable lakes, ponds and rivers, and there's no better way to cool off on a sweaty afternoon.

WATCH

The Moment *(Darcy Hennessey; 2017)* This documentary follows thrill-seeking mountain-bikers in the woodlands of British Columbia.

Seeing Canada *(Brandy Yanchyk; 2023)* Travel personality Brandy Yanchyk celebrates the attractions and cultural diversity of her home country.

Degrassi *(Kit Hood, Linda Schuyler; 1979–present)* The ultimate coming-of-age TV franchise unfolds in the Toronto school system.

North of North *(Stacey Aglok MacDonald, Alethea Arnaquq-Baril; 2025)* This Canadian sitcom offers a lighthearted take on Inuk life in small-town Nunavut.

Heartland *(Murray Shostak; 2007–present)* Horses, ranchers and personal problems lie at the heart of this long-running family drama.

Buffalo Pound Provincial Park (p171)

Words

Basics

Runners Athletic shoes

Toque A warm hat

Loonie/Toonie A one-dollar/two-dollar coin

Hang a Larry/Hang a Roger Go left/go right

Click Slang for 'kilometer'

Timmies Tim Horton's, a ubiquitous doughnut shop and favorite spot to refuel

Double-Double A coffee with two creams and two sugars

French Road Signs

Arrêt Stop

Voie Barré Blocked Path

Cédez le Passage Yield

Pas de Sortie Not an Exit

Centre Ville Downtown

Ne Dépassez Pas Do Not Pass

Entrée Interdite Do Not Enter

Bienvenue Cyclistes Welcome Cyclists

LISTEN

The Current with Matt Galloway
For the CBC, host (and cycling enthusiast) Matt Galloway breaks down current affairs.

Le P'tit Bonheur
(Félix Leclerc; 1989) Leclerc's playful French tunes are a pleasure to ride to.

The Bikepack Adventure Podcast
Québec resident Chris Panasky has explored dozens of countries by bike – and interviews fellow cyclists.

Oh What a Feeling: A Vital Collection of Canadian Music
(various; 1996) A who's who of Canadian stars.

READ

With You By Bike
(Katrina Rosen; 2019) A Canadian couple, struggling with their marriage, resolve to bike the world together.

A Short History of Canada
(Desmond Morton; 1983) The classic textbook remains informative and engaging.

Cycling From Sea to Sea: One Hundred Days Across Canada
(Jayden Beaudoin; 2024) A riveting ride across the continent.

Souvenir of Canada
(Douglas Coupland; 2004) The inventor of 'Generation X' waxes poetic about iconic Canadian products.

Bridge crossing, Meewasin Valley Trail (p157)

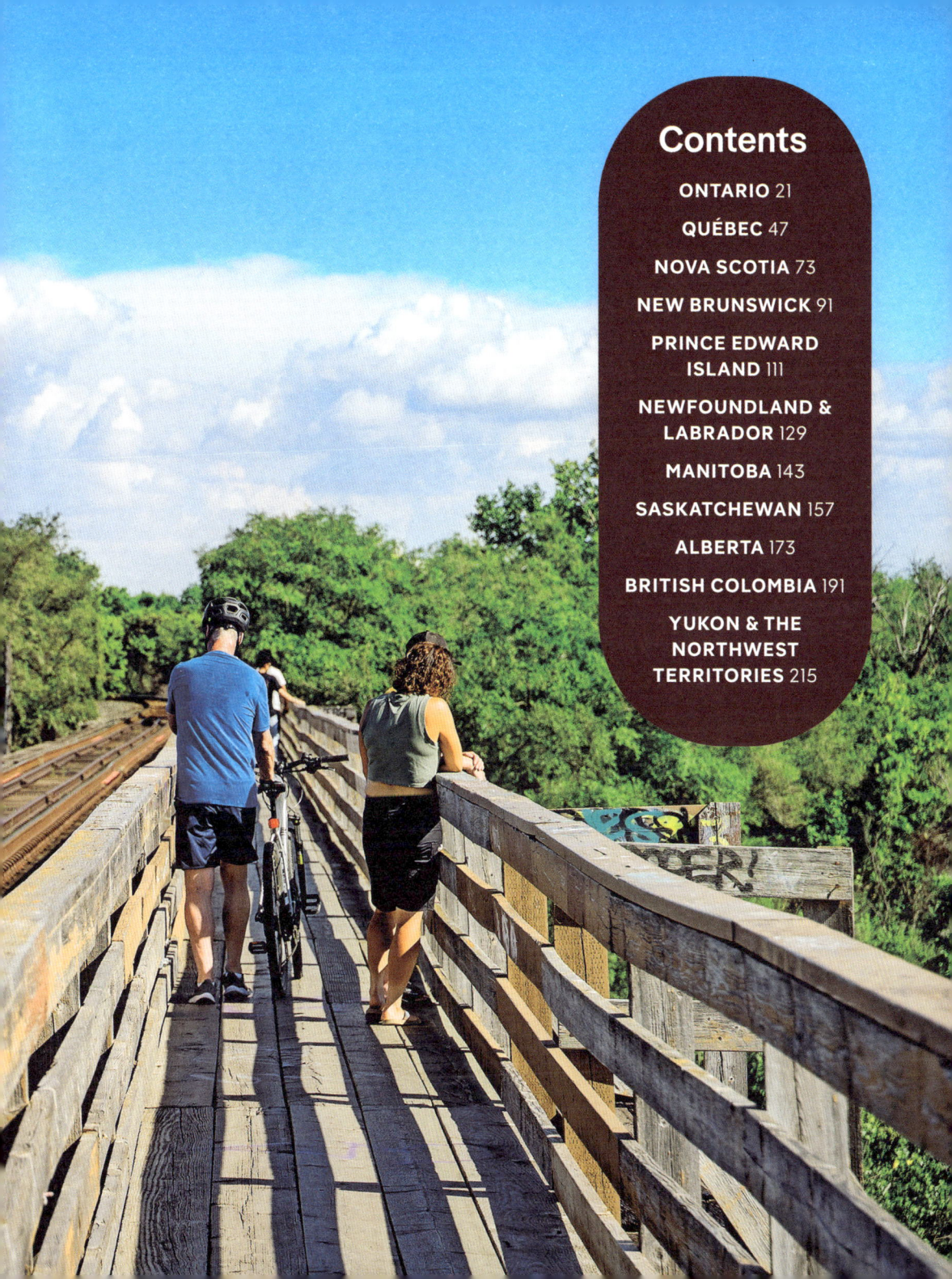

Contents

ONTARIO 21
QUÉBEC 47
NOVA SCOTIA 73
NEW BRUNSWICK 91
PRINCE EDWARD ISLAND 111
NEWFOUNDLAND & LABRADOR 129
MANITOBA 143
SASKATCHEWAN 157
ALBERTA 173
BRITISH COLOMBIA 191
YUKON & THE NORTHWEST TERRITORIES 215

Rideau Canal bike path (p26)

Ontario

01 Ottawa's Waterways

This easy loop ride on mostly paved paths takes you along the historic Rideau Canal along a flat and tranquil course, and returns to the city by the river. With historical references, wild birdlife and beautiful nature, this ride shows you Ottawa's quieter corners away from downtown. **p26**

02 Niagara Trail

A mostly gentle ride with a couple of challenging sections and traffic crossings, this ride takes you along the river, passing through parks, wineries, towns and monuments to reach Niagara Falls. There are several viewpoints along the way, and plenty of coffee stops if you need them. **p32**

03 Lower Don River Loop

One of the lesser-known cycle trails that takes you away from downtown along the tranquil Don River valley to visit some of Toronto's industrial heritage. Part nature trail, part paved bike lane, this is a day ride that gives you a different view of this modern metropolis. **p38**

Explore

Ontario

From cultural attractions in its cosmopolitan cities and heritage towns to natural wonders like Niagara Falls and a spread of forested parks with ever-changing seasonal landscapes alive with the wildlife, it is no wonder that Canada's capital province is arguably the most visited by international tourists.

There is no shortage of great bike rides in Ontario. Several long-distance trails such as the Trans Canada Trail and the Great Lakes Waterfront Trail traverse the province, leading to opportunities to explore more of Ontario on two wheels.

Ottawa

Canada's cosmopolitan capital is wonderfully vibrant, photogenic and cycle-friendly. Bike lanes crisscross download roads, and drivers are mostly friendly and understanding. It's located on the confluence of the Ottawa and Rideau rivers, and the city's waterways and access to surrounding nature trails make bike rides around town pleasant.

While the most obvious base would be around downtown, the Bayward Market area across the canal is a colorful alternative, with a large shopping mall for food supplies or additional clothing. Hotels, hostels and guesthouses all have a presence in Ottawa and you can eat well around the market with an array of international cuisines and street foods available. The light rail system is fantastic for getting around, but the best way would be to hire a bike to explore this city on two wheels.

Toronto

International travelers visiting Ontario are likely to arrive through Toronto International Airport first. This is Canada's most populous and global city, the epicenter for finance, technology and festivals. Despite high-rise offices and busy traffic, the city is well equipped as a base for cycling holidays. The Great Lakes Waterfront Trail joins Toronto on Lake Ontario all the way east to Québec, down to Niagara Falls and across the shore of Lake Erie; it then traces the waterfront of Lake Huron toward the town of Orillia on Lake Simcoe.

WHEN TO GO

While Ontario is a year-round destination and cycling is technically possible between March and November, early summer and early fall are the ideal seasons to go for a bike ride. While sunshine can be better guaranteed during midsummer, it is also the most crowded and comes with higher risk of wild fires that may close the bike trails.

There's no shortage of accommodations and dining options, and there are several bike-rental companies and touring companies to choose from. The city has invested in creating public leisure areas, including a large-scale project at the waterfront and port areas with walking and cycle ways, providing more future options for great bike rides.

Niagara-on-the-Lake

This small, former colonial township still retains its period charm characterized by its heritage wooden houses. Niagara-on-the-Lake is a perfect base for bike rides along the river, as well as visits to wineries of the region. Many visitors choose to stay here rather than the main town of Niagara Falls for its quieter lakeside atmosphere. On the edges of town, you'll also find vineyards with their own restaurants and accommodations.

Niagara-on-the-Lake is the start of the Niagara Trail. There are several bike shares and a couple of bike-tour companies in and just out of town, should you wish for a guide.

WHERE TO STAY

In the cities, you'll mostly find hotels and hostels. In rural areas around the province, especially near cycle trails, you are more likely to find mansion hotels, smaller guesthouses and campsites close by. Self-driving holidaymakers will find it more convenient to stay in a motel, although these are usually located away from town centers. There isn't a label for accommodations that may have facilities for cyclists, so it's always worth asking, as some place may allow you to take your bike into the room, or have an area in their car park to lock up.

TRANSPORT

Due to the size of the province, flying between distanced towns is common in Ontario. VIA Rail has daily long-distance connections between a set of destinations. Cities like Ottawa and Toronto have good bus, subway or streetcar systems for getting around town, but in smaller towns visitors will often hire a car for their journey.

WHAT'S ON

From food to film, music and comedy, there is a lot on around Ontario year-round. The province is home to many cycling events, from charity races to touring; the avid cyclist will always find an event to join.

Bluewater International Grandfondo

This annual event takes riders around the beautiful Lambton County.

Prince Edward County Grand Fondo

Take in cinematic views of vineyards and lake; the event ends in fun après-ride festivities.

Resources

Ontario By Bike *(ontariobybike.ca)* A great web resource for all cyclists, offering information, inspiration and suggested bike rides around the province around the province based on cycling style, terrain and ability.

Destination Ontario *(destinationontario.com/en-ca/things-to-do/cycling-and-mountain-biking)* For general inspiration, Destination Ontario has a quick guide to cycling and mountain-biking in the province.

01

Ottawa's Waterways

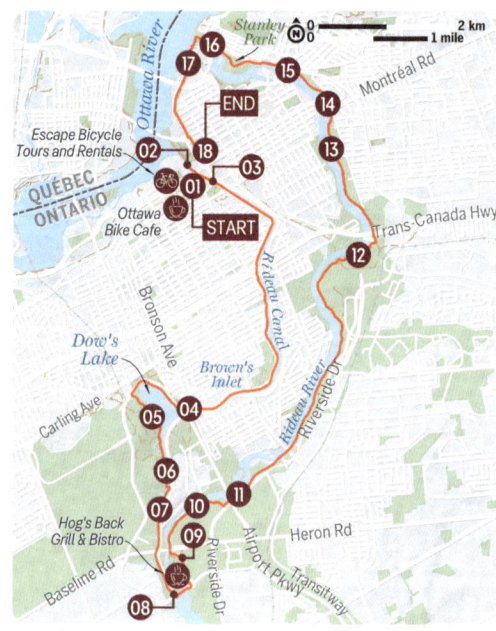

DURATION	DIFFICULTY	DISTANCE	START/END
1½hrs	Easy	24km	National War Memorial/ Byward Market
TERRAIN		Paved	

Elevation (m)

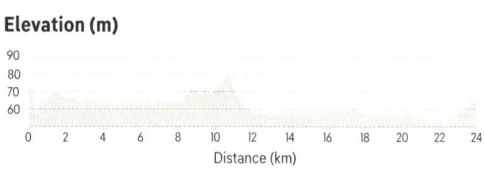

Every tour in Ottawa starts with the canal. The gentle multi-use path along the canal will take you away from downtown, and is installed with interpretation panels dotted along the way that tell the story of a particular point of interest or general historic facts. Learn the history of UNESCO heritage-listed Rideau Canal, built in the 19th century for military and trade, and considered the best-preserved slackwater canal in North America. Then return to Ottawa by the Rideau River, where you'll first enjoy the wild nature and birdlife that lives along it before passing the historic neighborhood of New Edinburgh and views of the Rideau Fall.

Bike Hire

Escape Bicycle Tours and Rentals *(escapebicycle tours.ca)* has an excellent range of bikes for rental and daily guided tours of Ottawa's surrounds. Rentals go from $12.70 for an hour to $37 for a day.

Starting Point

The bike ride starts at the National War Memorial in the heart of downtown, which is easy to find and has a path leading towards the canal bike path.

01 Starting from the National War Memorial, walk your bike across Elgin St toward the canal. Notice there is a downward ramp right by the crossing. Follow this down to the canal side.

02 Turn left first and follow the path under the bridge to reach Byward Museum; this small detour lets you see the series of eight locks of the canal. The Ottawa Locks is the end of the canal system, an engineering achievement around which

Best for

ART & CULTURE

National War Memorial

the city grew. Having learned all about it from the info boards, turn around and return on the canal path back under the bridge.

03 From here on, follow the canal in the upstream direction, passing the glass tulip–shaped Roger Center on your left and National Arts Center on your right. You are still within the vicinity of downtown, but on the canal you'll feel relaxed away from the traffic above. It gets quieter as you continue to ride along the canal, further away from downtown. Depending on the season, the trees that line the canal path may vary in color. As the canal bends and curls, ducking under several bridges and a number of parks, it makes its way toward Dow's Lake. There are a number of interpretation panels that describe how Ottawa developed and the importance of the canal for the communities.

04 Six kilometers in, you'll notice the waterway start to open up into a lake. Dow's Lake is an artificial oasis that was once a swamp, well known for its blooming flowers in spring and summer. The path will wind its way around the lake, letting you take in the tranquil surrounds as well as learn more about the lake and the operation of the canal through the interpretation panels along the path. There are public toilets at the pavilion here, open during the summer months.

05 As the lake curves around, the path approaches a small section of wilderness with some lovely viewpoints for photos. Garden and plant enthusiasts may wish to stop and visit the Arboretum and gardens on the right, as well as the city's Experimental Farm, one of five agricultural research stations set up in 1886 in Canada. Both are free to visit. Toilet facilities are available here.

06 From here, the canal path will take you to a lock station – Hartwells Lock. There are several picnic tables, and a washroom in the lockmaster's building, as well as potable water to fill your bottle.

07 When you are ready, walk your bike across the lock to reach the other side of the canal. Then continue the bike ride to your right.

08 You are nearing where the canal meets the Rideau River. The full canal system extends all the way to the city of Kingston, and you've just traced its final 10km. On reaching Hog's Back Bridge, the path will turn left and a ramp will take you onto the bridge. Cross the bridge, then carefully cross the road to join the path again.

09 There's a park area around Hog's Back Falls, a lovely place to linger where there is a little bistro cafe and washroom facilities. The park was developed around 1950 and is a popular nature spot for Ottawa residents. As you cycle through, there are historical displays and a heritage pavilion in the park, and

BEST BIKE RIDES: CANADA

☕ Take a break

As you cycle along the canal, you are never too far from a neighborhood should you need to stop for supplies. Exactly at the midpoint, as you join the Rideau River for the ride back, you'll find the HOG'S BACK GRILL & BISTRO, a lovely spot to rest, get a snack and enjoy the view. There is a public washroom, and a lookout point for a great view of the Hog's Back Falls.

on sunny days you'll see herons and cormorants fishing on the river. This marks the halfway point of your bike ride; you will be returning to Ottawa along the Rideau River. Like the canal path, the Rideau River Pathway is mostly paved and well managed, although you'll notice the difference in the environment. Where the canals feel organized and structured, the river path will take you through some of the wilder side of Ottawa nature, which you would have first experienced around Hog's Back Park.

10 Past the park, keep to the path on the right side of the river. There is a footbridge coming up, which looks tempting as there is a lovely view of the river from above. Visit it if you wish, although the path across the bridge goes nowhere and you'll need to return to this side to continue.

11 The path leaves the wilderness for a while and runs parallel to a highway between George Dunbar Bridge and Billings Bridge, although there are still some lovely views of the river along the path. Several access points on the right allow people to join the path from street level. To avoid confusion, follow the main path that hugs the river's shoreline.

12 There's a wonderfully natural section of the river path between the bridge crossing at Faircrest and a pedestrian and cyclist crossing near the motorway and Ottawa VIA Rail station, with access to the river around the footbridge for a good view of the river. From here on, the path will feel more urban, nearing the center of the city.

13 Coming up to the Adáwe Crossing footbridge, you'll find Rideau Sports Centre, where there is a small pub at the corner, should you need to stop for a drink or toilet break. It is also a chance to shorten your ride by crossing the bridge to return to downtown. However, it will mean missing out on some final surprises.

14 Soon the ride reaches the confluence of the Rideau and Ottawa Rivers. After the sports center, the river path ends at a road junction at Cummings Bridge. Keeping to the same side of the road, a cycle lane will take you across at the crossing, where you will follow it for a short 200m before it becomes the river path again.

15 Take care as you approach the next road bridge at St Patrick St – the path forks, and you want to follow it to the left, where it ducks under the bridge. This will

Skaters, Rideau Canal

Ice Skating on the Rideau Canal

The bike ride is the best way to explore Ottawa's canal in summer. But in winter the canal, stretching over 7km from downtown to Dow's Lake, transforms into the world's largest ice-skating rink. Imagine the world around you dusted with snow as the water along the canal freezes over, freeing everyone to skate in this open arena. This usually happens between January and March, when there have been more than 10 days of –10 to –20 degrees Celsius, allowing for at least 30cm of ice. It is then tested for safety before it is opened to public.

ONTARIO 01 OTTAWA'S WATERWAYS

The Anishinaabe Scout at Kìwekì Point

Visitors to the new Kìwekì Point will notice the prominent statue of the Anishinaabe scout, the Great River Man. The statue was created in 1918 and was once part of a larger work alongside French explorer Samuel de Champlain to show how Indigenous Peoples helped the newcomers to navigate the rivers. When Kìwekì Point was created, the statues were separated, placing the Anishinaabe scout in a new position as recognition of the skills and knowledge of the Indigenous Peoples of the Great Lakes. Kìwekì Point was designed in collaboration with the Algonquins of Pikwàkanagàn First Nations and Kitigan Zibi Anishinabeg, and Indigenous symbolism is part of the landscape throughout.

Kìwekì Point

now lead you to Stanley Park around the neighborhood of New Edinburgh. From here you could make a detour to visit Rideau Hall and its lovely gardens.

16 On the other side of Stanley Park, past the heritage Minto Bridge (a series of three truss bridges that connects the islands on the Rideau River with Ottawa), you will come up to a road crossing at Sussex Drive. It is recommended to walk across at the pedestrian lights, and walk the bike to the left using the footpath at the edge of the Ottawa River. Here you'll find Rideau Falls, a natural waterfall that drains the Rideau River into the Ottawa River. You need to walk your bike on the bridge connecting either side of the falls.

17 Join the bike lane on Sussex Drive and ride in the direction of downtown. Ignore the turnoff onto Macdonald-Cartier Bridge, and the cycleway will take you all the way to the National Gallery, with the big spider statue at its entrance. Another detour option from here is to visit Kìwekì Point behind the gallery for spectacular panoramic views of Parliament Hill and Ottawa-Gatineau with a circular walkway. Officially opened in 2025, this park features monuments, artworks and information panels on the history and wildlife of Ottawa.

18 This ride ends at ByWard Market area, one of Ottawa's oldest neighborhoods. Renowned for its diverse culinary options with flavors from all over the world, it is the perfect end for a snack, a meal, or simply to browse the shops and enjoy the energetic atmosphere.

TOP TIP:
Locking Up

Ask for a lock with your bike hire to give you the freedom of being able to visit some of Ottawa's attractions along the way. Although it is a relatively safe city, it's better to be prepared than sorry!

☕ Take a break

Back in town and have post-ride hunger? The inner cyclist in you will love the **OTTAWA BIKE CAFE**. Centrally located on Sparks St just a few steps away from the National War Memorial, the cafe serves a range of locally sourced food and drinks, and doubles as a bike workshop. Everything is bike themed – even some of the furnishing are recycled bicycle parts. There's a display of vintage bikes along the wall and a general friendly atmosphere.

02

Niagara Trail

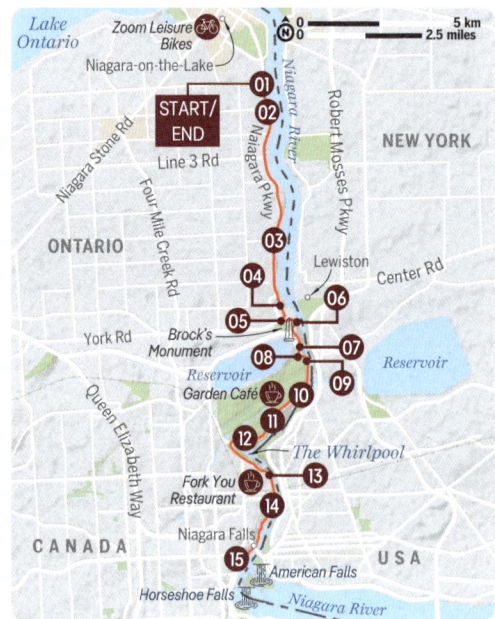

DURATION	DIFFICULTY	DISTANCE	START/END
3hrs	Hard	40km	Niagara-on-the-Lake

TERRAIN	Mostly paved

Elevation (m)

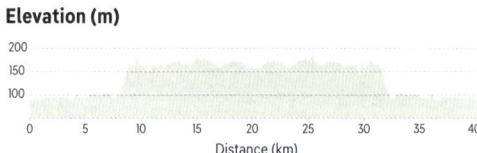

While most people visit Niagara Falls by car or coach tour, there is something about tracing the water flow of the jade green Niagara River to get there. From the quaint, pretty town of Niagara-on-the-Lake, in the heart of one of Ontario's great wine regions, this out-and-back bike ride will allow you to experience the nature, the communities and the slow emotional buildup of meeting the majestic falls by way of the bike. The Niagara Trail is part of the long-distance Great Lakes Water Front Trail. Although it has sections of sharp hills, it is mostly paved over and easy to follow.

Bike Hire

Zoom Leisure Bikes (zoomleisure.com) has both regular and e-bikes for hire. The main store is located in town at Niagara-on-the-Lake, with a delivery service to nearby locations also available.

Starting Point

This itinerary starts from McFarland Park car park on the junction of Niagara River Pkwy and E & West Line, just a short distance away from Niagara-on-the-Lake town center.

01 From the car park, the trail path runs along the side of McFarland House, built in 1800, one of the oldest surviving houses in the Niagara region. Join the trail here in the direction of south, with the car park to your right and the river to your left. For the first 7km of your journey, you'll be following the trail that winds its way among trees parallel to and between the main road, Niagara River Pkwy, to your right, and the river to your left. There are a couple of gentle inclines along this section of the trail but nothing too strenuous yet.

Best for ART & CULTURE

Laura Secord Homestead

02 Having left the start point behind, you'll soon come to a small neighborhood on the right. There is a small church and a country market, which is a good place to stock up on some locally grown fresh fruits, baked items and sandwiches. As you journey a little further down, you'll notice patches of vineyard begin to appear to the right side of the road, and you'll also pass by the first of several wineries along this road. Niagara-on-the-Lake is one of the most recognized wine regions in Ontario and this is a good chance for you to make mental notes on where to come back for some tasting.

03 Keep following the trail as it dips up and down and slowly becomes more of a sidewalk next to the road. You are still allowed to cycle here. Continue until you come to where the sidewalk ends, joining a junction that appears on the road. The main road bends to the right, with quieter Queenston St forking to the left, marked by the red-brick RiverBrink Art Museum on the corner. Turn left here onto Queenston St. From here, you'll be cycling on this quiet residential street. This is the small community of Queenston. Meander a bit if you like. A couple of side streets away from the main thoroughfare, you'll find historical Laura Secord Homestead; this was the home of Laura Secord, who walked a long way out of American-occupied territory to warn British troops of an imminent attack and became one of Canada's heroes of the War of 1812.

04 Back on Queenston St, there's an incline in your direction of travel, so take your time. Continue your journey until the street bends a sharp right. On the corner, you'll find Mackenzie Printery and Newspaper Museum. Turn right and cycle past the museum to come to the main road, where the segregated bike trail begins again.

☕ Take a break

GARDEN CAFÉ, which is at the car park of Butterfly Conservatory just shortly after the stretch of trail looking out to the power plants, has coffee and ice cream, as well as a range of quick eats such as soups, salads, sandwiches and wraps. It is conveniently located on the Niagara Trail as it bypasses the conservatory. There are bike racks for parking, and outdoor seating areas where you can keep your eyes on the bikes.

05 Join the bike trail, carefully navigating it to cross over York St and the main parkway at the corner as it rounds to the right, where you'll notice a trail entrance on the left into a forested area. It might be a good idea to stop and take some breaths here, as a steep climb is coming up.

06 This lush tree path soon becomes a battle for air on this very short but sharp climb through the trees before you emerge onto a small traffic circle. To your right is a staired path leading toward Brock's Monument inside Queenston Heights Park, where you could make a quick visit and use the public washroom in the park. You could get there by walking from this point, or continue on the trail with the bike; instead of following it to the left at the next road junction, follow the road to the right of the parking area for the parks.

07 Whichever option you choose, to continue the bike ride, get to the major road junction with road signs pointing to Brock's Monument to the right and Niagara Falls to the left. From here, the trail crosses the Niagara River Pkwy to the left and continues as a separate trail along the road. You'll notice a large building to your right, which is the immigration border for the bridge that crosses into the United States. We want to keep to the Canadian side, so keep on the trail, which goes under this border-crossing bridge, the Lewiston-Queenston Bridge. There's a nice viewpoint of the bridge just beyond this point should you wish to stop. The trail stops for 100m as it joins a gravel parking area before starting again, so do look out for cars.

08 Less than 1km past the bridge, you'll come to the first Niagara Falls attraction, the Floral Clock, which is often surrounded by tour buses. The trail itself stays on the quieter side of the road to the left and continues its way toward the falls.

09 Immediately after the Floral Clock, the surrounds will feel different. The trail is now entering a stretch across the power-generating plants of Niagara Falls, and you will ride under and next to rows of power lines and posts. Hydro power has been generated from the Niagara River and its falls for a long time, and this is a fascinating lookout to see the plants at work on both sides of the river.

Brock's Monument

Brock's Monument

Two hundred years ago the Niagara River, which forms a natural border between then British-ruled Canada and the United States, was not as peaceful as it is today. This monument commemorates the bravery of Major-General Isaac Brock, commander-in-chief of British forces in Upper Canada, who died in battle in October 1812, when the American troops crossed the Niagara River in an attempt to cut British supply lines.

Next to the monument is the Landscape of Nations, a park dedicated to the Haudenosaunee (Six Nations) Confederacy and Indigenous allies that fought in the War of 1812.

Hydro Power on Niagara

The power of water has long been a great resource, and for 100 years the Canadian Niagara Power Company generating station at the Horseshoe Falls has been harnessing the energy generated by the falls. When it first began to operate in 1905, Niagara Parks Power Station was the first large-scale power plant on the Canadian side of the Niagara River. Its construction was a feat of wonder for its time, featuring a stone exterior and low-profile architecture that blended into the surrounding natural environment. The plant was decommissioned in 2006. Today, it is a museum dedicated to preserving its heritage.

Horseshoe Falls

10 Passing the power plants, the trail merges with the road where a sign directs you to cross the road. Cross with caution, as cars do drive fast here. You are now at the car park of the Butterfly Conservatory, where the trail continues along it to the left. There is a cafe and washroom facilities here.

11 You'll only be on this side of the main road for a short while before you need to cross again as you pass Niagara Glen Nature Centre to the left. This is to avoid the tour-bus stopping area of the nature center. There are no indicators besides the fact that the trail ends and picks up across the road, so keep a lookout for these crossing points.

12 Coming up along the trail is a lookout point with an adventure-course area. This is a great opportunity to stop to admire the landscape of the Niagara River and take a break. The flow of the river's emerald green water – the color is attributed to dissolved salts and finely ground limestone through the power of the falls – continues to erode and shape the surrounding landscape today. From here, it is a short ride to the end of the protected trail, as you pass a helicopter port to the right and arrive at the car park of the Whirlpool Aero Car. To continue the bike ride all the way to Niagara Falls, cross carefully to the other side of the road and follow the direction of traffic.

13 The good news is that it's mostly downhill from here, and there is a shoulder on the road to keep a relatively safe distance with the flow of cars, although it does gets busier as you approach the next border crossing and into Niagara Falls proper. Take care for the next 3km.

14 You'll know you have reached the falls when you hear the sound of crashing water – and see casinos appear on the side of the road. Welcome to Niagara Falls. From here, you are free to continue on to view first the American falls, then the Canadian Horseshoe Falls a little further down the track. It can get very crowded here, so best to walk your bike. There are a number of roadside snack kiosks as well as restaurants and cafes in town.

TOP TIP:

Bus It

To shorten your trip or to avoid the car traffic approaching Niagara Falls, hop on a WEGO bus with your bike. A 24-hour pass is $13 (adult) and can be purchased online, from Niagara Falls bus station or any Niagara Parks shop.

15 When you are ready, turn around and follow the road back to the Whirlpool Aero Car. Rejoin the safety of the trail to return to Niagara-on-the-Lake, perhaps finally stopping to taste some wines on your way back.

☕ Take a break

The Niagara Trail ends at the car park of the Whirlpool Aero Car, signaling a good place to stop and rest. Although no food is sold here, near the ticket office there is a water-filling station to refill your bottles, and there are washroom facilities around the gift shop. For a bite to eat, the FORK YOU RESTAURANT, which serves Peruvian cuisine just 100m down the road next to the roadside motel, is recommended by locals.

03

Lower Don River Loop

DURATION	DIFFICULTY	DISTANCE	START/END
1½hrs	Easy	18km	Toronto Waterfront

TERRAIN		Mostly paved

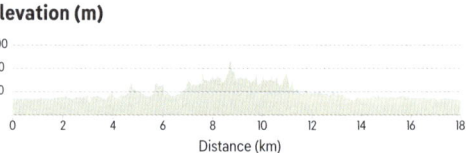

Taking the trail less traveled, this short loop bike ride leaves the bustling Toronto waterfront behind for a quiet spin in nature along the Lower Don Valley, Toronto's largest urban park. Along the way, you'll learn about the valley's industrial heritage at the brick works and paper mill, and enjoy the serenity of nature along the Don River. The ride allows you to experience the excellent bike lanes of Toronto before you return on the nature path, where there is public art along the trail to admire.

Bike Hire

Wheel Excitement Inc (wheelexcitement.ca) on Queens Quay at the waterfront has a range of bikes for hire, starting at $15 for an hour to $40 for 24 hours.

Starting Point

This itinerary starts on the cycle path at Queen's Quay Ferry terminal. However, you can start anywhere along the Toronto waterfront and join the same cycle path in the eastward direction.

01 To join this bike ride, you can start anywhere along Toronto's waterfront and follow the main cycle lane and travel eastwards, with the quay to your right and the city to your left. This lively neighborhood with hotels, residences, restaurants and shops is often busy with markets and festivals, which you can return to later for a visit. This cycle lane will come to a number of traffic lights before it eventually reaches the busy junction of Cherry St and Gardiner Expwy. You need to turn left here. Utilize the traffic lights to cross under the expressway onto Cherry St.

Corktown Common

02 Once you've traveled under the railway lines and the busy expressway overhead, having crossed two sets of traffic lights, take care not to accidentally turn onto the expressway ramp. Turn right onto Mill St just ahead.

03 At the end of Mill St, you come to a lovely leisure area named Corktown Common. The cycle lane will skirt around it and swerve to the left onto Bayview Ave. Follow this, as it turns to run in parallel with the rail line along the road. You will be cycling along this two-way cycle lane for a little while. Although the car traffic will seem busy, the cycle lane is safely segregated from the road so you can relax and go at your own pace.

04 Soon, you'll leave the urban area and pass Riverdale Park on the left, where there is an overhead crossing to the other side of the railway and river. Cycle under it to continue. The cycle lane joins up with the Bayview Multiuse Trail at the traffic-lights junction where Rosedale Valley Rd meets Bayview Ave on the left. This is a lovely tree-lined section that feels like you are finally escaping the car fumes. There is a slight incline here, and a narrow segment that hugs the pillars of the bridge as it dips under Prince Edward Viaduct, creating a blind spot, so watch out for pedestrians who might also be walking on the trail here.

05 The trail evens out and continues next to the main road, passing under a major road just before it bends to the right. You'll start to see a complex of brick buildings across the road to your left. This is the Evergreen Brick Works, a place of Toronto's industrial heritage. It was once one of the country's largest brick manufacturers, creating the foundation of many of Toronto's iconic buildings for 100 years. A set of traffic lights will allow you to cross to visit the site,

☕ Take a break

Evergreen Brick Works, within the Don Valley Brick Works Park, has its own cycle trails, children's playground, a garden shop, and a cafe serving great coffee, pastries and light meals. This is along the first segment of the bike ride and is a worthwhile stop if you want to learn about its history and have a coffee at the PICNIC CAFE. A farmers market operates on Saturdays. There are a couple of retail stores as well as public toilets on site.

where there are toilets and a cafe for a snack break.

06 Back on the cycle path heading north, there is a short rail crossing in front of you. Cross with care, avoiding getting your wheels caught in the railing. As you approach the road junction between Bayview Ave and Pottery Rd, follow the trail which turns a sharp right onto a short bridge across the railway line below. Immediately past this bridge, a tall chimney structure will come in sight to your right. Ignore that for now as you will return on the way back. Look to your left and follow a road crossing to join a section of the Lower Don Valley Trail.

07 A short ride on this part of the trail will allow you to experience the tranquil side of Toronto's nature valley. Follow this trail along the Don River for less than 1km, ignoring the first crossing to reach the second one. Turn right.

08 There is a curious stone structure among the shrubs. This is the Great Honey Kiln of 1800, a monument to Toronto's brick-making industry in the 19th century. You may also wish to explore the several side trails here to spend more time in nature. Otherwise, turn around here and return to the road junction the same way you came.

09 On reaching Pottery Rd, cross the road and turn left, toward the chimneys you saw on the way in. Another site of Toronto's industrial past, this is Todmorden Mills Heritage Site, the location of the first lumber mill in Toronto which grew into a community, marking the beginning of a booming industrial era. Todmorden Mills is now a theater and gallery. Stop here, walk the trails of its gardens, and visit the millers' homes to learn about the operation of the mills and the lives of the workers who once worked in these industries.

10 After a visit to Todmorden Mills, it's time to turn back, this time through the greenery of the Lower Don Valley Trail. Exit the mill and turn left. Just before the small bridge that crosses the rail lines, there is a trail to the left. Turn onto this trail.

11 This nature trail is paved but the condition is not perfect. The Don River and its valley had always been a place of gathering. It has provided the Indigenous Peoples of the valley (which included the Anishinaabe, Haudenosaunee

Don Valley Brick Works Park

Industries of Don Valley

The 18th century saw Don Valley develop into its industrial era, which played a vital role in the growth of Toronto. From the first sawmill at the location of Todmorden Mills in 1795 came the railway for the transportation of industrial goods and people, and the establishment of Evergreen Brick Works in 1889, which made bricks for the foundation of the city. It was from here that both the valley and Toronto boomed. Today, the Don River Valley is a parkland enjoyed by Toronto residents as an urban oasis, where nature is returning among the remnants of the past.

Queer History of Toronto

The Gay Day Picnic on Toronto Islands was considered the first formal Pride event of the city back in 1971, making Hanlan's Point one of the few oldest surviving queer spaces around the world. The queer community of Toronto gathered here during a time when homosexuality was illegal. To avoid trouble, a trip across to the islands from the city was a way to escape this institutional judgement. Today, it is recognized and respected by the City of Toronto as the oldest continually queer social space in Toronto, and is a beach where clothing is optional and where all sexuality is respected.

Distillery Historic District

and Huron Wendat) with clay to make pottery, fertile wetlands for agriculture and plenty of fish as a food source. As you bike along this trail, you'll encounter water birds wading along the shallows for fish and small wildlife scurrying undergrowth, and the high overhead rail and road crossings along this trail make it rather photogenic. Enjoy the slight downhill route among the trees.

12 As you continue along the trail, keep your eyes peeled for art and information panels. There are often temporary public art exhibits installed along this trail. Just after the trail passes under Prince Edward Viaduct there is a small, shaded resting circle to the right, with information boards on the local wildlife. The trail will come to an end at a wooden bridge crossing on the right. Cross the bridge and join the trail on the other side. Turn left.

13 You are now cycling close to the rail line. You will follow this narrow trail for about 1.5km until you reach Corktown Common. This time, taking the other side, follow the outer rim of the common where you will approach a junction with two underpasses across the rail line. Turn right and cross under the Bala Underpass, which will take you into the common grounds, equipped with playgrounds for children and picnic areas.

14 Turn left along the trail, which will take you to an exit of the common and back onto Mill St. You are now back in Toronto downtown. Instead of returning to the start point the same way, bike straight on when you reach the Cherry St junction – the cycle path continues, entering the city's Distillery Historic District to your left. Enjoy this well-managed cycle lane that is adorned with flowers in summer. This is the site of the former Gooderham & Worts Distillery, a complex of industrial buildings that has been transformed into a place of art, culture and entertainment. Stop and explore a little, then get back on the bike to continue on Mill St, near to the end of the ride.

15 At the end of the Distillery District block, cycle across Parliament St and past the parks on your left to come to Lower Sherbourne St. Turn left here.

TOP TIP:

Trail Closure

At the time of publication, the trail section between Bala railway underpass and the creek bridge crossing at Riverdale Park was closed for improvement works. Avoid this area by returning to Toronto by road instead of the trail at the end.

16 This road will take you straight back to the waterfront. Cross the streetcar tracks with care and turn right at the end. The map will stop at Queen's Quay Ferry terminal, but you can follow the waterfront for as long as you desire. Perhaps board a ferry with the bike and explore Toronto Islands, or continue along and explore the western part of the waterfront.

☕ Take a break

AMSTERDAM BREW HOUSE on Queens Quay back on Toronto's waterfront is a great place for a post-ride drink. Amsterdam is one of the branches of Toronto's original brewpub founded in 1986. This large venue has tables overlooking the quay and Toronto Island in the distance, and has a good menu with barbecue, burgers and pizzas. There's a lively and welcoming atmosphere, and cycling enthusiasts will love the bicycle-themed craft beers.

Also Try...

MARC BRUXELLE/SHUTTERSTOCK

Kate Pace Way

DURATION	DIFFICULTY	DISTANCE
1hr	Easy	17km one way

Named after retired winter Olympian Kate Pace, who was born in North Bay, this bike ride will take you from the North Bay waterfront toward the village of Callander. Start anywhere along the shore of Lake Nipissing, and you'll pass North Bay's museums, parks and outer residential areas, through a forest and wetland. This paved and mostly tree-lined leisure trail offers a bit of everything from quiet urban streets to birdsong-filled natural environments. The bike ride is easy and suitable for cyclists of all abilities, including children. There is a parking and toilet stop just before the trail reaches Callander, and an option to extend the ride with a short section along the gravel Cranberry Trail.

Toronto Islands

DURATION	DIFFICULTY	DISTANCE
30min	Easy	10km loop

Just a short ferry ride from Toronto's waterfront are a chain of islands collectively known as Toronto Islands (pictured above), a car-free environment with a compact residential community, several restaurants and cafes, a theme park, beautiful stretches of sandy beaches and possibly the best view of the Toronto skyline. Cycling a loop of the island is easy and stress free. You can take your bike on the ferry free of charge. There are three ferry points on the island departing from the same location at Queen's Quay, and you can be dropped off at one point and pick up the ferry from a different part of the island with the same ticket.

GUS GARCIA/SHUTTERSTOCK

Omemee Rail Trail

DURATION	DIFFICULTY	DISTANCE
2hrs	Easy	35km one way

To experience a lesser-visited landscape of Ontario, join this scenic section of the Trans Canada Trail (pictured above) between the towns of Peterborough and Lindsey. This well-maintained gravel trail is mostly flat and suitable for most. It crosses several bridges, including Doube's Trestle Bridge, and passes some of Ontario's lush farmlands and lakes. Those who wish to cut this trail short can stop at the village of Omemee, with beautiful views of the dam and its river, and places to stop to eat, before the return trip back to Peterborough.

At the time of research, this trail was closed from Orange Corners to Emily Park Rd due to fire damage on Doube's Trestle Bridge. An on-road detour is available and recommended.

Georgian Trail

DURATION	DIFFICULTY	DISTANCE
2hrs one way	Easy	33km one way

Along the shore of Georgian Bay, around two hours' drive north of Toronto, is a picturesque gravel trail that connects the towns of Collingwood, Thornbury and Meaford. The bike ride follows a trail with trestle bridges that was once the rail route of Northern Railway, taking in scenic views of the bay's landscape and the surrounding parklands, visiting marinas and beaches, with sightings of wildlife both on land and in water. Summer is a great season for this bike ride as the trail is lined with shrubs that bloom with flowers perfuming the air. Georgian Trail is well sign-marked, with signage boards displaying historic and environmental information. Bike hire is available at Collingwood, and the trail is suitable for all abilities.

Lachine Canal (p64)

Québec

04 Eastern Townships
A rural ride on the Estriade Rail Trail between Waterloo and Granby is pure bliss. Double the fun with a romp through Yamaska National Park. **p50**

05 Mont-Tremblant
When spring comes to Québec's ski capital, cyclists coast through mountain forest on the town's pristinely paved bike loop. **p54**

06 Old Québec
Explore the romantic old streets of Québec City, where stone storefronts and colonial battlements share the skyline with modern high rises and ample bike paths. **p58**

07 Lachine Canal
Cycle the length of Montréal along its 200-year-old canal system, then return along the St Lawrence River, Canada's most important waterway. **p64**

Explore

Québec

The moment you cross into Québec province, everything changes. Traffic signs are now in French. Fleur-de-lis flags rise over streets. Centuries-old stone buildings, built in the heyday of New France, anchor neighborhoods. Riding through Québec is like traveling through time, from colonial churches to repurposed factories to brutalist office towers, a dramatic succession of eras and artifacts. This region is also replete with cycling infrastructure – you could spend years exploring Québec's 12,000km of bike paths and dedicated lanes. Not only is Québec the second most populous province in Canada, it's also one of the most bicycle-friendly.

Québec City

Over the course of four centuries, Québec City has transformed from an austere outpost on the banks of the St Lawrence River to an urban masterpiece of stone and steeple. School groups travel here every day to walk the cobbled streets and ogle historic structures. For cyclists, Québec City is a 3D chessboard of alleys and slopes, paths and boardwalks. Find a room in Montcalm, explore the mythic Old City and savor some of the most beautiful skylines in eastern Canada. Sweat up hills and coast back down them, then replenish your energy in an authentic French bistro.

Montréal

Montréal is the second-largest city in Canada, and it behaves accordingly: it's diverse, action-packed and studded with skyscrapers. Eleven universities and scores of colleges keep this city youthful, and global restaurants and multilingual conversations reflect robust immigrant communities. In recent years, Montréal has become a promised land for urban bikers as well; the cycling network is a sophisticated mix of lanes and paths, totaling more than 1000km through Montréal's environs. Downtown is crowded with hotels and nightlife, and no matter what your post-ride stomach craves – poutine, tacos or falafel – Montréal serves it up right.

Mont-Tremblant

Nestled deep in the Laurentian Mountains, Mont-Tremblant is a happy oasis for outdoors-lovers of all stripes, and cyclists

WHEN TO GO

Québec is liveliest in summer, and seasonal institutions are dependably open in July and August. Late spring (May onward) and early fall (through early October) can be lovely as well. Lifelong Québecers may bike in all weather, and riding fat tires over snow and frozen lakes is a growing pastime.

in particular. This town is most famous for its ski resort, and millions of people converge here each winter to fly down slopes and lounge in lodges. Yet the warmer months are a fantastic time to visit as well, thanks to thinner crowds, lower prices and all the trail-riding you could want. As the main resort goes into hibernation, the spotlight moves to the actual town of Mont-Tremblant, a sporty little community of 11,000 souls. When you're finished tearing up singletrack, nab a pint and chat up fellow thrill-seekers.

Granby

The old mill town of Granby has long been considered a gateway to the Eastern Townships, and its center retains an Industrial Age character, with stately churches, brick storefronts and several attractive parks. The town has lots of amenities and chain stores, so it's a convenient place to headquarter as you pedal surrounding countryside, and you can choose from a range of local lodgings. Granby is generally quiet, a nice contrast to Québec's bustling cities and tourist attractions. You can also eat your fill, thanks to a long drag of pubs and restaurants.

TRANSPORT

Cars are convenient to all hub towns in Québec. Alternatively, VIA Rail Canada *(viarail.ca)* connects Montréal and Québec to the rest of the country; folding bikes smaller than 158 linear inches are allowed aboard for $25. Hop a shuttle to Mont-Tremblant from Montréal-Trudeau International Airport or a bus from Montréal (90 minutes). For Granby, check out Limocar buses *(limocar.ca)*.

WHAT'S ON

Tour La Nuit
Thousands of cyclists light up the streets of Montréal for one night each May. This all-ages event is part of the city's annual Go Bike Montréal Festival.

Grand Défi de Granby
(granddefidegranby.com) Each May, the Grand Défi draws thousands of cyclists to the Eastern Townships' second-largest town. This family-friendly ride around Granby offers routes from 2.5km to 45km.

WHERE TO STAY

Québecers are masters of hospitality, and in cities and towns, you'll have your pick of hotels, hostels and B&Bs. Rates are wide-ranging, depending on where you stay and at what time of year, and you'll find everything from no-frills motels on the edge of town to boutique inns in trendy neighborhoods. Québec is also rich in campgrounds; if you've brought your own car and equipment, you'll have plenty of places to pitch a tent. As more travelers bike-tour across the province, campsites have become an ever more popular place to hang your helmet. Wherever you stay, you can expect plenty of good eats nearby.

Resources

Bonjour Quebec *(bonjourquebec.com)* The province's official tourism site has activities, festivals and gorgeous photos.

Vélo Québec *(velo.qc.ca)* This exhaustive website is designed for every kind of cyclist and includes routes and trail conditions.

La Route Verte *(routeverte.com)* Your guide to Québec's trail system, the longest such network in North America.

04

Eastern Townships

Best for

ART & CULTURE

Yamaska National Park

DURATION	DIFFICULTY	DISTANCE	START/END
3½hrs	Moderate	50.5km	Granby

TERRAIN	Mostly paved, some gravel

The Eastern Townships are the rural heartland of Québec province, where a checkerboard of farms, forest and rolling hills extends about 430km from end to end. This is prime cycling country, thanks to an ambitious network of rail trails. The first-ever converted line was the Estriade, which runs straight from the village of Waterloo to the town of Granby; every summer day, cyclists of all abilities ride back and forth along this 24km route. A separate trail through the forestland of Yamaska National Park links up with the Estriade on both ends, forming a continuous loop.

Bike Hire

Sports aux Puces VéloGare (sapvelogare.com) stands right next to the Estriade trailhead in Granby. The store overflows with cycling gear and bikes for rent, and skilled mechanics can tune up your ride.

Starting Point

Start in Parc de la Tannerie, a lovely riverside greenspace on the edge of Granby. There's a sizable parking lot and top-notch information center right past the McDonald's.

01 Make sure to fill your panniers with water and snacks, as you won't find any convenience stores between Granby and Waterloo. Once you arrive in the Parc de la Tannerie, warm up on the flat path that leads out of Granby. This stretch passes through the town's residential outskirts, and it's routinely busy with cyclists, joggers and inline skaters; most pedestrians will keep to a dirt track on the side of the rail trail. Take in views of the placid Yamaska River as it feeds into Lake Boivin. When you reach a three-way intersection, stay straight

Elevation (m)

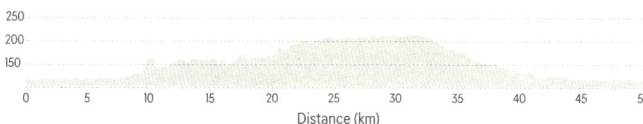

Breeze Through a Gallery

It's impossible to miss the giant pink elephant by the side of the road. Created by Jean-Yves Rhéaume and Marco De Muri in 2020, this bubblegum-colored pachyderm welcomes cyclists to the Estriade trailhead. And it's not alone – at least 50 sculptures are scattered along the bike path, a fine arts display known as Artria (artria.ca). The first works were installed as part of an International Sculpture Symposium in 1997, and more were added at successive editions. Today, this linear gallery extends all the way from Granby to Waterloo, and contributing artists represent 17 different nations. Spot monuments in concrete, stone and metal.

or turn left; either way, you're sticking to the Piste Cyclable La Granbyenne. Avoid turning right onto the Estriade; you'll be coming back this way later on.

02 Ride down one of the two tree-lined causeways around Réservoir Lemieux. These narrow stretches of land form a scenic circle around the reservoir, a popular circuit for hikers and runners. When you cross the small bridge over the Yamaska River, you might consider visiting the Centre de l'Intepretation de Lac Boivin *(8:30am-4:30pm Mon-Fri, 9am-5pm Sat & Sun; admission $7.50, under 6yr free)*, a nature center and trail network through local wetlands. Otherwise, continue east; the trail will curl its way into the countryside.

03 A small ranger station stands at the entrance to Yamaska National Park, where you can pay your $10 entry fee (free for children 17 and younger). Many riders will spend the day here; the main park area stands a respectable 10km away from Granby, and the grounds are packed with activities. Take a short detour to the beach, a popular spot with locals; a lifeguard watches over swimmers throughout the summer months. You can rent a bike or paddle a canoe on the calm waters of Réservoir Chonière; the artificial lake is a popular place for water sports, as well as an active habitat for ducks and blue herons. For passing cyclists, the many shaded tables make for a nice picnic or rest stop.

04 How did it become the Réservoir Choinière? A dam, of course – and you can ride right over it, thanks to a long dirt path along the water's southwestern edge. As you emerge from the trees, the grassy embankment offers generous views of the surrounding landscape.

05 The paved trail through Yamaska National Park is the most thrilling part of the journey, with its thick forest and rolling terrain. It's also the most challenging: you'll want a bike with dependable brakes and a decent cassette, as the climbs can be steep, and the trail weaves erratically through the woods. This segment feels a lot like mountain biking, but with smoother surfaces and gentler curves. The trail follows the reservoir's shoreline, although the views are obscured by ranks of trees. Zip along until you reach a small bridge over the stream; you'll ascend a long hill, then arrive at a fork in the path. Hang a right, toward Waterloo.

06 Arrive in Waterloo, a quiet little community that wraps around a lake of the same name. The bike path stops abruptly on the north side of town, but turn right on Rue Allen, then left on Rue Foster. This main drag will lead you into town; when you reach Rue Lewis, turn right and cross the bridge; there you'll pick up the Estriade Rail Trail, which stretches all the way back to Granby. Before you leave town, consider pausing at the End Path Lake View; just past the town cemetery, the trail splits off (to the left) and stops abruptly at the edge of the water.

07 A nice place to pause is the Parc Caboose (Caboose Park), a modest park with play structures and an actual train car permanently parked on the lawn. A bike rack allows you to lock up your ride and browse a handful of sculptures. There's also a bike pump, in case your tires need stiffening.

08 It's all downhill from here! The Estriade may feel flat, but you actually coast down 300m of elevation from Waterloo to Granby. This beloved route is smooth and fast, cutting through pastoral landscape. Stop about halfway at the Relais des Cheminots, a former railroad building with a water fountain, benches and restrooms.

☕ Take a break

Cyclists will be glad to find Waterloo in the middle of their loop; the town has a handful of restaurants, including the superlative gastropub MADAME FORTIN (madamefortin.ca). After lunch, cool off in the Plage Municipale (Municipal Beach) just 1km south of the bike trail. The sands are scarce, but it's a decent place to cool off on a muggy day. Get back in the zone by riding over the town's expansive pump track, just across the Rue Lewis bridge.

Yamaska River dam (p51)

Spin Around Granby

As you head east of Montréal, Granby marks the beginning of the Eastern Townships. The town is sizable, with a trendy downtown area along the Rue Principale and a few boutique hotels. The town sprawls westward, with chain restaurants, box stores and a good number of cheap rooms. What binds all this together is an impressive bikeway system, linking paths with separated lanes. The town boasts several bike shops, and you'll see cyclists pedaling the boulevards in all but the coldest months. Celebrate a long ride with poutine and a beer at one of Granby's many great restaurants.

05

Mont-Tremblant

Best for WILDLIFE

Mont-Tremblant resort

DURATION	DIFFICULTY	DISTANCE	START/END
1hr	Moderate	14.5km	Plage Municipale de Lac-Mercier

TERRAIN	Paved path, rolling forest

Mont-Tremblant is one of the most famous ski areas in Canada, and outdoor enthusiasts still flock here long after the snow has melted. For cyclists, a first-rate bike trail tethers the town of Mont-Tremblant to the resort area. Smooth pavement rises and falls with the dynamic terrain, delving deep into forestland and skirting river and lakes. The route feels longer and more remote than it is, and numerous hiking trails split off from the main path and disappear into the woods. Summer is the low season here, which means better rates and plenty of private time.

Bike Hire

Mont-Tremblant has several bike shops, and they're all exceptional. You can enjoy breakfast and a bike rental from Ocafé (*ocafevieuxtremblant.ca*), across the street from the bike trail.

Starting Point

You can begin your loop in many spots, but a great starting line is the Plage du Lac Mercier (Lake Mercier Beach), right in the middle of town.

01 Make sure to stretch before you leave the beautiful Lake Mercier waterfront, as you've got some decent hills ahead of you. You're starting in Mont-Tremblant-Village, a small commercial corridor that is geographically separate from the Mont-Tremblant resort. As you ride away from the lake, the paved trail plays peekaboo with Chemin du Village, the main road through town. You'll pass stores, restaurants and hotels as you ascend, along with the peaceful waters of Lake Moore. The two-lane path turns left into the woods, then crosses the road a half-kilometer later.

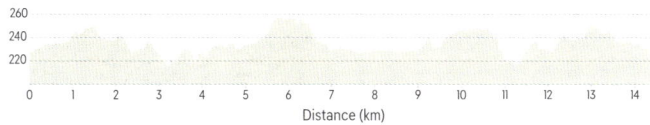

Panoramic Gondola

The gondola ride is the classic image of Mont-Tremblant, and all summer long these special cars glide up the mountain on their cables. This transport system is fundamentally designed for skiers, but anyone can benefit from the 360-degree views through the gondola's floor-to-ceiling windows. You are welcome to hike up the mountain and ride the gondola down for $12, though cyclists already putting in a few miles may prefer the more relaxing two-way journey ($32). If the resort is your main stop, you may also make time for Ziptrek Ecotours (tremblant.ziptrek.com) with its five-cable course and longest runs in Québec.

02 At the T-intersection, you'll take a right into the forest. The path becomes a roller coaster of ups and downs, and the Laurentian Mountains will loom large beyond the evergreen spires. This route is well paved and popular, but the deeper you go, the fewer cyclists you're likely to see.

03 Follow a hairpin turn toward the Devil's River, where you'll cross the wood planks of a pedestrian bridge. Continue down the path, which will now follow the river's gentle rapids on your right.

04 At the three-way intersection, veer right, keeping to the river. You can technically go either way, since the path forms a circle, but many prefer this counterclockwise route. Coast down a curving slope under a highway bridge, known as Pont Beauvallon, and follow the undulating landscape eastward.

05 The bridge that crosses the Devil's River is one of the most gorgeous spots on this route. The lumber-covered floor is plenty wide, and high wood guardrails rise on either side. Crossing the bridge isn't necessary for this route, but you'd be crazy to skip it; the river rushes below and the banks billow with foliage. If you have time to spare, you'll find additional trails on the other side, which wind their way toward Mt Saint-Bernard.

06 The path turns north and soon intersects with Chemin Duplessis, a busy road that leads into the resort area. The path parallels the road for about 1.5km, then you arrive at Mont-Tremblant's main entrance. There's been some recent construction work on the path, so if you run into orange cones or a 'détour' sign, feel free to take the road instead.

07 At the resort, you'll ride across a wide square, where European-style high rises welcome crowds of skiers in the colder months. You're now halfway through your circuit, so this is a natural place to stop, look around and grab a refreshment. Many riders will treat this as their main destination for the day, thanks to the many summer activities that take place around the resort. Visit the Tremblant Information Center, located on this square, to see what's open. Once you're ready to press on, proceed down the path, which flanks the road Chemin des Voyageurs, toward the waterfront.

08 Lac-Tremblant is a beautiful body of water, and on a calm summer day the glassy surface reflects the mountainous skyline all around. There's a small boardwalk that extends toward the lake; take a moment to ride to the end, where a platform looks out on the peaceful scene. Just around the corner is Parc Plage, a tiny slice of beach that opens during the summer months (late June to late August). Humble though it is, Parc Plage has an on-site lifeguard, just enough sand for sunbathing and lake water deep enough to submerge your body. Entry is a steep $9 for visitors 13 and older, but the lake is a refreshing break for sweaty cyclists who remembered to bring swim gear.

09 If you have some extra energy, a patch of marshland lies directly in front of the resort area; the bike path forms a mini-loop around it, running along Chemin Duplessis and Chemin des Voyageurs. You'll cover some of the same ground, but the views of the buildings, mountains and cattails are worth another lap – and some snapshots.

10 Pedal away from the resort, along Chemin des Saisons. The path breaks away from the road and re-enters the forest. You'll pass the manicured lawns of a golf course, Golf Le Géant, on your left, but trees quickly swallow up your view. Ride until you reach the same three-way intersection, this time taking a right, back toward the town of Mont-Tremblant.

11 The paths back to Lake Mercier should look familiar now, but as the saying goes: what goes up must come down. The ride through town is a long downhill route, and you can pick up a lot of speed on this smooth path. The descent is blissful, and on low-traffic days you might forego the path altogether and just bomb down the road.

☕ Take a break

The Mont-Tremblant ski village boasts a healthy dining scene, with everything from pubs to pizzerias to sushi. A standout is LA DIABLE MICROBRASSERIE (microladiable.com), a brewpub with a nice selection of craft beers, ciders and cocktails. Carnivores will scarf down La Diable's lamb and bison burgers, and the fillet of grilled salmon is a particular treat. This spot is open every day and located about 130m down the main street from the resort's entrance.

Mont-Tremblant bike path

56 BEST BIKE RIDES: CANADA

Vélo Mont-Tremblant

Riders in Mont-Tremblant are wise to affix some thick tires, because this little district is beloved for its mountain biking. The forests yield a vast web of dirt paths and singletrack, much of which overlaps with the paved bike trail. To find this network in its entirety – and connect with local riders – check out Vélo Mont-Tremblant *(velomontremblant.com)*. Here you'll find comprehensive maps, racing clubs and up-to-the-minute trail reports. In the Laurentians, mountain biking is a four-season pursuit, thanks to fat bikes and a diehard off-roading community. Many routes are gentle, but more demanding rides require technical skill.

06

Old Québec

Best for

HISTORY

St Louis Gate

DURATION	DIFFICULTY	DISTANCE	START/END
80 mins	Moderate	11km	Montcalm

TERRAIN	Paved streets and paths

In short, Québec is one of the most beautiful cities in North America. The atmosphere of Vieux-Québec (the Old City) feels more like musketeer-era France than modern Canada, and travelers come from around the world to stroll these narrow streets and admire the preserved architecture. It's also a great city to explore by bicycle, thanks to its manageable size, ample bike paths and mesmerizing maze of blocks. This route will acquaint you with Québec's historic center, as well as parks and trails along the gorgeous St Lawrence River.

Bike Hire

àVélo was the first bike-share system in North America with a fully electric fleet; just download the app. For more traditional rentals, visit Cyclo Services *(cycloservices.net)* down the hill on Rue St-Paul.

Starting Point

Get situated on the sidewalk of Rue St-Louis, in the fashionable Montcalm neighborhood. Fuel up with breakfast and coffee at one of the many local eateries.

01 Montcalm is a great place to headquarter in the city – you're situated among cafes, global restaurants and a row of affordable hotels. It's also an ideal place to start your circuit around Old Québec. Set your wheels on the pavement of Rue St-Louis and aim your handlebars east. Traffic is busy but slow in this bohemian neighborhood, and you'll start by rolling downhill. Conserve your energy, though: you'll have some big climbs at the end of this route.

Elevation (m)

Distance (km)

02 Before you leave the neighborhood, hang a left onto Blvd Honoré-Mercier. You can't miss it, as the road enters a park area directly in front of Québec's palatial Parliament Building. Make a trip around the traffic circle and admire the elegant Fontaine de Tourny. While this fountain was originally cast in 1855 and perfectly fits the antique ambiance, it was first installed in this spot in 2007, after a rigorous restoration process, to celebrate the city's 400th anniversary.

03 About 100m further down Rue St-Louis, you'll pass beneath the castle-like St Louis Gate. You can fly through this stone masterpiece without a second thought, but do consider (carefully) taking an immediate left, into Esplanade Park. Here you can roll your bike up a ramp onto the old wall, which offers a nice preview of the Québec skyline. These walls once protected the upper city; below, the stone structure built into the grassy hill is the old powder magazine. These former ramparts are worth a short stroll, though riding on the wall is not permitted. While you're admiring the battlements, you may consider a stop at the Citadelle. This star-shaped bastion stands on Québec City's highest hill, looking as imposing as it did in the 18th century. The museum inside (adult/teen/child $22/8/free) contains thousands of military artifacts, from the colonial period to the present day, as well as rebuilt walls and barracks. For cyclists, even the outside is a pleasure to explore; paths snake their way around the former moat, so you can take an extra spin around this panoramic prominence.

04 Zoom down Rue St-Louis, into the Old City. This is where Québec really starts working its magic: a cyclist could spend hours exploring these narrow backstreets and ogling the centuries-old facades. This main street curves past rows of bistros and shops, and you should find it easy to keep up with staggered motor traffic. Note that these 17th-century streets have no shoulders at all, and cyclists are not permitted on the sidewalks. On busy summer days, this corridor is flooded with tourists on foot – and a good number of fellow cyclists – so be mindful of people in the street as you proceed into Québec's dense center.

05 The Place d'Armes is a splendid old park across from the Château Frontenac, and you might call it the 'middle' of Old Québec, as several major streets converge around it. This is another great place to stop, get your bearings and people-watch. Later, you'll likely

BEST BIKE RIDES: CANADA

☕ Take a break

BRASSERIE INOX *(brasserieinox.com)* is one of the pillars of Montcalm nightlife, and a wide range of patrons convene here for superlative craft beers, greasy treats and hockey games on giant TVs. A favorite local haunt since 1987, INOX is a fitting place to celebrate your ride around town. Yet you could also start here; the restaurant opens at 11am on most days (Mondays at 3pm), so you're welcome to house a European hotdog or vegan chili before you venture out.

want to come back here to browse shops and take in Québec's animated nightlife scene.

06 The most hair-raising segment on this loop is cruising around Côte de la Montagne (Mountainside St) which cuts a dramatic boomerang down a steep slope. Squeeze those brakes: this incline is no joke, and drivers tend to accelerate fast up this hill. In just a few blocks, you'll pass a half-dozen remarkable sites. Seconds before you turn onto Côte de la Montagne, you'll breeze past the Notre Dame de Québec Basilica Church on your left. As you gain momentum, you'll fly beneath the understated Prescott Gate, which also serves as a pedestrian bridge; tourists will likely wave or snap pictures from above. Ease around the tight curve, where you'll spot the Escalier Casse-Cou on your right; this picturesque stairway is a shortcut to the car-free shopping district below. In the final stretch, you'll see the Québec City Mural covering an entire wall. This photorealistic painting by 12 local artists depicts different characters from the city's history, and it blends so seamlessly into the urban landscape that it's earned the French name *Trompe l'Oeil* (Optical Illusion).

07 Now it's time to take a spin along the Québec City waterfront. Turn left onto Rue Dalhousie, being careful as you cross this busy motorway. Follow the bike lane until you reach the water, when the lane intersects with the Rue du Littoral (Coastal Way), a bike path that parallels the shore. Turn left onto this path, then follow it around the block and back along the street. The Rue du Littoral will quickly lead you into the Vieux-Port, a former industrial area that has been transformed into a grassy public park. In the warmer months, you can stroll around the urban gardens of Jardins du Bassin Louise; otherwise, the Vieux-Port is a nice place to sit down, have a snack and view the ranks of boats in the marina across the water. This park is your halfway point; from here, you'll start a circuitous journey back.

08 Backtrack through the Vieux-Port, along the Rue du Littoral and down Rue Dalhousie. You'll bike past the Place de Canotier (Boaters' Plaza), a park and boardwalk on the water; on hot days, children charge through the expansive splash pad. The bike path twists its way along the Rue des Traversiers, until it begins to parallel Boulevard Champlain.

Dufferin Terrace and Château Frontenac

Château Frontenac

The most iconic landmark in French Canada is the Château Frontenac, the fairy tale–like hotel built in 1893 by the Canadian Pacific Railway. With its high walls and many conical roofs, the château looms high above the old city and is visible from miles away. The complex remains an active luxury destination, with 610 guest rooms and suites, but you are free to admire its epic architecture from the Dufferin Terrace, a sprawling promenade out front. The terrace boasts six gazebos, tower viewers and the upper station of the Funiculaire cable car. The views here are among the best in the province.

Funiculaire

No visit to Québec City is complete without a ride on the Funiculaire. This little train system carries passengers up and down a 59m slope, from the Château Frontenac to the car-free Rue du Petit Champlain below. Designed by William Griffith, this two-track system has operated continuously since 1879, though the mechanism changed from water-balance to electric in 1909. You are technically allowed to bring your bicycle aboard, though it's usually too crowded inside the little car. Not to worry; the ride takes less than a minute each way, and you can lock your bike on the street.

Funiculaire

09 Boulevard Champlain is one of the most important roads in Québec City, and it follows the river for nearly 7km, running between the Pierre Laporte Bridge and Samuel de Champlain Promenade, downtown. The bike path follows suit, cutting a straight line between unvarnished industrial parks (on your left) and wooded cliffs (on your right). Like the Fontaine de Tourny, this bikeway was installed to commemorate the city's quadricentennial.

10 After about 3.5km of straightforward riding, you'll arrive at a minor cross-street called Rue de l'Anse au Foulon. Turn right to cross Boulevard Champlain; here, l'Anse au Foulon becomes Côte Gilmore, a street that climbs the hill back to Montcalm. But there's no need to huff up this steep, narrow motorway; the bike path breaks off to the right, toward a convenient bike ramp. Before you pedal away, though, check out the Escalier du Bois-de-Coulonge (Coulonge Woods Staircase). This stairway has 294 steps in all and cuts through the forest, making for a pretty picture.

11 The path will take you east, in the direction you came from, for about 300m, when you'll turn onto a ramp up the hill. Follow an acute S-curve, feeling the burn as you go. One good thing about this relatively tough climb is that the view of the river gets better as you go higher. Watch out for cyclists going the opposite way; it's easy to pick up speed, and there are several blind spots.

12 At the T-intersection, turn left. You are welcome to keep right; the path continues due east, and this route takes you on a pleasant pedal through the trees. But veering left leads directly to the Plains of Abraham, where you can complete your circuit.

13 Today, the Plains of Abraham is a pleasant public park crosshatched with paths. The grounds are carefully landscaped, and joggers and picnickers take advantage of the benches and mown lawns throughout the spring and summer. Small children could bike in circles around this park all day, and anyone can enjoy the stone viewpoint in the southeast corner, which opens up on the St Lawrence River below. What isn't obvious to a passing cyclist is that the Plains of Abraham was also an important battlefield, where French and British armies fought for control of the Citadelle. It was here that French forces were defeated after an hour of fighting on September 13, 1759, which signaled the slow collapse of New France and eventual founding of Canada. You might ponder the significance of this fateful ground as you wrap up your ride, or you may just enjoy the view of Québec's handful of skyscrapers. The standout: the Hôtel de Concorde Québec, a concrete tower with a rotating restaurant at the top.

14 Back in Montcalm, celebrate a successful excursion with a gourmet meal and a craft beer from a local brasserie. You'll have plenty to choose from.

TOP TIP:
E-bikes

Québec City is exactly the kind of place e-bikes were made for. Québec's hills are long and steep, and a little pedal-assist goes a long way. At the very least, traditional cyclists should bring a bike with dynamic gearing.

☕ Take a break

You could spend weeks eating your way through Vieux-Québec, though its restaurant scene skews toward haute-cuisine. Peckish cyclists may drop into LE BUFFET DE L'ANTIQUAIRE *(lebuffetdelantiquaire.com)*, an old-school diner on Rue St-Paul, just a stone's throw from the Vieux-Port. This place has red leather booths and a row of stools along the counter, but the grub is top-notch: Feast on eggs benedict, meatball-infused *ragoût de boulettes* and decadent slices of cake. On hot days, the milkshakes are divine.

07

Best for

FOOD

Lachine Canal

DURATION	DIFFICULTY	DISTANCE	START/END
2hrs	Easy	31km	CNR Wellington Bridge

TERRAIN	Mostly paths, some streets

Lachine Canal

Montréal has earned a global reputation for cycling, thanks to a sophisticated grid of protected lanes and multi-use paths. The largest city in Québec is a glittering metropolis of skyscrapers, public parks and cafe-lined streets. Montréal's cycling superhighway is the Lachine Canal, a smoothly paved bike trail that runs on both sides of the historic waterway. Once a throbbing industrial corridor, the Canal Lachine is now a buzzing linear park. Each summer day, thousands of cyclists pedal from one end to the other, but ambitious riders can continue along the verdant banks of the St Lawrence River.

Bike Hire

Download the Bixi app *(bixi.com)* to access the city's popular bike-share system. For a more traditional rental, Ma Bicyclette *(mabicyclette.ca)* is located right on the bike path.

Starting Point

Montréal is so well connected with bike routes, you could start anywhere in or around the city. The eastern tip of the Lachine Canal makes for a natural kickoff.

01 Get your bike ready on the north side of the canal. Before you start, look across the water at the Farine Five Roses sign; this massive advertisement was first put up in 1948, and it's one of the most iconic landmarks in southwest Montréal. Five Roses Flour is still a major Canadian company, and the sign speaks to the Lachine Canal's industrial past.

Elevation (m)

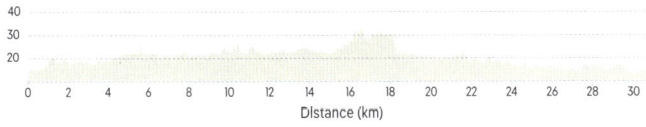

French artist Ankhone. You will pass this massive artwork on your right; you can circle the building to see this jazzy abstract painting in its entirety.

06 Cross the narrow Atwater Footbridge to the south side of the canal. This bridge is usually busy with urban dwellers, thanks to the nearby Marché Atwater. It's also pedestrian-only, so make sure to dismount and walk your bike down the designated lane.

07 At the Côte-St-Paul Lock, you'll cross the canal again, riding over an island to reach the north side of the canal. This lock isn't quite as glamorous or well trafficked as St-Gabriel, but it works great for fording the waterway.

08 The next 5km are flat and straight, giving you ample time to take in the postindustrial greenscape. This corridor ushered in the Industrial Revolution in Montréal, and the row of factories produced everything from nails to timber to granulated sugar. Many of these buildings are husks of their former selves, though manufacturing still hums along the canal.

02 As you ride southwest, you'll spot an island on your left with rusted steel trestles; this is CNR Wellington Bridge, which used to turn sideways to facilitate passage for both trains and barges. It's one of many striking spans you'll spot on your ride.

03 Head west, down the trail. In summer, this two-lane bikeway is mobbed with riders. Follow cycling etiquette and be conscious of those around you, especially in the first few kilometers. You're likely to spot clusters of kayakers paddling down the waterway as well.

04 The St-Gabriel Lock is perhaps the most famous of the canal's five locks. The machinery still works flawlessly, raising and lowering the water level, and the central island has been converted into a park area that hosts regular gatherings and events.

05 Hangar 1825 is an old industrial building along the river that is now covered in a four-sided mural by

09 At Dollard Ave, you'll cross the canal one last time. A ramp takes you onto the highway bridge and across the water; take a moment to appreciate the Gauron Bridge and LaFleur Bridge, whose steel structures were built next to each other in 1912 and 1959. These former bascule bridges are now permanently lowered, but they

BEST BIKE RIDES: CANADA   **65**

☕ Take a break

True to its name, the art-infused coffeehouse CAFE MA BICYCLETTE attracts a steady stream of cyclists, and not just because there's a sizable rack outside. The spotless cafe has cozy indoor and outdoor seating in the summer, and the menu is thick with quality coffees and nibbles (the vegetarian bahn mi is to die for). It's located right on the trail, so you can grab a quick refresher and spend hours among likeminded riders. If the name rings a bell, these are the same folks who rent bikes just a half-kilometer down the way.

could once be raised 50m in the air in only three minutes.

10 For the next 2km, follow the south side of the canal to Chemin du Musée (Museum Trail), a busy motorway that effectively marks the end of the Lachine Canal. But the fun is far from over: the path continues into René Lévesque Park, a peninsula that thrusts a further 1.5km into the St Lawrence River.

11 The park is a narrow strip of land dotted with trees and sculptural works. Perhaps the most famous public art project is the boot-shaped *Site/Interlude*, composed of boulders and metal frames, by Irish-born artist David Moore. Pedal to the end of the path, where it turns 180 degrees, back toward the city. Here you'll find an opening in the shrubbery with a view of the St Lawrence and a couple of benches. This viewpoint faces west, and if you time it right, it's a splendid place to watch a waning sun.

12 To keep things simple, many riders may decide to ride back along the Lachine Canal. They already know the way, and it's easy cycling back to the starting point. Others may even call an Uber, satisfied with the ground they've covered. But some of the best sights on this circuit are yet to come; once you double back along René Lévesque Park, take a right onto the bike path that runs alongside Chemin du Musée.

13 Chemin du Musée feeds into Blvd LaSalle, and the bike path will parallel the boulevard for the next 11.5km. The first leg is a blissful ride through wooded parkland, a nice blend of trees and sod. One word of caution: in summer, this route is known for its shadflies (also known as mayflies). These moth-sized bugs swarm around the riverbank and dive-bomb into shirts and faces. They don't bite, and they have little interest in people, but you're wise to wear sunglasses and keep your mouth closed.

14 As you ride parallel to Blvd La Salle, consider a pause at Quenneville Bay, a tiny inlet that lies at the end of the Canal l'Aqueduc. There's a pretty wooded area here, La Béhane Park, and a boardwalk that extends into the water. You can walk your bike to the end of this walkway, where an observation deck looks out on the bay. (This is another favorite spot for sunsets.) Across the park is the headquarters for Rafting Montreal *(raftingmontreal.com)*, a popular white-water tour company.

Lachine Lock

The Lachine Lock

At the western end of the canal is the Lachine Lock, the anchor point of several surrounding parks. You can lock up and stretch, or you could cross the bridge to Monk Park, a pleasant green space that occupies its own little island. Go straight along Chemin Iroquois and you'll find the end of a narrow peninsula, with its photogenic views of the water. The illuminating Musée de Lachine is close by, but it was closed for renovation at the time of research.

Verdun City Beach

This little crescent of sand looks like it's been here forever, as do the crowds of swimmers on a sweltering afternoon, but the city installed this beach in 2021. Sunning here and wading in the St Lawrence are free, and a lifeguard supervises during the warmer months. There are several places to lock up your bike nearby, and if you've pedaled this full circuit under a high sun, goodness knows you deserve a dip. The park around it is attractively laid out, and you're just a few blocks away from some of this neighborhood's coolest brasseries.

Verdun City Beach

15 The path will pass Vague à Guy, one of the most magical spots along the St Lawrence River. Vague à Guy is often translated as the Eternal Wave, and this small stretch of water ripples in just the right way, mimicking a swelling wave. This is a favorite destination for surfers, who can paddle out and pop up on their boards, standing upright for minutes at a time. River surfing is popular across Canada, and Vague à Guy is so close to the riverbank that spectators will gather to watch surfers hang ten. The viewpoint is right on the bike path, with benches set up.

16 At about the halfway point down Blvd La Salle, you'll find a large stone cottage, the Maison Nivard-de-St-Dizier *(maisonnivard-de-saint-dizier.com)*. First built in 1710, the house is a prime example of French Colonial architecture, and it contains a well-curated history museum with rotating special exhibits. The museum is free to enter and worth a visit; but if you're in the zone and don't feel like stopping, the exterior makes for a nice picture on the go.

17 The path curves around the Verdun Dancing Terrace, a popular pavilion where scores of people come together to try out salsa, bachata and tango. You'll hear the music long before you see the dancers, and you can expect to spot a class in session on any warm day. Many of the sessions are free, and if you arrive at the start, you can lock up your bike and join in.

18 After about 11km along the Blvd La Salle, arrive in Verdun, a vibrant neighborhood on the edge of the St Lawrence. The main attraction on a summer day is Verdun Beach, but this park is full of other activities as well: a skate park, basketball court, baseball diamond, bocce course, outdoor swimming pool and dog run, among other amenities. The bike path runs past the Verdun Auditorium, a storied venue for hockey games, and finally intersects with Blvd Gaétan LaBerge, which marks the end of the St Lawrence River Trail.

19 Take Rue Gilberte-Dubé one block west, where you turn right on Wellington St. Follow the bike route (both lanes on the right side of the street) for 2.5km until you again reach the Lachine Canal.

20 Ride over the Wellington Bridge, the still-operational motorway next to the CNR Wellington Bridge. Use the bike lane as you cross, then follow the ramp to the bike path. You're now back where you started. This little area is well trafficked and often hosts festivals and events, but it's not a dependable place to celebrate. Hungry? You can ride just a couple more blocks to Rue Notre-Dame, a multi-neighborhood corridor full of dining and nightlife. If you still have energy to burn, you could also ride Rue Commune straight into Old Montréal, the city's cultural heart. Finally, you could head northeast, through the industrial zone of Cité du Havre, toward the islands of Île Notre-Dame and St Helen's Island. Both islands are connected by bike-accessible bridges, and the paths just keep on going.

TOP TIP:
On the Metro

One way to zip around Montréal is by metro, and cyclists are usually allowed to transport their bikes in the rearmost car. You may run into problems at rush hour or holidays; try to time your subway rides during off-peak hours.

☕ Take a break

The longtime nexus of the Little Burgundy district is MARCHÉ ATWATER, an art deco marketplace dating back to 1933. Unlike so many institutions in southwest Montréal, this busy complex was always a market, and vendors have continuously bagged fine meats, farm-fresh produce and aromatic flower bouquets from these very stalls. The market is a place to warm up and sip steaming drinks in the winter. Vendors spill out into the parking area to sell wares in the bike-friendly months. Just a short distance from the Lachine Canal, this place is the ideal spot to fuel up.

Also Try...

PIERRE DESROSIERS/SHUTTERSTOCK

P'tit Train du Nord

DURATION	DIFFICULTY	DISTANCE
4½hrs	Moderate	83km

The 'Li'l Train of the North' may sound adorable, but this rail trail is formidable: the full bike route runs 234km from urban Montréal through the Laurentian Mountains, including a stretch through Mont-Tremblant. The rolling forests and glassy lakes make much of this landscape feel like true wilderness.

A complete journey takes most riders three or four days, but if you don't have that time to spare, a celebrated segment lies between the villages of Mont Laurier and La Macaza. This sylvan wonderland is beloved for its railroad artifacts, winding gravel surfaces and enchanting mountain views. Both Macaza and Mont Laurier have a range of accommodations; you can bike from one town to the other or sample smaller stretches in between.

Île d'Orléans

DURATION	DIFFICULTY	DISTANCE
3½hrs	Moderate	67km

Île d'Orléans (pictured above) is an island just downstream from Québec City. Its western shore is so close to the city that you get a splendid view of the downtown skyline. The island is beloved for its whitewashed colonial villages and many vineyards, and the smoothly paved perimeter road is a real treat for road cyclists.

A full loop will take most of a riding day, and you'll have to share the two-lane highway with passing cars and trucks. But the pace here is also pleasant and relaxed; autoroute 368 roughly traces the island's shores, and two-wheeled travelers are treated to gentle climbs and descents through gorgeous farmland. For an abbreviated route, you can take an inland shortcut along Rte du Mitan.

PAOLO BOSIO/SHUTTERSTOCK

Estriade

DURATION	DIFFICULTY	DISTANCE
5hrs	Easy	99km

The Estriade bike path connects Granby to Waterloo, but the full route is much longer, extending to the sizable town of St-Jean-Sur-Richelieu. If you're already staying in Granby, consider this long westward ride through Québec's countryside.

Converted from an old railroad line, the Estriade is basically flat and ramrod straight from Granby to the little town of Farnham. There, the path's direction shifts a few degrees and continues directly to St-Jean-Sur-Richelieu. You'll travel a good distance – a 'metric century,' if you cycle the whole way and back – but the riding is nearly effortless, and the scenery is as peaceful as a landscape painting. The Estriade is also handy for bike-touring across the province, and St-Jean-Sur-Richelieu is a handy place to spend the night.

Parque National de la Jacques-Cartier

DURATION	DIFFICULTY	DISTANCE
25mins	Moderate	6km

Just 40 minutes by car from Québec City, the forested river valley of the Parc National de la Jacques Cartier (pictured above) is a multisport playground. Locals love this national park for its rich woods, frothing rivers and lattice of hiking trails.

Cyclists can ramble all through the park, by smooth road or dirt path. A nice place to start is the Discovery and Visitors Center, a cozy structure with restrooms, a general store and ample parking. A smooth motorway takes you north to the confluence of the Jacques Cartier and Sautauriski Rivers; veer along the Sautauriski, where the road turns to dirt, then into a riverside trail. To get the most out of this route, a mountain or gravel bike is ideal.

Mahone Bay (p82)

Nova Scotia

08 Salt Marsh to Atlantic Trail
A ride through history and nature on a combination of two trails taking in the beautiful Salt Marsh landscape, over causeways surrounded by water that is vibrant with birdlife, to finish at a beach popular with surfers at the end of the Atlantic Trail. **p76**

09 Bay to Bay Trail
On the journey end of the longer Rum Runners Trail, the Bay to Bay Trail is a scenic, tree-lined multi-use trail that links the colorful, UNESCO-listed town of Lunenburg to the lively community of Mahone Bay, with some remnants of the old railway en route. **p80**

10 Landscapes of Grand Pré
This is an easy day ride on a former rail line between Kentville and Grand Pré; experience the power of the tidal waters and learn the culture and agricultural heritage of the Acadians, with opportunities to stop for wine tasting and great dining around Wolfville. **p84**

BEST BIKE RIDES: CANADA

Explore

Nova Scotia

There is a lot to love about Nova Scotia, the heart of Atlantic Canada, with its varied landscape and 13,300km of coastline. The soft white sandy beaches on the Atlantic shores, the rolling hills and coastal cliffs of Cape Breton Island, the lush agricultural landscape of the Annapolis Valley and the forests and lakes of the mountainous inland all wrap around the history and heritage of Mi'kmaq, Celtic, Acadian and modern settler cultures. Among all of these wonders are some great cycling adventures. From former railways to epic cycling routes, there is a bike ride for every cyclist in Nova Scotia.

Halifax

Most international visitors are likely to arrive in Halifax, Nova Scotia's capital, as their first port of call. Its international airport has connections to Europe and the US and is a major cruise stop, as well. It's the hub of tourism, commerce and transport for the province.

Although populous, Halifax has the charm of a smaller town and a strong sense of community. The city is friendly and well serviced by public transport in and around the center. It is also the main hub of Nova Scotia's long-distance Maritime Bus network (maritimebus.com).

There are a range of accommodations options from budget lodging to luxury hotels, and plenty of museums, historical landmarks, parks and galleries to explore for a couple of days. The lively waterfront boardwalk is packed with boutique shops, markets, cafes, bars and restaurants. Downtown Halifax offers more galleries and museums, including Halifax Citadel, with arguably the best view of the city.

Lunenburg

Popular for its colorful fishers' houses and UNESCO heritage status, Lunenburg was once a hub for rum-smuggling operations during the Prohibition era. A Maritime Bus service connects Lunenburg with Halifax once a day, although most visitors come by coach on a day tour from Halifax. It is worthwhile staying here for the night, to enjoy the quiet mornings and sunset hours on the harbor after everyone leaves. There are a number of museums and art galleries in town, or take

WHEN TO GO

Traditionally, May to October is the best time to visit Nova Scotia, when the Atlantic climate is warmer and stable, and cycling facilities and services are open. The tourist season peaks in the heat of midsummer in the months of July and August, when wild fires can affect the region, so it is best to follow any warnings issued by the local government.

the opportunity to sail on the Bluenose II ship for a scenic trip on the water.

Lunenburg is a great base to cycle the Rum Runners Trail, a multi-use trail created along the railway that was once at the heart of the smuggling operation (p81). There is also a gravel trail leading toward Bridgewater where there are several other heritage trails. The excellent bike shop in town has quality bikes for hire and recommendations for a day's ride.

Guesthouses and motel-style accommodations are available in and on the edge of town, and there is a wide selection of dining venues from excellent seafood restaurants to a lovely sushi eatery and European-style bakery. There's an array of boutiques, two supermarkets for self-catering holidaymakers, and a weekly farmers market (May to September) for fresh local produce.

TRANSPORT

Most people visiting Nova Scotia will hire a car, although it is possible to travel around by public transit. If you use Halifax as a base, Maritime Bus has a good network of long-distance journeys around Nova Scotia, with most services able to take your bicycle as long as it is packed in a bag. It is recommended to book your tickets online prior to your trip.

 WHAT'S ON

Gran Fondo Baie Sainte-Marie

(granfondobaiesaintemarie.ca/en) The only regular cycling event in Nova Scotia cycles through the coastal villages along the shores of Saint Mary's Bay in the Municipality of Clare.

Halifax Busker Festival

(buskers.ca) One of the most fun and colorful of the many festivals held throughout the summer months.

Lunenburg Folk Harbor Festival

(folkharbour.com) Folk music by the sea.

 WHERE TO STAY

In larger cities and towns like Halifax and Lunenburg, there's a range of accommodations options for all budgets. Book early at these popular hot spots as they are likely to be full well in advance. In smaller towns like Kentville, accommodations will mostly be in motels or private rental and guesthouses, which can be a more personal experience with friendly hosts who can advise you on what to do and where to eat.

For the more adventurous, there is a network of both national and private camp sites around the province, some with cabins for a glamping experience.

Resources

Tourism Nova Scotia
(novascotia.com) General travel information and itinerary inspiration on Nova Scotia.

Cycling Nova Scotia
(cyclingns.ca) A local organization and community of cyclists to promote cycling, organize events and advice on cycling around the province.

Maritime Bus *(maritimebus.com)* A good bus network around Nova Scotia.

08
Salt Marsh to Atlantic Trail

Salt Marsh Trail

DURATION	DIFFICULTY	DISTANCE	START/END
1½hrs	Easy	20.4km	Salt Marsh Trail Head

TERRAIN			Gravel

The Musquodoboit Railway that crosses the Cole Harbour salt-marsh landscape once transported industrial and material goods and passengers between Dartmouth and surrounding rural areas to Musquodoboit Valley. After the decommissioning of the railway, the causeway on the shallow waters of the estuary became a protected landscape, and is home to a diverse range of wildlife. From the salt marshes to the sandy beaches of the Atlantic, this out-and-back bike ride combines the best of two of Nova Scotia's popular rail trails, which form part of the overall Trans Canada Trail.

Bike Hire
Hire your bike from I Heart Bikes *(iheartbikeshfx.com)* on the Halifax waterfront with prices starting from $60 for the day for a hybrid bike. Road, gravel and e-bikes are also available.

Starting Point
The Salt Marsh Trail begins at its junction with Bisset Rd at Cole Harbour, with a small car park at the trail head and links with Cole Harbour Heritage Trails.

01 From the car park, head east and follow the tree-lined trail for about 500m. This is a lovely introduction to one of Nova Scotia's favorite trails on the former railway.

02 The beauty of the Salt Marsh Trail soon comes into view as you approach the first causeway across this marshland, where trees begin to thin and water is seen on each side of the path. At this point, there is a small picnic area, a

Elevation (m)

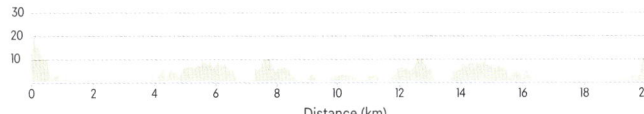

The Blueberry Express

Despite being mainly used for transportation of beach gravel, limestone, forestry/sea products and general merchandise for the communities, the Musquodoboit Railway was nicknamed Blueberry Express for the baskets of blueberries from the surrounding farms that were being transported for sale in Dartmouth and Halifax. Is it also believed that, as wild blueberries are abundant in the region, when the train made slow progress with many stops along the way, the passengers would rush off the train to pick blueberries from nearby bushes. Look around the woodland areas – you may still find bushes of wild blueberries.

toilet and another information board to tell you more about the history of the Cole Harbor Salt Marsh.

03 You are now cycling through the special environment of the salt marsh, where the meeting of land and water creates a landscape that supports a unique ecosystem. Normally filled with freshwater, the marsh is flooded by saltwater from the coast twice daily, inviting a diverse range of wildlife that is on show here.

04 Several causeways, along with short bridges, link the small islands across the marsh. Follow this one as it weaves a curly line across the water. From herons to geese to warblers to eagles, it is worth taking it slow to enjoy the array of birdlife that inhabits this environment.

05 While you are cycling on the causeway, there are several interpretation panels along the way providing wildlife, historical and environmental information. They are great to give you new perspective on the surrounds.

06 After roughly 3km of pedaling along the causeway, the Salt Marsh Trail enters another tranquil woodland section with water views on the left. The trail officially concludes at a road junction with W Lawrencetown Rd, which is marked with a trail board on the side. This is a good point to turn back along the Salt Marsh should you wish to return to the start. The next part of this ride will begin across the road where the Atlantic View Trail immediately begins.

07 Cross the road carefully (beware of incoming cars) and join the Atlantic View Trail by cycling through the named wooden gate. This once abandoned railway bed formed the part of the Musquodoboit Railway that joined onto the section with Salt Marsh Trail, providing access to the sea as well as more woodland communities beyond.

08 You'll notice a slight difference in climate along this part of the ride – as you get closer to the coast, the air is cooler and the surroundings lusher. The beginning of this trail takes you across a body of water that is still part of the marshes, often alive with ducks on both sides as you approach a small farm on a small hill to your right. Ride at leisure past the farm until you come to a road junction. Carefully cross the road here and continue along the trail.

09 Take a slow meander along this section that is lined by trees until you come across another road junction. Keep your eyes and ears open for birds of prey circling this section in the sky. At the road, cross with care. You are almost there.

10 The trail takes you across another body of water connected by a bridge. This is part of the estuary that flows out to sea. Ahead of you stretch the beaches on the Atlantic, giving the trail its name, although at this point the view is blocked by sand dunes between you and the water. To get there, you'll need to cross a busy road. The trail continues on the other side.

11 Another wooden gate marking the Atlantic View Trail welcomes you to Lawrencetown Beach. To your right is the beautiful sandy beach. Stop here for a refreshment break or to relax on the beach a little. Bike racks are available near a sandy path to the beach by the surf school, where there is also a small food kiosk and toilets. The Atlantic View Trail continues along the coast to eventually end at Duncan's Cove Beach several kilometers later. Those with extra energy can continue to explore.

12 When you are ready, follow the same way back, first along the Atlantic View Trail and then joining back onto Salt Marsh Trail to return to the start.

☕ Take a break

Bring enough water and snacks with you for the journey before you reach the trail head at Salt Marsh Trail, as there are no refreshment stops until you reach the beaches. If the surf school is open, there is a small kiosk selling cold drinks and snacks at the end of the Atlantic Trail at Lawrencetown Beach. There is also a public toilet here. Note the kiosk is cash only.

Salt Marsh heron

A Paradise for Birds

The estuary around the Salt Trail, washed with both fresh and saltwater and surrounded by woodlands, is alive with birds and other wildlife. This is one of the best places for bird-watchers with ducks, mallards and geese that take advantage of the safe and biodiverse landscape all year round. Eagles and ospreys can often be seen circling the sky for prey. Songbirds such as finches and sparrows, and shorebirds such as warblers, sandpipers, yellowlegs, willets, plovers and herons wade the waters and hunt for food, while cormorants and goldeneyes dive for their catch.

09

Bay to Bay Trail

Lunenburg

DURATION	DIFFICULTY	DISTANCE	START/END
2hrs	Moderate	29km	Lunenburg downtown

TERRAIN	Mixed gravel/road

A bike ride that invites you to relive the smuggling days of the Prohibition, this is an easy day ride on a route linking one harbor town to the other, utilizing the Bay to Bay section of the Rum Runners Trail, and returning by road along the coastline to enjoy views across the water. A mostly flat ride with variations of woodland nature and coastal scenery, this is a lovely day out suitable for those more comfortable riding on roads with traffic.

Bike Hire

Rent a bike from the Lunenburg Bike Shop (lunenburgbikeshop.com) from $60 per day, with a range from hybrid, gravel, road and mountain bikes available. E-bikes will cost more.

Starting Point

Start anywhere in center Lunenburg; in this case, in front of the bike shop where there are several access points to the Bay to Bay Trail from town.

01 From the front of the bike shop, ride away from town center and turn left on Kempt St, then right onto Pelham St. There is a slight incline but don't worry, most of the ride will be easy going once you are on the trail.

02 Toward the end of Pelham St, turn left onto Sawpit Rd. In about 150m, you'll see the Bay to Bay Trail cross your path. Turn left onto the trail.

Rum Runners

When Nova Scotia's fishing fleets faced decline in the 1920s and '30s, the province's maritime workers sought alternative ways to earn a living. Around the same time, Prohibition was introduced nationally; under the law, the sale of alcohol was banned in the country, but its export wasn't prohibited. The legal loophole opened a new industry. Fishers and boaters became 'rum runners'.

Taking advantage of the concealed harbors and the established maritime industry along the coast between Halifax and Lunenburg, alcohol was shipped into the United States. A railway link was used to transport the goods between Halifax and Lunenburg.

Elevation (m)

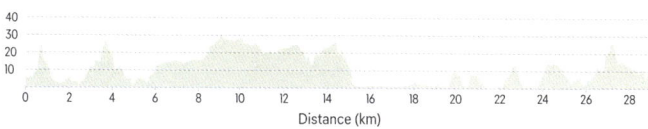

03 You are now on the Bay to Bay Trail, a gravel trail that was once a railway line. This section takes you across Lunenburg's back harbor through residential areas and the quieter side of town.

04 After the trail crosses Kissing Bridge Rd, it curves left as if returning to town. Keep following it until you reach a trail junction, where you will need to make a sharp right-hand turn.

05 Follow the trail until you come to a set of stairs. You will need to get off the bike to navigate the stairs and emerge close to a major road junction of Maple Ave. The trail continues across the road where there is a signboard with information about the trail. Cross the road carefully here to rejoin the trail.

06 After the initial steep descent on a short ramp, the rest of this trail is flat and easy going, lined with a light forest of mostly white birch trees and several creeks along the way.

07 Until Schnares Crossing, the trail follows the main road that leads in and out of Lunenburg. Then it branches into the forests, where it becomes a delightful ride filled with natural scenery for the next 14km.

08 You'll start to notice signs to Mahone Bay to your right, but ignore them. To take full advantage of the Rum Runners Trail and the beauty of the bay, follow the trail, crossing various road junctions that continue to point to Mahone Bay until you come to a trail junction, decorated with skeletons of railway machinery.

09 The trail junction has a large signpost indicating the various destinations you can reach by following the trail in different directions. Follow the trail to the right toward Mahone Bay and Chester.

10 Technically, you are now on the Dynamite Trail, the next section of the Rum Runners Trail from Bay to Bay. It's only a short ride now to the junction with Clearway St. Cross this, continuing until the next junction with Clearland Rd. Turn right onto the road.

11 At the end of Clearland Rd you will find yourself on one end of Mahone Bay's lovely waterfront, with a small car park with flagpoles in front of you and the visitor information building to your right. Turn right, and follow the road to enjoy a nice vista across the bay and the stretch of waterfront houses and docked boats in town.

12 Follow the road until a roundabout, passing two historical churches on your right, and turn left to continue on the main road along the shore. You can now take some free time to explore the town or have a rest by the water.

13 When ready to return, follow the bay's outline to your left and continue on the main road, Lighthouse Route. This scenic route is a delight to bike on but you will be cycling on roads with traffic for the next 8km or so.

14 Following Lighthouse Route, you are treated to a scenic ride all the way back. Take care as you approach Madders Cove. You want to leave the main road and turn left onto Madders Cove Rd, with beaches and water views along the way. Although quieter, it is also narrower, so still keep your guard up for traffic passing.

15 Approaching Hermans Island, turn right onto Hermans Island Rd at the four-way junction. Follow this road for about 1.5km until a sharp right-hand turn. Ignore Prince Inlet Rd, which seems to go straight on, and turn right.

16 This road ends back on Lighthouse Route. Turn left here, then immediately right onto Schnares Crossing Rd so you can rejoin the safety of the trail. Turn left onto the trail and follow it back to Lunenburg.

☕ Take a break

Have water ready for the initial part of the journey as there are no tap or kiosk facilities on the trail. Once you reach Mahone Bay, you can rest and refuel. There are several cafes with outdoor patios so you can keep an eye out on your bike, as well as grocers for picnic supplies. Sit-down meal options are aplenty too, from pizza and barbecue to seafood. There are toilets at the marina.

Lunenburg

Lunenburg

It's hard not to be charmed by the tiered structures and colorful houses of Lunenburg's old town, considered to be the best surviving example of 18th-century British colonial settlement, preserved in its original layout as established in 1753 in North America. Designated as a UNESCO World Heritage site in 1995, citing its Outstanding Universal Value, Lunenburg continues to safeguard and preserve the wooden houses that characterize the town. Consider visiting the Fisheries Museum of the Atlantic on the harbor to learn more about the town's rich maritime history through its fisheries and rum-running legacy.

10

Landscapes of Grand Pré

DURATION	DIFFICULTY	DISTANCE	START/END
2hrs	Easy	32.5km	Kentville downtown

TERRAIN		Gravel

Harvest Moon Trailway

This is an easy, out-and-back bike ride on a former railway that forms the trail end of the longer-distance Harvest Moon Trailway, through the tidal plains of Minas Basin that feeds the fertile UNESCO World Heritage landscape of Grand Pré and its wine region. You'll encounter the tidal system as you ride along the estuary, learn about the Acadians at the Grand-Pré National Historic Site and have the chance to stop by wineries for tasting along the way, and enjoy a bit of dining and shopping at vibrant Wolfville.

Bike Hire

Valley Stove & Cycle (valleystoveandcycle.com) is a bike shop in the heart of Kentville with friendly and knowledgeable staff. The store has bikes for hire, as well as sales of accessories and snacks.

Starting Point

The rail trail begins on an elbow on Justice Way, which is 200m from the town center. For ease, the directions here begin at the bike shop.

01 Once you've got your bike, immediately turn left on the main road at the shop front onto Bridge St. There are no bike lanes here, so watch for traffic during this short stretch. When you see Kings County Museum on your right, pass Webster Ct and turn right onto Justice Way at the next turn.

02 Follow Justice Way until where the road bends, where you'll see the beginning of the rail trail between trees straight ahead, marked by signage that might be hidden behind

The Acadians

From 1680 the Acadians settled at Grand Pré for its potentially fertile salt marshes. For 70 years before their forced exile, the Acadians utilized their knowledge of farming using dykes and the aboiteau wooden sluice system and a drainage network that managed an ever-changing tidal marshland into agricultural farmland, a method known to be the first of its kind in North America.

Since 2012, the landscape of Grand Pré was inscribed on the UNESCO World Heritage list for its unique cultural, agricultural and archaeological elements of the Acadian traditions, and acts as a memorial of their deportation in 1755.

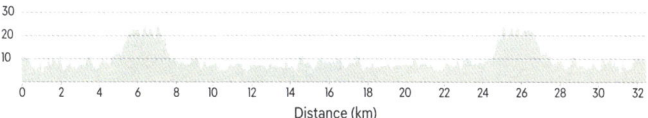

branches. Join the trail here. This is a lovely railway lined by trees at first, then farms to one side most of the time. After crossing a short bridge, follow the trail for about 2km before the landscape opens up to show the beginning of the marshes.

03 As you approach an overhead car crossing, a deep trench created by the tide appears on your left. This is the Cornwallis River. Depending on the time of day, this could be in the form of dried up red earth or mud plain gushing with water from the Basin, a great experience of the landscape that is shaped by one of the most extreme tidal ranges in the world.

04 Continue to follow the trail, which occasionally crosses service roads where you may encounter traffic as you pass by New Minas and its small industrial area. There are no obvious signs of the direction of the trail except for the railway tracks that run along as a reminder of the trail's history. Keep on the gravel trail but do look out for car and truck traffic here.

05 Leaving New Minas there is a short stretch of lovely scenery ahead of you, with the river on your left, and wild, overgrown vegetation on your right. Continue on until the town of Greenwich, where you'll need to cross a road that may be busy with traffic. Take care here.

06 Not far from Wolfville now, the trail will lead you along the back of town with hints of a busy center behind the buildings with a mural of the town and access road to the town center.

07 Unless you are in need of a break, leave visiting Wolfville to your return journey. Continuing on the trail you will come to a wooden viewing point on what was once a dock in Wolfville. There are interesting information boards to tell the story of Wolfville as a shipping community in this tidal mud land. The trail continues at the end of the boardwalk, and for the next section along you'll start to notice detour signs to two wineries that are near the trail. Grand Pré as a wine region may not be well known, but the locals do pride themselves on having the first appellation in Nova Scotia. Pop in for tastings if you like; otherwise continue on the trail to soon reach Grand Pré.

08 The trail ends at the junction with Grand Pré Rd, where you'll find Grand-Pré National Historic Site. There is a small trailside bike maintenance station, and bike parking at the entrance to the site so you can take a couple of hours to visit and learn about the Acadians. There is also a small shop selling water and limited snacks, and toilet facilities in the main building. A short hike up the hill from the site takes you to the landscape of Grand Pré View Park. It is worth the trip as the view is magnificent.

09 When it's time to turn back, return to the rail trail in the reverse direction. The return journey will take you into Wolfville for a short ride along its high street, where you can choose to rest up for a drink or a meal, or to simply soak in the atmosphere and get back to Kentville by rejoining the trail again.

A Surprising Wine Region

Nova Scotia is believed to be Canada's first wine region, although this fact remains unofficial, and grapes are believed to have been grown along the East Coast since 1600s. However, it wasn't until 2012 that the province established its first appellation, Tidal Bay, to signify the crisp white wine produced in the landscape of Grand Pré. The designation is awarded only to wines made from 100 percent Nova Scotia–grown grapes, and will have to pass a blind tasting for its flavor and be approved only if the wine fits the palate profile. Visit Grand Pré Winery, the oldest farm winery in Atlantic Canada, to try this wine.

10 Instead of returning the bike straight away, pay a visit to the Kentville Historical Society on Station Lane, and check out the railway mural on the building of a funeral home opposite. For more time on the bike, the Miner's Marsh Trail is a lovely loop among nature.

☕ Take a break

Wolfville is home to a number of great brewpubs where you can enjoy a cold local beer with delicious seasonal cuisine. Try the KING'S ARMS COMMONS for a good range of local and international beers with a great bistro menu. Do order the lobster roll in season: it is just the fuel you need for the ride back.

Grand-Pré National Historic Site

Also Try...

COLIN D. YOUNG/SHUTTERSTOCK

Cabot Trail

DURATION	DIFFICULTY	DISTANCE
2-4 days	Hard	300km

Considered one of the best rides in the country, this is an epic full road trail that has lured road cyclists to the shores of Cape Breton Highlands (pictured above) with its challenging terrain with breathtaking views. Starting from the town of Baddeck, known to be the home of Alexander Graham Bell, the inventor of the telephone, it follows the road that circles Cape Breton Island, joining coastal towns, harbors and park trails. This is one where you can take as long as you like, as there are accommodations options along the way. Taking your time means you can go for a leisurely swim at the wonderful Ingonish Beach, visit markets, stop for seafood chowder or fresh oysters, and even look for whales off the coast. A must for road cyclists looking for the ride of their lifetime in Nova Scotia.

Rum Runners Trail

DURATION	DIFFICULTY	DISTANCE
1-3 days	Hard	119km

Extending on the Bay to Bay Trail itinerary, the Rum Runners Trail runs from Halifax to Lunenburg and can be attempted in both directions. The seven joined sections that make up the full trail are almost completely flat and sheltered by trees, and the trail takes you along the fishing towns that once worked as a network of smuggling operations during Prohibition.

Choose to smash it out in one day or to slow down and enjoy the views and the seafood. There are sleeping options in most towns along the way, and plenty of culinary experiences to be had. Some tour operators and bike shops offer shuttle services for the one-way journey to make your bike rides stress-free.

DANITA DELIMONT/SHUTTERSTOCK

Northumberland's Coastal Trail

DURATION	DIFFICULTY	DISTANCE
2-3 days	Hard	110km

Starting from the historic town of Pictou where strong Scottish roots are still celebrated, this mostly on-road bike ride journeys through villages, farms, heritage sites, flower meadows and vineyards with coastal views of the Northumberland Strait. Have a night's rest in Tatamagouche, a lively community with galleries, museums and restaurants. Along the route, there are several detour opportunities to visit some of the lesser-visited corners of Northumberland, such as the first rock salt mine in Canada at Malagash Peninsula or a short ride to Cape John, a working lobster harbor, before finishing up at the village of Pugwash, former home of Nobel Peace Laureate Cyrus Eaton, who received the prize for sponsoring an international peace conference calling for nuclear disarmament.

Harvest Moon Trailway

DURATION	DIFFICULTY	DISTANCE
1-3 days	Moderate	110km

The Harvest Moon Trailway is a long-distance bike trail built on a former railbed, connecting the seaside town of Annapolis Royal, home to the first European settlement in North America, to the UNESCO World Heritage site of Grand Pré. An easy flat trail along the Annapolis River passes railway bridges and the picture-perfect towns of Berwick, Kentville and Wolfville (pictured above), with access to many of the area's treasures such as farmers markets and wineries, emphasizing the importance of agriculture in the valley. This is a place rich in Acadian heritage, and several interpretive panels and boards along the way provide stories of local history and culture. This is a beautiful extension to the Landscapes of Grand Pré bike ride.

BEST BIKE RIDES: CANADA

Fundy National Park (p109)

New Brunswick

11 Fundy Trail Parkway

Designed as a top North American scenic drive, the Fundy Trail Parkway was completed in 2019 and is an ideal e-bike route. Even with electric assist, the many hills make it challenging. The scenery on the way out changes on the way back as the world's highest tides surge and ebb in the Bay of Fundy. **p94**

12 Moncton's Riverfront Trail

Moncton's Riverfront Trail out-and-back route will appeal to families. Interpretive signs and small monuments make for an educational ride. Cycling across a marsh beside a muddy river and through mature forest lends itself to family photo opportunities. Ice cream is your reward. **p98**

13 Fredericton Two Rivers Ride

Here's New Brunswick's best urban ride, but with plenty of woods and canopy cover. The first half is an out-and-back riverside city ride. The second half loops on two sides of another river. A former railway trestle separates the two. **p102**

Explore

New Brunswick

With two wildly differing Atlantic Ocean coastlines just 25km apart and a riverside capital city at its heart, New Brunswick's landscape presents a unique set of cycling opportunities. Trail variety is a given. Of the three selected here, one is in a provincial park along clifftops for grand views of the Bay of Fundy where the world's highest tides sculpt the shoreline. The second follows a muddy river over open marsh before plunging into forest. The third parallels city streets and a mighty river across a former railway trestle past taprooms, cafes, shops, museums and historic sites.

St Martins

The community of St Martins is the closest settlement with services to the Fundy Trail Parkway ride. Both are enclosed in the coastal municipality officially known as Fundy-St Martins. A little confusing, but the salient point is that little St Martins, with its campgrounds, country inns and seafood restaurants, is your base for this ride. Historically, it was the sea caves that lured visitors. At low tide with vast swathes of ocean bottom exposed, you can walk over seaweed-carpeted rocks to the caves. At high tide, local company Bay of Fundy Adventures (*bayoffundyadventures.com*) leads kayaking excursions from the tiny port to the caves and beyond. Campgrounds, cozy inns, seafood restaurants and the attractive covered wooden bridge keep visitors here. Begun in 1998 and completed in 2021, today the Fundy Trail Parkway competes as St Martins' biggest draw.

Moncton

New Brunswick's largest city is known for its central location between two distinct coastlines (thus its nickname, Hub City), each with its own unique geological, historical and cultural identity. Because of the Acadian roots of the city and province, you're as likely to be greeted in French as much as English on the streets, in hotels and restaurants, and at attractions. While Moncton has a number of small parks, it's the Riverfront Trail that easily qualifies as the best place to ride a bike. For easy access to the trail and to be closest to the best restaurants and activities other

WHEN TO GO

Peak season is July and August when all attractions are open and restaurants have expanded hours. Accommodations are more expensive and can be fully occupied, so book early. Temperatures are rarely too hot for cycling, but the climate in May, June, September and early October is ideal, and prices are lower than in peak season.

than cycling, it's best to stay within five or ten blocks of the starting point, which is in the downtown area.

Fredericton

The provincial capital's downtown is hugged by a bend in the Saint John River or the Wolastoq ('Beautiful River') in the local Indigenous language. For millennia, the Wolastoqiyik thrived beside these wide, calm waters. Not long after the first settlers arrived in 1785, the strategic location became a British colonial stronghold. Today, those dual roots are exposed at historical sites, heritage buildings and restaurants across the city. As a university town, Fredericton buzzes with a youthful energy that fuels its nightlife, festivals, arts scene and outdoor activities, including cycling. Stay on the riverbend, walking distance from most sights and services, including two bicycle rental shops. Ride straight from a shop to the nearest trail that leads to and over the river.

WHERE TO STAY

From charming country inns to historic B&Bs to national park campgrounds, accommodation options meet every budget and preference, even in tiny St Martins next to the Fundy Trail Parkway. Two of three rides in this chapter begin in cities – Fredericton, the capital, and Moncton – where the options are plentiful, some right on the cycling route. Hotels and other accommodations are more expensive in peak season and can be fully booked. Reserve early or travel outside peak season.

TRANSPORT

The best way to reach New Brunswick is by car from Québec, Maine or Nova Scotia. Flying into Fredericton, Saint John or Moncton, rental cars are available, but may be fully booked in July and August, so book early. It's possible to do bike rides in Moncton and Fredericton without renting a car at the airport.

WHAT'S ON

Harvest Music Festival
(harvestmusicfest.ca) Every September, New Brunswick's biggest festival fills the streets of Fredericton, the capital, with blues, jazz, rock, food and vendors. Whole streets shut down, but the cycling paths are open.

New Brunswick Highland Games
Bagpipes and drums resound across Fredericton every July, warming up athletes in Scottish events like the caber toss and hammer throw.

Resources

Tourism New Brunswick
(tourismnewbrunswick.ca) The official tourism website has mountain-bike and cycling sections.

Moncton (moncton.ca/en) The city's official website is designed for visitors as well as residents.

Fredericton Tourism (frederictoncapitalregion.ca) Has a downloadable trail map.

Fundy Trail Parkway (parcsnbparks.ca/en/parks/35/fundy-trail-provincial-park) This park's website has tide charts and trail details.

11

Fundy Trail Parkway

Best for

COASTAL VIEWS

Fuller Falls

DURATION	DIFFICULTY	DISTANCE	START/END
4hrs	Hard	42km	West kiosk

TERRAIN	Paved road, hills

It's all about the coastal scenery on the Fundy Trail Parkway out-and-back ride that snakes along the edge of the Bay of Fundy where the world's highest tides sculpt the shoreline. From the first kilometer to the last, with views from the many clifftop lookouts down to the beaches and streams, there's no New Brunswick route that offers a higher concentration of 'wow' moments. This is a ride that you'll feel grateful is an out-and-return route because you'll get to experience the views twice, at different stages of the 12-hour tide cycle.

Bike Hire

2nd Wind Cycle (*2ndwindcycle.com*) rents e-bikes at the western entrance to the trail. Riders have to be 16 or older. For younger riders who want mountain bikes, Outdoor Elements outlets in Sussex and Alma are a 40-minute drive away.

Starting Point

Park at 2nd Wind Cycle, 8km from St Martins and half a kilometer before the park's west entrance kiosk. This is an out-and-back route, so you'll end here as well.

01 Departing from the rental shop, round the corner to Fundy Trail Parkway's west kiosk. In high season from late June to late August, the gate opens at 8am and closes at 8pm. From mid-May to late June and late August to mid-October, the hours are 9am to 5pm. Entry is free for cyclists, but report at the kiosk upon arrival. Automobiles must stick to the slow 40km/h speed limit the entire route, and traffic is typically light, so it's a safe cycling environment. You're on an electric bike, so the many hills along the route will be relatively manageable.

Meet the Parkway Champion

Mitchell Franklin saw the potential of what is now the Fundy Trail Parkway long before it became a park. However, he struck out repeatedly in his efforts to convince officials of its many scenic, geological and historic riches. Finally, in 1994, he convinced then premier Frank McKenna to join him on a drive to the end of the gravel road from St Martins at Fox Rock, today the first lookout. It was a glorious day with the sunshine sparkling off the Bay of Fundy. So impressed was the premier, he promised Franklin on the spot that the parkway would be built.

Elevation (m)

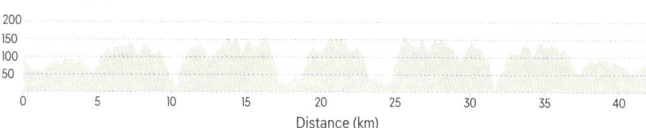

02 The first stop is just 600m from the kiosk at Fox Rock Lookout. Though not the park's best view, it's the one that convinced New Brunswick premier, Frank McKenna, in 1994 to dedicate government resources to building the parkway. Just 350m further, the view from Fownes Head Lookout leaves you with a better appreciation of the forces at work in the bay. You'll have to hike 1.5km to a viewing platform to see the flowerpot rock – a pinnacle so named for the tuft of small trees growing on its top – which stands alone as evidence of how the tides erode the adjacent cliffs. From here, you can see the park's shoreline curving away into the distance. Back on the road before it leads inland, a third stop at Melvin Beach Lookout is tempting.

03 The horseshoe-shaped, 2.4km route to Pangburn Beach Lookout gets you to the same view from the other direction. Down wooden steps is Fuller Falls, viewed from a platform. The brook drops from the forest onto a slant of rock and then runs down a steep gully to the shore. Melvin Beach stretches from here 1km to the northeast. If half a dozen people are on the beach, consider it crowded. Continue on, stopping at Black Point Lookout and Hearst Lookout for more views of the shoreline and the bay. The latter is named for William Randolph Hearst, the American newspaper magnate who built a sawmill here on the Big Salmon River in the early 20th century to produce paper for his businesses. A park lodge and riverside trail are named after him as well.

04 Cycling another 3.7km, you'll pass three more lookouts and observation decks. Stop if you have time, but if you're pressed, continue on to bigger attractions, starting with Big Salmon River. This is the site of the park's interpretive centre and the park's only restaurant, along with trails, a waterfowl observation deck at the river mouth, and the fun Big Salmon River Suspension Bridge parallel to the paved road. The wooden deck of the suspension bridge is hung by cables over the river, so it swings and bounces lightly as you walk across. The river beneath is great for swimming in waters warmer than the bay itself. If you have lots of time, consider walking the moderately challenging Salmon River Lodge Trail (3.7km one way) that leads from the bridge once you reach the other side.

05 From the river, the road twists and turns repeatedly past more lookouts. Expect steep climbs and drops for 8.7km until you reach another major stop, the Long Beach Interpretive Centre down at sea level. If you decide on this as your final stop, consider it a fine choice. At the small interpretive center, you might bump into volunteer Beverly Franklin, the daughter of Mitchell Franklin, the man who conceived of the parkway. Here are changing rooms, small exhibits, and water for people and pets, as well as the finest of the park's seven beaches.

06 Any of the next four lookouts can be your turnaround location, the last being Isle Haute Lookout. Though not the end of the park, it's the last stop before the road turns inland away from coastal views. Isle Haute is an island far away on the Nova Scotia side of the bay, but its steep cliffs make it visible on a clear day. From here, retrace the parkway route back to the west kiosk and the bike-rental shop, enjoying the same lookouts as before. This time, the scenery will be quite different, given that the tides will have likely dramatically dropped or risen.

☕ Take a break

Dining choices are limited to a single restaurant, so unless you packed a picnic (a great idea, given the many ideal picnic locations with a view), FRESH AT FUNDY at Big Salmon River is your only choice for food. It serves basic sandwiches, burgers and fries, fresh fried-fish tacos and chowder in a lumber camp–style restaurant with picnic tables. It's worth checking out just for the historic photos with informative interpretive panels lining the walls.

Big Salmon River Suspension Bridge

Walton Glen Gorge Falls

If you're up for extending your ride 6.7km to the extreme eastern end of the parkway, lock your bikes at the Walton Glen Falls parking lot and hike the easy 1.2km trail to the wooden deck lookout platform teetering over a gorge and the falls tumbling 40m over the opposite rockface. It's oversold in promotions as New Brunswick's Grand Canyon, but the comparison gives you a sense of the dramatic views here. With nothing but forest in every direction to frame the steep-sided gorge and falls, the place has a kind of peaceful permanence.

12

Moncton's Riverfront Trail

La Bikery Cooperative

DURATION	DIFFICULTY	DISTANCE	START/END
3hrs	Moderate	26km	La Bikery Cooperative
TERRAIN		Flat, gravel	

Here's an easy out-and-back route for the whole family that begins and ends at the bike hire on the edge of downtown. With almost no altitude gain and a combination of paved and gravel surfaces, the Riverfront Trail suits cyclists at any skill level. Much of the route crosses open marshland, so prepare for possibly sunny and windy conditions to fully enjoy the views of the chocolate milk–colored Petitcodiac River and its slick, muddy banks exposed between tides that fill and drain the channel twice daily. The motivation to do the entire out-and-back riverside ride is the little ice-cream shop (p100) at the turnaround point.

Bike Hire

The colorful La Bikery Cooperative at 120 Assomption Blvd sits steps from the trail and rents bikes ($15 per hour, up to $45 for eight hours) suitable for most riders ages eight and up.

Starting Point

Either walk to La Bikery Cooperative from a nearby hotel or drive to the parking lot. After picking up your rental, cycle onto the adjacent trail.

01 To start, rent a bike at La Bikery Cooperative; you won't miss the trailside building because of its bold murals. The Riverfront Trail runs beside the muddy Petitcodiac River across from the bike shop.

02 Turn left onto the trail to begin your ride. Here you'll see the Irish Family's Memorial, a group of stones set in a circle with a Celtic cross at the center as a tribute to the Irish

Tidal Bore Surfers

A few skillful athletes have surfed the tidal bore, waves carried by the tides 29km inland from the Bay of Fundy to Moncton. In 2013, JJ Wessels and Colin Whitbread of California managed to stay on their boards for the entire journey, setting a North American record for the longest distance ever surfed. Thousands lined the riverbanks to watch the achievement as the two pros dodged 'death rocks' to stay with the bore. The stamina required to surf the bore and avoid the dangers means this challenge is only for the most experienced.

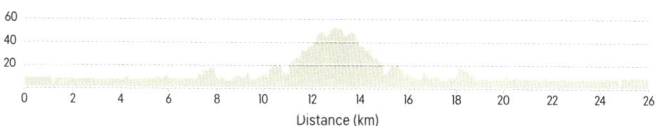

immigrants who contributed to building Moncton and nearby communities. Half a kilometer from the bike shop, you'll see Treitz House, Moncton's oldest building, built in 1769, on your left. Inside are small exhibits about the history of Moncton, but the building also serves as a visitor information center. Next to Treitz House stands the Moncton 100 Monument in the shape of a three-masted sailing ship with a statue of Joseph Salter, Moncton's first mayor. On the opposite side of the trail, a wooden observation deck juts over the riverbank for the best views of the twice-daily tidal bore. It's a natural phenomenon created when the world's highest tides in the Bay of Fundy push a low wave some 29km upstream to Moncton.

03 Continue on past Château Moncton to another viewing platform where Humphry's Brook flows into the Petitcodiac River. Before crossing the trail's covered bridge, check out Settlers Landing on your left, marking the spot where the first settlers landed here on June 3, 1766. Just beyond the bridge on the right stands yet another monument, this one to French settlers. The Acadian Odyssey Monument consists of a cross and a block of granite covered in brass plaques that tell the story of the 'Grand Derangement' or 'Great Expulsion', when British colonial forces expelled some 10,000 French Acadian settlers from Atlantic Canada in the mid-18th century. Although many died on route to other lands, including Louisiana where their descendants are known as Cajuns today, many others eventually returned, including to the Moncton area.

04 Just beyond the Acadian monument, the trail turns south out onto the marsh, which widens considerably, especially in comparison to the narrow way between the river and the city up to this point. Benches are placed along this long stretch for resting and gazing out over the marsh toward the river, now in the distance. The occasional interpretive sign provides information about the marsh's ecosystem. A single outhouse sits beside the trail 6km from the bike shop. Halfway along, the trail skirts the backs of residential neighborhoods until it crosses Fox Creek. Here, the Riverfront Park Tower gets you 3m off the ground for a better view of the creek, the marsh and the Petitcodiac, now beside the trail again. It's a nice place to sit, refuel and rest at almost the halfway point. It has a roof that provides shade after cycling exposed to the sun on the open trail. Check out the interpretive sign here that illustrates how the construction of dikes assists with flood control.

05 A couple of kilometers on, the trail turns sharply away from the river into forest and past a subdivision beyond which it meets Rt 925, also known as Dover Rd. It's a quiet rural road with light traffic and wide shoulders for safe cycling. Turn left and cycle 1km to the Esso gas station at the end of the road where you can claim your reward – an ice-cream cone from the little Dover Highway Eats takeout. The last couple of kilometers are mostly uphill, so if you'd rather forego ice cream and avoid the elevation gain, turn around when you come to the subdivision. The cooling effects of the sweet treat will give you that extra energy for the return ride back down Dover Rd and onto the Riverfront Trail.

06 To extend your time on this outing, plenty of dining options await back in Moncton. In addition to the many chains, the trail ducks around the deck of the restaurant at the Château Moncton. Just beyond is Classic Burger where the massive menu presents every option you can imagine from a burger shack. It also has a deck overlooking the river, and if your timing is right, you'll witness the tidal bore making its way upstream.

☕ Take a break

On the return ride, just 100m before the bike shop, look to your right for the **RIVERFRONT CAFE AND MARKET**, which makes a perfect final stop before turning in the bikes. They make the usual espresso-based coffees and build sandwiches to satisfy that appetite you've worked up. While there, browse the Starving Artist Gallery and Gifts for pottery, paintings and other artwork to take home as souvenirs of your riverfront ride.

Riverfront Trail

Hub City

Moncton came by its nickname – the Hub City – honestly. Located at the geographic center of Canada's Maritime Provinces (New Brunswick, Prince Edward Island and Nova Scotia), Moncton is skirted by both the Trans-Canada Highway and the region's railway line. It's also home to New Brunswick's largest airport. Events like the HubCap Comedy Festival lean on the city's reputation as a vibrant center. For visitors, Moncton makes a convenient base to explore southeastern New Brunswick. The shoreline known as the Acadian coast to the east and the Bay of Fundy coastline to the west – each blessed with a national park – is within an hour's drive.

13

Best for

FOOD

Fredericton Two Rivers Ride

DURATION	DIFFICULTY	DISTANCE	START/END
3hrs	Easy	17.3km	Delta Hotels Fredericton

TERRAIN	Flat, paved and gravel

Gibson Trail

Explore two rivers in one easy outing that includes a loop in this out-and-back ride. The route shoots between the shoreline of the Saint John River and downtown streets, bringing cafes, restaurants, shops and taprooms within easy reach. The trail passes historic buildings, Fredericton's original craft brewery and New Brunswick's finest art gallery. It's a blend of safe, urban cycling and peaceful trails beneath shade trees. Across the Bill Thorpe Walking Bridge, the route loops along a pair of trails on either side of the Nashwaak River through a mature forest canopy back to the starting point.

Bike Hire

The Radical Edge *(radical edge.ca)* and Savage's Bicycle Center *(sbcoutlet.com)* in the downtown both rent bikes. Both are a short ride or walk to the South Riverfront Trail.

Starting Point

From either bike-rental shop, ride or walk your bike to the South Riverfront Trail or 2km to the trail's start behind the parking lot at the Delta Hotels Fredericton.

01 To complete the full route, set off from the start of the South Riverfront Trail. You'll find it between the parking lot at the Delta Hotels Fredericton and the Saint John River. On sprawling, publicly accessible grounds just beyond the hotel, pause at Government House, the residence of New Brunswick's Lieutenant Governor. It's a grand stone building with green, copper roofs and the look of an English estate. Continue on beneath the Westmorland Bridge that carries vehicle traffic

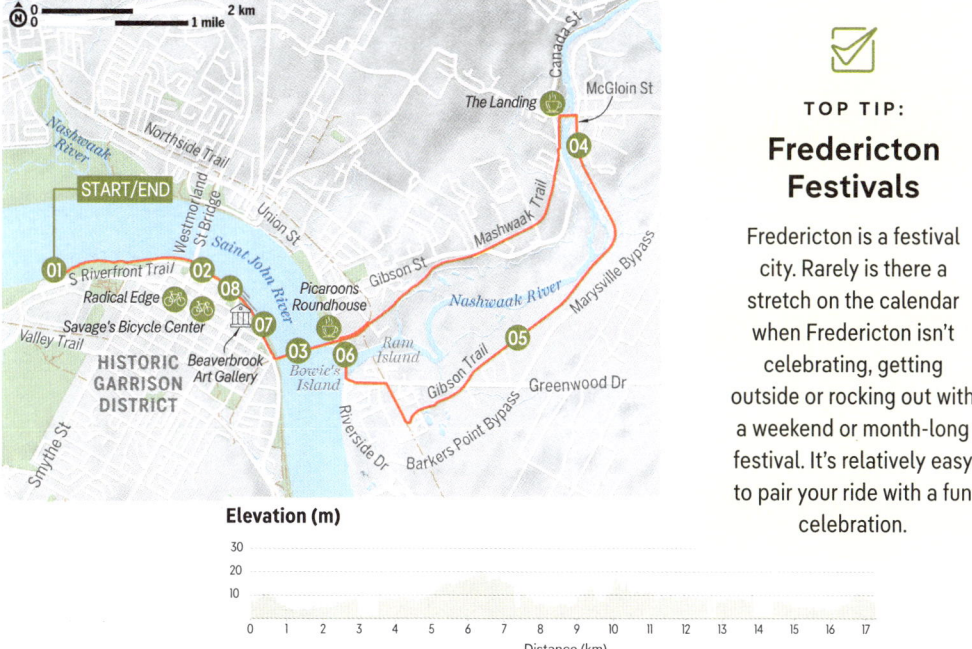

TOP TIP:
Fredericton Festivals

Fredericton is a festival city. Rarely is there a stretch on the calendar when Fredericton isn't celebrating, getting outside or rocking out with a weekend or month-long festival. It's relatively easy to pair your ride with a fun celebration.

across the river. On your right across a busy highway, you'll see buildings and green spaces that make up the Historic Garrison District harkening back to the founding of Fredericton. British colonial history resonates among old barracks, city hall, the courthouse and other heritage buildings, especially when Carleton St is lined with vendors every Thursday during the Garrison Night Market. The city's public library, the New Brunswick Sports Hall of Fame and the Fredericton Region Museum are here next to the grassy lawn called Officer's Square. Inside the museum, rooms are filled with exhibits interpreting the history of the city, and strangely, a large exhibit dedicated to a UFO expert with Fredericton roots. Quirky and delightfully amateurish, the exhibit is remarkable for its content and for the man it honors. Nuclear physicist Stanton Friedman took on UFOs with a passion beginning in 1958, researching and making presentations on many incidents. His work got him inducted into the UFO Hall of Fame in Roswell, New Mexico.

02 Beside the trail between the Westmorland Bridge and the Bill Thorpe Walking Bridge, you'll see the first of many art installations. The first is *Watermark*, a series of posts before a set of concrete footings that reach across the river and once supported a bridge, now gone. Next is an anchor from a Canadian navy ship named for *Fredericton*. Behind Beaverbrook Art Gallery, you'll find several whimsical art installations followed by more conventional statues and a fountain. One is of Lord Beaverbrook and another of Scottish poet Robbie Burns.

03 Cycle onto the Bill Thorpe Walking Bridge, a former railway trestle, now with wooden decking rather than rails. Ride slowly, both as a courtesy to pedestrians and to enjoy the experience and the view. On the opposite northern shore, the bridge leads directly onto the paved Nashwaak Trail that parallels the small river of the same name. This is where the loop section of the route begins, out on the Nashwaak Trail on one bank of the Nashwaak River and back on the Gibson Trail on the

☕ Take a break

At the Crocket St Bridge, THE LANDING is run by coffee experts the Mill Town Roaster. They serve some of the best espresso drinks around. Stacked sandwiches, smoothies, tea beverages, craft beer and pastries will tempt you to extend your mid-ride break, especially with their shady patio overlooking the river calling you away from the trail. Mill Town shares the riverside building with cycling experts the Radical Edge, the same folks who may have rented you a bike.

opposite bank. Once the Nashwaak Trail passes between a couple of small industrial sites, it briefly hugs Kaine Creek, an arm of the Nashwaak River, before skirting the back yards of a few houses, then plunging into forest. When it reaches the Nashwaak again, the trail ducks beneath Canada St. This is where the Landing, a blue historic building, houses one of several Mill Town Roasters' cafes and a Radical Edge bike shop outlet. Stop for a coffee and a treat on their spacious outdoor patio beneath a shady tree before walking your bike onto and across the bridge. A small island splits the river at mid-span.

04 On the other side of the bridge, find the Gibson Trail, which leads back to the Bill Thorpe Walking Bridge. The trail begins a block from the bridge. To find it, turn right off the bridge onto McGloin St. As McGloin St swings left, you'll see Marysville Heritage Centre followed immediately by the entrance to the gravel-surfaced Gibson Trail, which will return you to the Bill Thorpe Walking Bridge. Before you hit the trail, take a few minutes to look around or longer to cycle around this little neighborhood, Marysville, once an industrial town. The long, four-story brick building on your left was a cotton mill – one of the largest mills in Canada – built in 1883–85 and operating until 1975. This is Marysville Place, now government offices. The mill, and the neighborhood around it, is a national historic district because it's 'among the earliest and most complete Canadian examples of an integrated industrial/residential community.' The mill was the centerpiece of an entire 19th-century model community built by Alexander 'Boss' Gibson, who named Marysville for his wife and his daughter, both named Mary. If you cycle around a bit, you'll see some of the 24 duplex tenement houses Gibson built for his workers.

05 The Gibson Trail runs through the wilder side of the Nashwaak River. You'll cycle 3km over marsh, then under forest canopy before you see another building. Over Greenwood Drive and through a parking lot, a wetland called Hyla Park Nature Preserve is on your left. It's not a very large wild space, but it is Canada's first park dedicated to amphibians, established in 1995 'for the purpose of protecting and preserving the gray tree frog *(Hyla versicolor)* and its habitat for future generations.' Six other species of frogs and toads live here as well. Just beyond Hyla, the trail takes a

Bill Thorpe Walking Bridge

Who was Bill Thorpe?

William Wellington (Bill) Thorpe (1933–2006) means far more to Fredericton than his years as a teacher, coach and city councilor – even deputy mayor – would suggest. A dedicated athlete passionate about the outdoors, he dreamt of turning the local abandoned rail system into a network of city trails. He founded the Fredericton Heritage Trust and the Fredericton Trails Coalition. Two years after his death, the 1905 railway bridge he envisioned as a modern walking bridge was named after him. At last count, over 600,000 walkers, hikers and cyclists use the bridge every year.

Dalí meets Indigenous Art

Even Salvador Dalí fans might be surprised to find one of his large master works in Fredericton. The Beaverbrook Art Gallery is named for Lord Beaverbrook. His wife, philanthropist and art collector Lady Dunn, was a personal friend of the artist who promised her a painting for the Fredericton gallery. The perspective in *Santiago El Grande*, a painting practically bursting with motion, is beneath a rearing white horse carrying James, the patron saint of Spain. The painting opened the gallery in 1959 with one heck of a splash. Today, intricate contemporary Indigenous art blazing with color pairs well with Dalí.

Beaverbrook Art Gallery

90-degree turn and runs straight back to the Nashwaak River Trail Bridge. Continue on over the bridge and along the Gibson Trail until it intersects with the Nashwaak Trail. From here, it's only a few hundred meters until you're back on the Bill Thorpe Walking Bridge.

06 Just as you reach the bridge, you'll see the Picaroons Roundhouse on your right. Declared a national historic site in 2008, the building where railroad locomotives were serviced has strong links to 'Boss' Gibson as well. Constructed at what was the Gibson Railway Yard by the same construction company that built the brick cotton mill in Marysville, the half-million bricks used to build it in 1885 came from Gibson's brickyard. Picaroons purchased the roundhouse in 2013 for $100 and began renovations to transform it into a brewery and taproom.

07 Over the bridge, the Daily Espresso cafe at the southern end of the Beaverbrook Art Gallery is a cheery place awash in light from tall windows, suitable for a stop near the end of the return leg of the cycling route. The Beaverbrook is a top-tier Canadian gallery, so be sure to leave time for a look through its many rooms. There's the famous Salvador Dalí painting *Santiago El Grande*, the impressive 'Grandfather canoe' built locally of birchbark in 1820, bold contemporary artworks by top Canadian artists, a significant historic collection and always a few engaging temporary exhibits. The permanent collection, established in 1959 with 300 works from Lord Beaverbrook's private collection, has grown to 5000 works and includes paintings by Thomas Gainsborough, JMW Turner and Joshua Reynolds. Among the gallery's historic Canadian artworks are paintings by 'Group of Seven' artists and many by Cornelius Krieghoff, a prolific painter who depicted 19th-century life in Québec.

08 From the Beaverbrook, it's an easy ride on a paved cycling path back to the starting point. Alternatively, this is the best place to leave the trail, if you want to cut your ride short by 2.7km. Cycle the city streets or walk your bike along the sidewalk back to a bike-rental shop, three blocks to Savage's or four to the Radical Edge.

☕ Take a break

PICAROONS ROUNDHOUSE is New Brunswick's original craft brewery. The brick building has a patio overlooking the river where you can pop in for a pint. There's also a cafe and a restaurant onsite for bites and alternative drinks. Picaroons is part of the Taproom Trail *(frederictoncapitalregion.ca)*, a collection of craft-beer taprooms around the city pulled together into a challenge. To participate, pick up a Taproom Trail passport at Fredericton Tourism or a participating taproom; get it stamped at six locations to receive a bumper sticker (or collect eight for a T-shirt).

Also Try...

GREENSEAS/SHUTTERSTOCK

Sugarloaf Cycling Park

DURATION	DIFFICULTY	DISTANCE
2hrs	Hard	1-5km

A ski center in winter, Sugarloaf Provincial Park in northern New Brunswick morphs into a prime mountain-biking destination in summer, complete with lift service to the trails. Beginners and expert riders alike have options for a fun day on 25km of trails. You can rent bikes onsite and head out onto trails like the 1.2km Supa Sweet, loaded with features, or the 2.3km Sugar Mama Trail for an easy downhill ride. The longer 4.8km Panorama Trail leads across relatively flat cross-country dirt tracks beneath shady forest canopy. Several moderate trails like the 1.9km Grumpy Grizz are hybrids of difficult technical trail and easier cross-country trails. Some trails include berms, but they're mostly downhill.

Rockwood Park

DURATION	DIFFICULTY	DISTANCE
2hrs	Easy	1-5km

The port city of Saint John developed Rockwood Park (pictured above) into the city's prime outdoor recreation area. Ten lakes, 2200 acres of forest and 55 trails and footpaths leave lots of room for easy, family-friendly fun, including swimming, hiking and cycling. Trails range from singletrack routes and rocky routes for more experienced mountain-bikers to wide gravel or paved trails for leisurely cycling. The paved 2.9km Fisher Lakes Drive and the wide gravel 3km Zoo Trail are among the easiest routes. Trails are multi-use, so watch for hikers, dog walkers and runners sharing the way. Head to the Interpretation Centre to pick up a park trail map and find out how to rent bicycles.

DANITA DELIMONT/SHUTTERSTOCK

Fundy National Park

DURATION	DIFFICULTY	DISTANCE
1-4hrs	Moderate	1-26km

One of New Brunswick's two national parks, Fundy has paved roads, gravel roads and cycling trails to choose from. Head to the Chignecto Recreation Area, the mountain-bike hub of the park, to try a couple hundred meters of challenging track with built-in berms and rollers. Other forested trails and open roads are relatively flat for easy riding, including the 1.5km Cygnus, 1km Ursa Major, 0.7km Ursa Minor and 1km Orion. The 5.6km East Branch Loop and 3.5km Maple Grove are among the park's moderate cycling trails. The difficult 13km Bennett Brook Trail is the longest and leads to a dam along steep switchbacks. Rent bikes from the park's official outfitter, Outdoor Elements (outdoorelements.ca).

Acadian Peninsula Veloroute

DURATION	DIFFICULTY	DISTANCE
3hrs	Moderate	70km

With 610km of connected trails and cycling paths, New Brunswick's only official cycling route is more a collection of 14 cycling circuits than a single path, making it possible to link together many combinations of rides. The collection of routes crisscrosses the Acadian Peninsula, including remote Miscou Island. Take several days to cycle large parts of it or spend a few hours in one area. For the easiest ride, try some of the 70km of paved cycling path in the Caraquet area (pictured above) through coastal and forest scenery. Here you'll pass fishing boats, spot wildlife and ride through French Acadian communities that proudly paint their red, white and blue colors on everything from mailboxes to entire buildings.

BEST BIKE RIDES: CANADA

Prince Edward Island

Scale: 50 km / 25 miles

Locations

Gulf of St Lawrence (northwest)

Northumberland Strait (south)

Kings County:
- East Point
- North Lake
- South Lake
- Elmira
- Harmony Junction
- Souris
- Naufrage
- Greenwich
- St Peter's Bay
- Midgell
- Albion Cross
- Newport
- Georgetown
- Gaspereaux
- Cape Bear
- Cardigan
- Montague
- Murray River
- High Bank
- Little Sands
- Murray Harbour
- Pictou Island
- Vernon Bridge
- Orwell
- Caledonia
- Wood Islands
- Eldon

Queens County:
- Mt Stewart
- Dalvay by the Sea
- Brackley Beach
- Rustico
- North Rustico
- New Glasgow
- New London
- Cavendish
- Prince Edward Island National Park
- Charlottetown
- Springton
- Victoria
- Borden-Carleton
- Confederation Bridge
- Hillsborough Bay

Prince County:
- Park Corner
- Malpeque Bay
- Margate
- Indian River
- Kensington
- Summerside
- Miscouche
- Hog Island
- Lennox Island
- Bideford
- East Bideford
- Tyne Valley
- Mount Pleasant
- Wellington
- Bloomfield
- Woodstock
- St Anthony
- O'Leary
- Miminegash
- Campbellton
- Cape Wolfe
- West Point
- Skinners Pond
- Tignish
- Seacow Pond
- North Cape
- Cape Kildare
- Cascumpec Bay
- Egmont Bay
- Cape Egmont
- Mont Carmel
- Bedeque Bay
- Seven Mile Bay
- Cape Tormentine
- Murray Corner
- Port Elgin

NEW BRUNSWICK

NOVA SCOTIA

Markers: 14, 15, 16

Confederation Trail, Montague (p122)

Prince Edward Island

14 Gulf Shore Parkway (West)

A beautiful coastal cycling trail along the red sandstone coast of Cavendish. Fully paved and segregated from traffic, this undulating trail with small climbs will get your heart pumping, all the while accompanied by fantastic views of the Gulf of St Lawrence. **p114**

15 St Peter's Bay to Lighthouse

Considered by locals as the most scenic section of the Confederation Trail, this easy bayside trail takes you from St Peter's Bay to the village of Morell, before continuing toward the lighthouse. With farms and wildflower meadows on your left and the bay on your right, this trail definitely lives up to its reputation. **p118**

16 Three Rivers Trail

Between Cardigan, Georgetown and Montague is the heritage Three Rivers section of the Confederation Trail. Take a nice bike ride along the tree-lined trails that are alive with wild creatures, and visit the three towns, each with unique stories to tell. **p122**

Explore

Prince Edward Island

Canada's Atlantic island with landscapes that inspired *Anne of Green Gables* and a delicious culinary scene, PEI is not just a great holiday destination, it is also a cycling paradise. The island's extensive Confederation Trail network, built on decommissioned railway lines that once brought the islanders to join the Confederation, reaches from the far east end of the island to the far west, taking you to less-visited corners of the island. With over 250 interpretive panels installed along the trail, presenting architectural, historical or natural-environment information, the bike rides are both recreational and educational.

Charlottetown

Whether you are arriving by air from international or Canadian destinations or by coach from nearby Nova Scotia or New Brunswick, you are likely to be arriving in Charlottetown. This is also where you'll find all the services you need for your trip around Prince Edward Island, including car hire, bike hire and the bus transit system for getting around.

If you are staying for a couple of days of sightseeing, stay around the downtown area to fully appreciate the historic monuments, cultural museums and general lively atmosphere of this small city and the fantastic dining scene. The colorful merchant houses at Peake's Wharf are where you'll find some great seafood options, including excellent lobster rolls when in season. Around downtown, accommodations range from five-star hotels to guesthouses, each with their own character and charm, and there is no shortage of places to eat and drink. From steak houses to Peruvian, Vietnamese, sushi and Italian, there is a restaurant for every taste. The Founder's Food Hall & Market by the Visitor Information Center is a good place to start, or check out the lively historic Victoria Row and its array of pubs and restaurants. Do also try PEI's own Cows Ice Cream. The main shop is on Grafton St, with several outlets around the city.

The Confederation Trail branches into the heart of the city, and a couple of bike paths take you to nearby towns, making it easy to explore on two wheels.

WHEN TO GO

Although cycling is possible all year round, the best time to visit is during the warmer months between June and October. Visiting in early fall around mid-September is beautiful as the summer wraps up its last blooms and fall colors begin to appear. It will also be quieter, with fewer people on the trails.

Summerside

The second-largest city on Prince Edward Island lies toward the western part of the province and is mostly known as a quaint seaside holiday town. Summerside has several museums and cultural attractions, with a good number of hotels and guesthouses, cafes and restaurants, and grocery stores. The Confederation Trail comes through here, making Summerside a good hub town from which to explore the Cavendish coast on the Gulf Shore Parkway bike ride (p114). A couple of hotels in the downtown area have bike rentals for guests, which is convenient for viewing the many heritage murals around downtown, or to explore the nature trails of Rotary Friendship Park. The town's airport has no scheduled commercial flights, so getting here largely requires getting a coach or hire car from Charlottetown.

TRANSPORT

Most visitors hire a car on Prince Edward Island, although it isn't impossible to get around without one. T3 Transit (t3transit.ca) operates bus services around the island, with its hub at Royalty Crossing in Charlottetown. The city bus services around Charlottetown accept cash or prepaid tickets only, and can take bikes on their front rack. Rural services should be booked online ahead of travel.

 WHAT'S ON

PEI Gran Fondo
(granfondo-pei.ca) Every summer, Prince Edward Island hosts this amateur cycling event that tours 150km coast to coast on the island over two days.

PEI International Shellfish Festival
(peishellfish.com) Known for its quality seafood, this is a celebration of the island's great feasts from the sea. With four days of culinary contests and tasting, it's one for the foodies.

Resources

Visit Tourism PEI
(tourismpei.com/pei-confederation-trail) Has a good page about the Confederation Trail, including maps and suggestions of accommodations, dining and bike-rental options.

Discover Charlottetown
(discovercharlottetown.com) Great ideas on what to do, where to eat and where to stay.

 WHERE TO STAY

While there are many hotels and guesthouse options in Charlottetown, holiday accommodations in rural areas can be limited and it is difficult to find somewhere to stay in summer if you don't book ahead. The most popular styles of accommodations on Prince Edward Island are tourist homes and cottages for longer stays, but you can also find guesthouses and small-scale motels and hotels for the one- or two-night sleeps. Many have bicycle-parking facilities, although not all are secure, so do ask before booking. Camping is also a popular option for those cycling multiple days on the Confederation Trail.

14

Gulf Shore Parkway (West)

Best for

COASTAL VIEWS

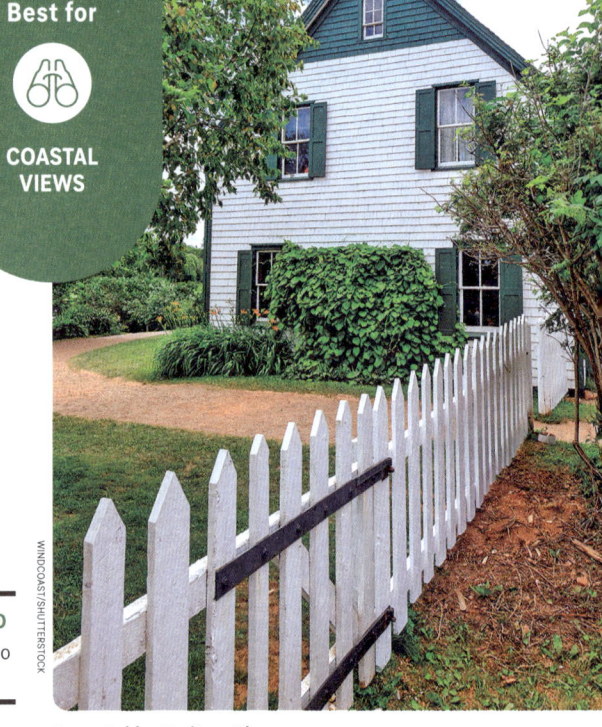

Green Gables Heritage Place

DURATION	DIFFICULTY	DISTANCE	START/END
1hr	Easy	20km	North Rustico Harbour

TERRAIN		Paved	

Taking in views of the coastal cliffs and sandy beaches along the Gulf of St Lawrence, the western stretch of the Gulf Shore Parkway is an easy out-and-back 20km ride from North Rustico Harbour to Cavendish. This paved, two-way multi-use trail joins several accessible beaches along the way, and ends at a car park and viewpoint where the ancient red sandstone cliffs can be viewed across the bay. Although the trail rises and falls with the curves of the cliffs, you can take your time without stress of traffic, and rest at one of the several benches with bike racks along the way.

Bike Hire

Outside Expeditions (getoutside.com) rents bikes at the edge of North Rustico Harbour. Adult bike rental starts from $20 for an hour to $45 for a day. Kids bikes, tandems and e-bikes are also available.

Starting Point

The start of this trail begins at North Rustico Beach car park. If joining from the bike hire, follow a gravel trail about 200m away on the road to the start.

01 From the North Rustico Beach carpark, face west with the sandy beach to your right where you will see the start of the paved section of the Gulf Shore Parkway trail. Join this trail at your leisure.

02 There is a gentle incline to start, which is a good introduction to what the rest of the trail's topography will be like. After around 30m, the legs get a rest on a quick descent before the trail climbs again.

Anne of Green Gables

Lucy Maud Montgomery wrote *Anne of Green Gables* in 1908, basing many of the landscapes on places she knew and loved around Cavendish and her own experiences from where she grew up. The Green Gables Heritage Place is an original 'Green Gables' house once owned by the Macneill family, who were cousins to Lucy Montgomery. The woodlands surrounding it has been landscaped to bring the setting of the story to life, and the visitor center has a great exhibit on Montgomery's life and career and the impact her story had, as well as an appreciation for the coastal environments at Cavendish.

Elevation (m)

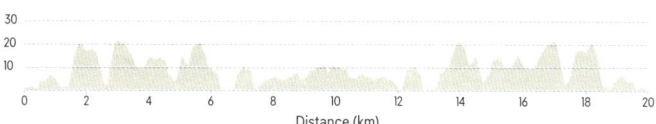

03 Enjoy this well-paved trail as you share it with walkers and other cyclists. The trail will rise and fall for a few kilometers yet. This roller coaster will give you an appreciation of the rolling cliffs you'll soon see on the horizon appearing to your right.

04 Although the views of the beaches and coastal cliffs are alluring, do take time to look to your left as well. The landscape is scattered with wild woodlands and farm estates in between, with character-filled wooden farmhouses surrounded by meadows that face the sea. This is the landscape that inspired LM Montgomery's *Anne of Green Gables*, and is particularly pleasant to cycle through.

05 Around the junction of Church Hill Ave is a nice scenic section with a lake on the left side of the road and the sea to your right. There is access to the beach here where you can see the distant red sandstone cliffs coming up. Take a breather here, as a steeper climb is about to start.

06 Bike on. The steady ascent lasts around 800m. The trees on both side of the trail thicken, creating a good area for birds to nest, so keep your eyes peeled for bald eagles that frequent this part of the coast. You are now entering the landscape that is both geographically significant and historically important, which you'll have a great view of just a little beyond the peak of this hill as you start to descend again. This will be your experience along this trail, as it rises and falls along the coast and has you rise and fall with it.

BEST BIKE RIDES: CANADA   **115**

07 At about the trail's halfway point is Cape Turner, where you will notice a small turnoff toward the shore among the trees. The views are stunning and there is a toilet and an information board about the surrounds here.

08 Another climb is coming up, lasting another 800m, and at the top of this one you're rewarded with sweeping views of the Gulf of St Lawrence and the famous Cavendish coast landscape. There is a small roadside parking area for cars and a bench along the trail here, should you wish to stop and appreciate the surrounds – but it will be mostly downhill and flat from here to Cavendish, so you may want to push on.

09 At the bottom of the hill, another small parking area appears for the vantage point to view a sea stack called 'The Cactus Pot.'

10 Continue to follow the trail for the next 3km or so to reach a large car park. This is the end of the trail and a good place for a picnic break. At one end of the car park you'll find the Oceanview Lookout, where there are several information boards with geological and historical facts about this area that are worth a read.

11 On the far side of the car park you'll find a trail that takes you to the Cavendish Dunelands, which is also worth visiting for views of the sand dunes, the ocean and a couple of freshwater lakes. Note that you need to walk your bike here. You can also choose to extend your ride from here to visit Cavendish, follow the bike path toward the center of Cavendish for refreshments and perhaps to visit the Green Gables Heritage Place for some *Anne of Green Gables* inspiration.

12 When you are ready, turn around and follow the Gulf Shore Parkway trail back to North Rustico to complete your bike ride.

☕ Take a break

There are no opportunities for food and drinks until you get to Cavendish, so stock up on supplies from North Rustico before you depart. On reaching Cavendish, there's a Tim Hortons and a couple of take-out places on the main road. Alternatively, if visiting the Green Gables Heritage Place, there is a cafe onsite, and toilet facilities.

Cavendish cliffs

Cliffs of Cavendish

The red sandstone cliffs of Cavendish have been the work of nature for over 250 million years and are scientifically and historically important for many reasons. A vast variety of wildlife is active along this stretch of coast, including swallows, eagles, foxes and kingfishers. Fossils from the Permian period, such as giant ferns and Dimetrodon, have been found in these fragile cliffs, and the ever-changing formation of the cliffs is evidence of environmental and climate impact on nature. In recent years, more frequent storms and rising sea levels have hastened the erosion of this landscape.

15

St Peter's Bay to Lighthouse

St Peter's Bay

DURATION	DIFFICULTY	DISTANCE	START/END
2½hrs	Moderate	34km	St Peter's Bay Landing
TERRAIN		Gravel	

Widely considered the most picturesque section of the entire Confederation Trail, this is an out-and-back bike ride that will take you along the gentle gravel path over the estuaries and wetlands of St Peter's Bay before cycling to the beach at the St Peter's Harbour Lighthouse. Expect to be charmed by the calm waters with its countless rows of mussel farms and water fowls wading and hunting near the shallow edges, decorated by wildflowers lining the path in colors of yellow, purple and red. Then on to a short ride with traffic, to the lighthouse looking over a white sandy beach.

Bike Hire

Confederation Trail Bike Rentals (confederationtrail.ca) is right near St Peter's Bay Landing where this trail begins. Adult bike hire is $50 per day. Kids bikes, kids tag-along bikes and e-bikes are also available.

Starting Point

The trail starts at the road junction from St Peter's Landing and the highway. Take care crossing the roads as they can get very busy with traffic.

01 From St Peter's Bay Landing, head toward the road junction with the highway and turn right toward the bay, with the water on your right onto the gravel path. Immediately you'll be taken by beautiful views across the bay and the mussel farms it harbors.

02 A small white church with a green roof will appear on your left. This is St Peter's United Church, a historic place built in 1886 and recognized for its Gothic Revival architectural style.

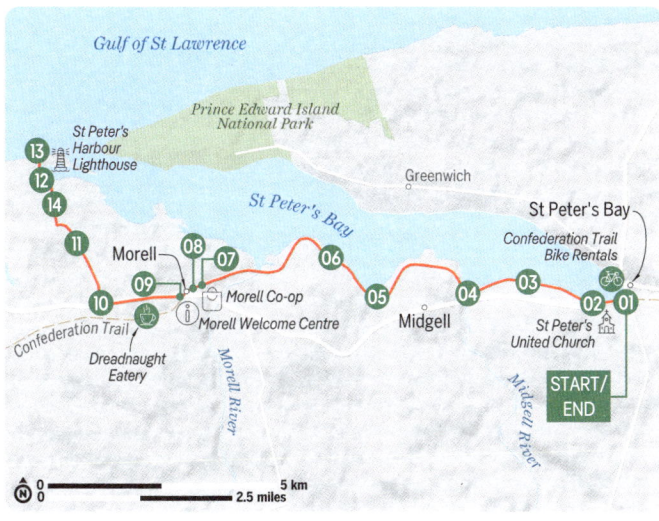

The Confederation Trail

Prince Edward Island is known as the Birthplace of Confederation. The Charlottetown Conference of 1864 was held to discuss uniting British colonies in this part of North America into one political entity. It was the first step toward a united Canadian Confederation.

The Confederation Trail is so named thanks to the network of railways that helped the islanders, who originally opposed the idea despite having hosted the conference, and joined the Confederation six years after the formation of Canada. More can be learned about this complicated political history at the newly renovated Confederation Chamber at the Province House National Historic Site in Charlottetown.

Elevation (m)

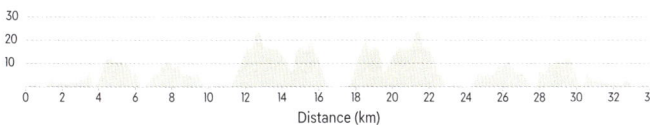

03 For the next 10km, you'll be following the most scenic part of the Confederation Trail. Mostly flat, the gravel trail is easy to follow, with bridges connecting land across various bodies of water. The trail will cross several farm access roads where you may encounter cars and tractors, so proceed with caution.

04 Notice the vibrant birdlife that calls this bay home as you approach the first bridge at Midgell. Stop at the information boards to learn about the majestic great blue herons, the symbol of Prince Edward Island. If you are lucky, you might see one hunting in the shallows of the rivers.

05 Continuing on, still following the gravel path lined with trees, you will be surrounded by meadows and farmland. It's not far to come to the next bridge, with more information boards and scenery of the bay.

06 Gently rolling on, the trail wraps around the small hamlet of Dingwell before coming to the third and final bridge. This particular bridge over Morell River is the longest trail bridge on the Confederation Trail, at 70m long. At this point, you can start to hear the traffic on the nearby highway as you approach the town of Morell, which has a visitor center with toilets.

07 The first road you'll come across in Morell is Red Head Rd. Immediately to your left is a signboard for a nature walking path, which is a short walk into the woods by a small lake that might make a nice walk to shake those bike-riding legs out. To continue the bike ride, cross the road carefully to join the trail again at the opposite side.

08 This small urban section of the trail passes a small co-op shop on your left. This is where you can pick up some supplies for the remainder of your trip. The bike ride will leave the safety of the Confederation Trail and join the traffic from this point.

09 On reaching the junction with Veterans Memorial Hwy and Benny Lutz Lane, turn right onto the highway for a short while. Although traffic can get heavy and speedy on this stretch of the road, there is a wide shoulder you can cycle on, keeping you safe.

10 Cycle for 2km to reach Bristol, and turn right onto St Peters Harbour Rd. You are now off the main highway onto a residential area with less traffic, which you'll stay on for another 2km until after a left bend on the road. Here you'll find the gravel Lighthouse Rd branching off to your right. Turn right here. This turn can be difficult to spot as it is unpaved and feels more like a track or trail than a road.

11 Take this gravel road all the way to the end. Take care of its many bumps and look out for the occasional traffic that ventures this way. Nature gets wilder as you get nearer to the water and the lighthouse comes into view. Notice the sudden change in the landscape, where the water seems to be everywhere, overgrown with reeds that line your path.

12 The end of the path is by the lighthouse. St Peter's Harbour Lighthouse was built around 1878 and moved positions several times to meet the ever-changing coastline of the island. Decommissioned in 2008, it is now a Federal Heritage Site.

13 The beach beyond the lighthouse is fantastically soft and white, and is a great place for a picnic. There are bike racks at the entrance to the beach, or you can choose to walk your bike through the boardwalk onto the sand.

14 From here, follow the same route back to Morell to rejoin the Confederation Trail back to St Peter's Bay.

☕ Take a break

There is a co-op supermarket in Morell where you can pick up picnic supplies to have at the beaches of the lighthouse. For those wanting a larger meal, try the family-owned DREADNAUGHT EATERY food trailer serving fish and chips, lobster rolls, burgers, pulled pork and salads. It is a gentle ride to Morell from St Peter's Bay but do make sure you have a drink bottle with water with you.

St Peter's Harbour Lighthouse

Indigenous Peoples of St Peter's Bay

There's definitely a charm to St Peter's Bay that has drawn settlements of people as early as 8600 BCE. Archaeological finds at Greenwich Peninsula found traces of settlement by three different ancient indigenous cultures, the Paleo-Indian (8600-3500 BCE), the Archaic 'Shellfish' People (3500-1000 BCE) and the Algonquin, the ancestors of the Mi'kmaq People who are native to the eastern, Atlantic regions of Canada. St Peter's Bay's name under the Mi'kmaq tradition is Poogoosumkek Boktaba, meaning 'a place to dig for clams,' evidence of the bay being an established source for fish and shellfish.

16

Three Rivers Trail

Montague

DURATION	DIFFICULTY	DISTANCE	START/END
3hrs	Moderate	38.5km	Montague

TERRAIN	Gravel

The first rail journey between Montague and Georgetown took place in 1906. This is a branch section of the Confederation Trail that takes in the nature and environment of the Three Rivers, a lush and fertile part of Prince Edward Island, with its lands nourished by the flow of the Montague, Brudenell and Cardigan rivers. Although it's a long day's out-and-back ride, the trail is mostly flat, crossing several farmlands and industrial plants. The apple trees that are known to line the Confederation Trail are especially prominent on this section, making it a beautifully green and occasionally fragrant bike ride during blossom season.

Bike Hire

The only option in Montague is an e-bike rental at the marina, with rentals starting from $40 for a short ride. Credit card and ID are required for bike rentals.

Starting Point

The start of the trail is right by the waterfront marina, just after a small car park, where there is a large turntable of the former railway still visible.

01 From the start of the trail next to the large concrete turntables, ride away from Montague with the town on your left and the bay to your right. This is the Montague River, the first of the Three Rivers. Soon, you'll pass several residential houses to your right before crossing Swans Lane, where the trail will follow the river for the first 2km before it curves north toward the town of Brudenell.

The Three Rivers

Originally known as Samkook by the Mi'kmaq People, meaning 'the land of sandy shores,' the Three Rivers refers to the geological river system of Montague, Brudenell and Cardigan rivers that flows into Cardigan Bay. Jean-Pierre Roma established a fishing trade post settlement here at Brudenell Point to boost French presence on Prince Edward Island in 1732, and his estate is now a museum. Another notable figure is Andrew MacDonald, one of the fathers of Confederation, who was born here at the Three Rivers. Today, the Town of Three Rivers refers mostly to Montague, and the surrounding area is now a protected landscape.

Elevation (m)

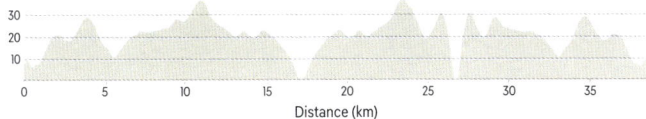

Distance (km)

02 There are a couple of road crossings ahead that occasionally have industrial traffic and fast cars, so take care as you proceed. The first crossing is Robertson Rd. Those interested in historical museums could make a detour here and turn right onto the road to visit Roma at Three Rivers National Historic Site at the end of the Brudenell peninsula. If you choose to do this, you could return by Brudenell Point Rd, where you can join the trail again at the next junction.

03 There is a gentle incline to the trail, and several more along the way, although nothing too strenuous that would take your breath away. After you cross Brudenell Rd, where there are a couple of industrial businesses, you will reach a vantage point at the bridge crossing the second of the Three Rivers, the Brudenell River. Stop here to appreciate the nature of the river and the forests that surround it, and try to spot ducks, herons, beavers and other wildlife that lives among this wilderness.

04 From here, the trail curves around to follow the river's flow toward the bay through forests on your right and farmlands on your left. Take care at the road crossing at Georgetown Rd coming up, with a large farming-supply business at the junction corner, and another crossing shortly after at Park Rd. These roads can be busy as they are the way in and out of Georgetown by car.

05 You are now approaching one of the trail junctions. Montague Junction has a

BEST BIKE RIDES: CANADA

shelter and several trail information boards, one about the Trans Canada Trail, and the other one about apple trees. After a little rest, follow the signed direction and cycle toward Georgetown.

06 Follow the trail all the way to the beach of Georgetown. The trail crossing at Bovyer Rd can be tricky as the trail joins diagonally across the road, so look for the trail entrance before crossing the road to be safe.

07 As you get closer to the end of the gravel trail at Georgetown, there is a small picnic table with a lovely view toward the harbor on your right. The gravel trail ends where it meets a small road with a gate. Cross this side street and join onto a paved trail.

08 Now you're on a path that cuts across a park with a small kiosk (not always open) and a children's play area to the end, where there is a restaurant on a headland looking out to the bay. Cycling along, you'll have the beach on your right and the town of Georgetown on your left. At the end of this path, there is a blue plaque with information on the history of the Three Rivers, as well as several benches facing the water.

09 Rest up here, and take in the view of the beach and the harbor – it's a glorious sight. When you are ready, head back in the direction you came from. Rejoin the Confederation Trail to return to Montague Junction.

10 Back at the junction, turn right in the direction of Cardigan to visit the third of the Three Rivers. This is a short detour. There is a heritage museum by the marina to learn more about the history of this area, and if the timing is right, have lunch at Clam Diggers restaurant.

11 It's time to get back, so find the trail again and follow the gravel back to Montague. You have started and ended at the end of the line. On arriving back, you could check out the railway turntable remains by the marina and read the information to learn about why a branch line of the railway eventually came to Montague.

☕ Take a break

There are no refreshment facilities while on the trail, so buy some snacks and drinks before departing for the day at the supermarket (Atlantic Superstore) in Montague. There is a small picnic area at the trail junction as well as along the beach area in Georgetown. CLAM DIGGERS restaurant at Cardigan is widely recommended and is an option for a sit-down meal; otherwise return to Montague for a post-ride drink and meal at the town's BOGSIDE BREWING.

Confederation Trail

Where Did the Apple Trees Come From?

Traveling along the Confederation Trail you'll notice a curious abundance of apple trees. Not entirely wild, nor entirely cultivated, but entirely relevant to the fact that the Confederation Trail was established on the now-disused railways, and apples, being a fruit that was easy to pack and eat on a train journey, were often brought along for the ride by passengers. Once eaten, the core would be thrown out the window to each side of the tracks, and over time the seeds germinated and grew into the trees that continue to drop their fruits on the track after all these years.

Bikepack the Confederation Trail

Stage 1: Charlottetown to St Peter's Bay

DURATION	DIFFICULTY	DISTANCE
4hrs	Hard	58km

Start anywhere from Charlottetown's Confederation Trail and head north. You'll pass the airport before the trail turns eastward. The first section of the trail will have you weave in and out of Charlottetown's suburban and trade areas. The trail follows the highway so it is difficult to leave the city behind until you pass Mount Stewart, where the nature begins. There is a small cafe attached to the town's library at Mount Stewart, should you feel hungry; otherwise the trail continues through a forestry section before arriving at Morell. Here you can join the return journey of the St Peter's Bay to Lighthouse trail all the way to St Peter's Bay, where you can indulge in a seafood dinner at the Landing.

Stage 2: St Peter's Bay to Elmira

DURATION	DIFFICULTY	DISTANCE
3hrs	Hard	45km

From St Peter's Bay, follow the Confederation Trail eastward. This is a stage with views of trees and small hamlets along the way. At the halfway point, you can branch off at Harmony Junction to visit the seaside town of Souris (additional 8km one way). Use the opportunity to stop for a meal and stock up on supplies, as there will not be many facilities until you reach Elmira (pictured above). On reaching the trail's end, you can choose to cycle on for another 5km to the lighthouse at East Point, or rest up for the day at your accommodations. Your best option is to look into North Lake Harbour where there is a motel and a campsite.

MEUNIERD/SHUTTERSTOCK

Stage 3: Elmira to Montague

DURATION	DIFFICULTY	DISTANCE
5½hrs	Hard	75km

This stage leaves the Confederation Trail to start by following the Island Walk Trail, where cycling is also allowed. From Elmira, cycle toward South Lake to join the trail that zigzags in and out of the coastline and the inland towns toward Souris, Howe Bay and Cardigan. This is where you'll join back onto the Confederation Trail to finish at Montague. This is a long day, but you'll be rewarded with wonderful scenery, wildlife and a chance to visit these heritage towns and Amish villages along the way. The Island Walk Trail isn't always a dedicated trail, and some parts of it follow the road, so watch for traffic.

Stage 4: Montague to Charlottetown

DURATION	DIFFICULTY	DISTANCE
3hrs	Hard	48km

This is the last stage to complete the loop back to Charlottetown. Cycle toward Victoria Cross from Montague on the road to reach the town of Uigg, where you can join a section of the Confederation Trail in the northward direction. The trail will wind itself in and out of woodlands and farmlands before reaching Mt Herbert, where the trail ends at a road junction. From here on, it is on-road cycling shared with traffic until you reach Hillsborough River Bridge. There is a two-way dedicated cycle lane on the west side of the bridge, taking you back to the city, where you can rejoin the Confederation Trail for a grand finale at your destination in Charlottetown (pictured above).

Bonavista (p132)

Newfoundland & Labrador

17 **Bonavista Peninsula Ride**

This breezy route takes in a bit of everything that the Bonavista Peninsula is famous for, including quintessential Newfoundland coastal scenery, a historic lighthouse, sea stacks with nesting puffins, dramatic rock formations and a 19th-century plantation, with plenty of places to enjoy a picnic along the way. **p132**

18 **Bell Island Loop**

Once known for its iron ore mining, hilly, scenic Bell Island is now a popular tourism destination and an easy getaway from St John's. This route around the island's periphery takes in the lighthouse and historical sights, with the chance for a detour to visit the sea stacks at Grebe's Nest. Cafes en route offer the chance for a waterside lunch. **p136**

Explore

Newfoundland & Labrador

This is Canada's remote, northeastern frontier, with vast pine forests, bird-covered sea stacks and fog-draped fishing villages. You will need to reset your inner clock to adjust to laid-back local rhythms, and your external clock to match the province's 30-minute GMT offset. Newfoundland, where the rides in this chapter are located, is also famous for its music, pub and theater scenes. What 'the rock' lacks in dedicated bike paths is compensated for by the warmth of its welcome – it's hard to visit without being addressed as 'm'dear' at least once – and its many opportunities to combine cycling with hiking.

St John's

Newfoundland's main port of arrival has several bike-rental shops, a low-key but dedicated cycling scene and a range of hotels, including a hostel and a campground. While it is not the most bicycle-friendly city, once away from downtown there are some fine nearby rides. Pedego rents e-bikes and offers bike tours, while nearby Freeride Mountain Sports rents mountain bikes for 24-hour periods, making longer or multiday itineraries feasible. Both shops are on Water St, which has many eateries and – during summer peak season – several traffic-free sections. To transport your bike from St John's to or from a trailhead, try renting a minivan taxi, many of which accept bikes; useful contacts here include Jiffy Cabs and City Wide Taxi, or try an Uber XL.

Bonavista

Bonavista is a 3½-hour drive north from St John's at the end of the Bonavista Peninsula. If you can only visit one place outside of the capital, this is a good choice thanks to its bike-rental shops, large supermarket and array of hotels, both in Bonavista and in nearby towns.

Twillingate

This town, where one of this chapter's rides is located (p140), is known as a hub for iceberg spotting and whale-watching, as well as for its hiking trails *(rockcuttrails.ca)* and its good selection of crafts at the Artisan Market. A hostel, a campground, several homey hotels, good dining and a well-stocked supermarket round things out. Twillingate is an easy 1½-hour drive from Gander International Airport, where there is also vehicle rental.

WHEN TO GO

The province's best cycling is from May to September, when the weather tends to be drier and sunnier, but bring a rain jacket just in case. These months are also whale-watching season, with sightings generally peaking in July and August. May and June bring the chance to see icebergs. Late autumn and winter are infamous for strong winds, especially in the east.

Corner Brook

Newfoundland's second-largest town after St John's is about a 45-minute drive from Deer Lake Regional Airport (where you can rent a vehicle) and about an hour's drive from Gros Morne National Park. It makes a useful starting point for exploring western Newfoundland, primarily because of its good cycle shop, Cycle Solutions, which offers a range of rentals plus shuttle service and car carrier-rack rentals (all of these should be arranged in advance). If you need to spend the night, there is a modest array of mostly midrange hotels and a campground. Note that most cycling in western Newfoundland is along roads. Main arteries can have considerable traffic during summer peak season, but side roads are generally quiet. Throughout, distances are long and many areas are hilly, making this region a better bet for experienced, confident cyclists.

TRANSPORT

St John's International Airport receives domestic and international flights. You can also fly into Deer Lake, near Gros Morne National Park, or Gander (335km northwest of St John's). DRL buses (which take disassembled bikes for a fee) connect major settlements, including St John's, Gander, Deer Lake, Corner Brook and Port aux Basques. Elsewhere, you'll need a vehicle.

WHAT'S ON

Pippy Park Winter Bike Festival
(bicyclenl.com) This fun event on snowy but groomed singletrack is held each March in and around Pippy Park in St John's.

Long Range Enduro
(wccanl.ca/enduro) A challenging community-oriented ride that is held in August in western Newfoundland's Humber Valley between Deer Lake and Corner Brook.

Royal St John's Regatta
(stjohnsregatta.ca) Join in the festivities at this early-August St John's classic – a provincial public holiday.

WHERE TO STAY

Outside of St John's, where you will find a full range of places to stay, most Newfoundland accommodations are either at campgrounds or in small, family-run motels or B&Bs. At some of the larger chain motels in St John's you should check in advance about bike policies, but it is generally not a problem to find somewhere to keep your bike overnight. Throughout the province, accommodations fill during the summer peak season, especially in St John's, and especially in July and August when the city hosts several music festivals and sporting events.

Resources

Bicycle Newfoundland and Labrador *(bicyclenl.com)* The province's official cycling organization.

Ordinary Spokes *(ordinaryspokes.ca)* St John's–based community cycling group.

West Coast Cycling Association *(wccanl.ca)* Focal point for mountain biking in western Newfoundland.

Avalon Mountain Bike Association *(ambanl.ca)* Avalon Peninsula mountain-bike resource.

T'Railway *(trailway.ca)* Updates and info for Newfoundland's T'Railway.

BEST BIKE RIDES: CANADA

17

Bonavista Peninsula Ride

Best for
WILDLIFE

DURATION	DIFFICULTY	DISTANCE	START/END
2hrs	Moderate	25.9km	Bonavista/ Mockbegger Plantation

TERRAIN	Gentle hills, mix of tarmac & packed gravel

Puffins, Elliston

With its rich marine environment and seabird-filled coastline, it is easy to see why the original Beothuk inhabitants and, later, the Italian sailor Giovanni Caboto, were attracted by what is today known as the Bonavista Peninsula. The name supposedly comes from Caboto's exclamation of 'buona vista' when he first sighted land after a five-week sail across the North Atlantic, and there are indeed many 'good views' – of summer's puffins, craggy sea stacks, tiny islands and colorful houses, especially along the coast-hugging sections of this route.

Bike Hire

Rent bikes in Bonavista town at Coastal E-Bikes (coastal-e-bike-bonavista.com) or at nearby Bicycle Picnics Cafe & Bistro (facebook.com/bonavistapicnicscafe; hybrid bikes), which will also pack you a picnic lunch.

Starting Point

Start on Mockbeggar Rd, along the coast and in between Bonavista's two bike-rental shops. Both shops offer free parking nearby and the route's end point is just down the road.

01 Start on Mockbeggar Rd, which overlooks Bonavista Bay on the western edge of town, and follow this up and around to your right, staying close to the coastline and enjoying the views. After about 500m, you will see the appropriately named Long Beach to your left. Don't miss reading the sign detailing the effects of the 1755 Lisbon (Portugal) earthquake that were felt all the way across the Atlantic here in Bonavista. Continue following the still very quiet road along the coast, staying left at the fork in front of the large, yellow Swyer's Fresh Foods and then winding your way through a small

The Beothuk

When Giovanni Caboto spotted Bonavista in 1497, the area was already home to the Beothuk People and their ancestors, who lived mainly in the area between Bonavista Bay and Notre Dame Bay. While there are few traces remaining today of the Beothuk, one of the best places to get an introduction to their way of life is at the seasonal Beothuk Interpretation Centre in Boyd's Cove. It is about 300km northwest of Bonavista off Rte 340 and an easy stop if you are combining cycling in Bonavista with a visit to Twillingate.

Elevation (m)

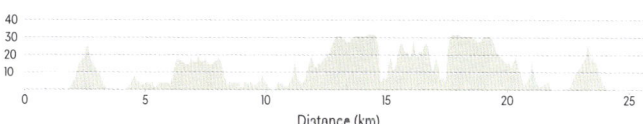

neighborhood. Just before the 2km mark, there is another tiny fork where you can take either side. The roads join together again at Red Point Rd, which then merges with Cape Shore Rd.

02 Follow Cape Shore Rd, enjoying the increasingly lovely sea views to your left, until just after the 7km mark, where you will see the Cape Bonavista lighthouse – one of the ride's highlights – just ahead. It is well worth paying the $6 admission fee to go inside. On the lower floor are period furnishings and information about life as a lighthouse keeper. Up in the tower, you can see the original (now restored) lighting system, which was fueled by seal oil. Inside the lighthouse ticket office (which is just before the lighthouse) is another small, free museum. Just offshore are massive sea stacks favored by puffins and other nesting seabirds and just below the parking area (to the left of the lighthouse access road) is Landfall Park, with walking trails and a statue of Giovanni Caboto. On all sides, the views from the cape are wonderful.

03 Once you're finished at the lighthouse, retrace your route for about 3km, again passing Landfall Park until you see a wide, mostly smooth but occasionally potholed dirt road on your left, fringed by a horse farm and sheep pastures. Turn here and follow this road east to Dungeon Provincial Park – another highlight. From the viewing platform, you can look down on what was once a large, enclosed cave (the roof now collapsed) with two openings to the sea and get an idea of the power of waves, wind and erosion

BEST BIKE RIDES: CANADA   133

over the millennia in shaping Newfoundland's coast. Dungeon Provincial Park is part of the larger Discovery Global Geopark (*discoverygeopark.com*), which incorporates other sites on the Bonavista Peninsula and attempts to show the region's many layers of both geological and human history.

04 From the Dungeon, continue east and then southward, still following the dirt road, past Lance Cove until about the 13.6km mark and the junction with the tarmac Spillars Cove Rd. Turn left here and follow the lightly travelled road until its end. There is a parking lot to your left. Continue straight on with your bike over a somewhat rougher but rideable dirt path for about 400m, turning left at the small footpath junction at around the 16km mark. (This footpath is part of the Klondike Hiking Trail connecting Spillars Cove with Elliston.) Just ahead of you to the left is a huge rock formation rising up from the sea known as the Chimney. The air here is filled with the sound of seabirds and crashing waves – it is a wonderful spot.

05 Retrace your steps back to Spillars Cove Rd and past Dungeon Provincial Park to Cape Shore Rd. Turn left onto Cape Shore Rd and retrace your steps back to town, enjoying the fine views as you approach Bonavista.

06 The cycling route's end point is at Mockbeggar Plantation, where you can visit a late-19th-century plantation house and learn about the area's role in Newfoundland's history. (Entry to the site is included in the Cape Bonavista lighthouse ticket.) After returning your bike, finish by exploring the harbor area – about 500m down from the plantation – on foot. Call in at Ye Matthew Legacy museum, where you can visit the scale model of Giovanni Caboto's 28m caravel, the *Matthew*, and watch the fishing boats in the harbor. Nearby are several cafes, including Bicycle Picnics Cafe & Bistro and Mifflin's Tea Room.

☕ Take a break

About 50km southwest of Bonavista is the village of Trinity, with beautifully preserved historic houses and an active theater scene, whale-spotting tours (try Trinity Eco-Tours or Sea of Whales) and a short hiking trail to the top of Gun Hill. Afterwards, enjoy homemade soup at the VINTAGE GRIND CAFÉ or a hearty waterside dinner at DOCK MARINA. About 10km up the road on the edge of Trinity East is the trailhead for the Skerwink Hiking Trail.

Cape Bonavista Lighthouse

Cape Bonavista Lighthouse

If you climb the tower of the Cape Bonavista lighthouse, you can get a close-up look at the workings of a catoptric lighting apparatus. With this system, seal or whale oil was used to fuel lamps, whose light was then reflected by polished silver parabolic mirrors that concentrated the light into a strong beam. Catoptric lighting was used at Cape Bonavista until 1962. In contrast to modern lighthouses, the system at Cape Bonavista required daily – sometimes even hourly – maintenance, including refilling the oil, checking the length and positioning of lamp wicks and frequently polishing the reflecting mirrors.

18

Bell Island Loop

Best for

COASTAL VIEWS

Bell Island Lighthouse (p138)

DURATION	DIFFICULTY	DISTANCE	START/END
3hrs	Hard	25.6km	Bell Island Ferry Dock

TERRAIN	Hilly & mostly paved

Bell Island – only 34 sq km in area and with just 2000 residents – earned an outsized reputation in the late 19th century due to its iron ore mines. Today it is a scenic, off-the-beaten-track place filled with quiet corners where you can see seabirds, spot whales (sometimes), step back in history and cycle or hike. The island's main draw is its coastline, rimmed by high cliffs, rock formations and sea stacks. It is also full of historical sites, most of which are accessible on a bike. Allow at least half a day for exploring, and ideally longer.

Bike Hire

Mighty Bear Resort rents e-bikes and will meet you at the ferry. Freeride Mountain Sports *(freeridems.com)* in St John's has mountain-bike rentals. There's no charge to bring bicycles on the ferry.

Starting Point

The loop starts and ends at the ferry dock and can be done in either direction. Going clockwise lets you save the lighthouse views for the end.

01 From the Bell Island ferry dock, you will be glad to have an e-bike when you see the very steep hill ascending to town. After cruising (or pedaling) up, turn left onto signposted Memorial St, where things get a bit easier.

02 Continue along Memorial St for 650m until you see Cemetery Hill Rd leading left. Follow this down toward the water, where there is a battery with two cannons that were used for defense during the WWII U-boat attacks on the island.

Global Iron Ore Hub

During the early 20th century, Bell Island became globally renowned for its iron ore production and the population swelled to over 12,000. During WWII, local mines played such an important role in Allied war efforts that German U-boats launched several attacks on nearby iron ore–carrying ships. One attack accidentally struck a pier, making Bell Island one of the few North American sites to receive a direct wartime hit. The local iron ore industry flourished until the late 1950s, when changing global markets and increasing competition sent it into permanent decline. To learn more, don't miss the museum and mine tour (bellislandminetour.com).

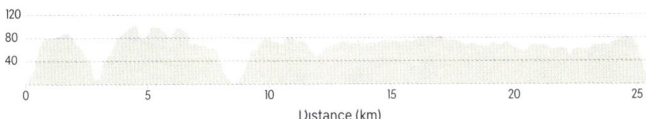

03 Back on Memorial St, continue to about the 6.2km mark where there is a signposted turnoff to the left leading down a small, unpaved lane toward the coast and the old Community Cemetery, which has gravestones dating to the early 1800s. Just beyond this turnoff to the right is the small Sacred Heart Grotto.

04 Again back on the road, which is now called Lance Cove Rd, continue to the 7km mark and the left-hand turnoff onto Lance Cove Beach Rd. This takes you down to a small beach (one of the few spots on the mostly cliff-clad island that can be directly approached from the water) and the moving Seamen's Memorial, honoring sailors killed during the 1942 U-boat attacks targeting iron ore freighters. Just up from the memorial is Rose Castle Inn & Cafe, with outdoor terrace seating overlooking the sea – a perfect spot for a break.

05 Back on the main route, continue toward the southwestern tip of the island and then bend back northeastward. You will now find yourself on a sparsely traveled inland road (Middleton Ave) paralleling the coast. After passing the airfield turnoff, you will see Hunts Hill Rd to your left at about the 17.3km mark. Here you have a choice. Many locals will tell you not to miss Grebe's Nest. If you are cycling with others, feeling adventurous and the weather is dry (as parts of the route are slippery when wet), you can try this detour. Otherwise continue straight along the tarmac road, proceeding as per Step 6 (following). For the Grebe's Nest detour: turn left onto Hunts Hill Rd and then take the third left onto Carter Ave. This soon turns into an unpaved track taking you down to a rocky cove. Ahead of you to your left, look for the small entrance to a low tunnel that has been blasted through the rock and is supported by wooden beams. It can be accessed with a bit of scrambling. This low and dark tunnel, which was built in the late 1960s by local fishers, takes you to Grebe's Nest, a charming hidden cove surrounded by cliffs and looking out to sea stacks. This is also one of the best spots for appreciating Bell Island's geology, with its impressive rock formations. Note that there is nothing obvious along this route to which you can lock your bike. After enjoying the beauty and solitude of Grebe's Nest, retrace your steps back to the main road.

06 Continue along the main road (now called West Mines Rd) for about 5km after the Hunts Hill Rd turnoff. Wabana's Main St is to your right. Ignore it and go left on Railroad St – the Bell Island Community Museum and Number 2 Mine Tour site is straight ahead to your left; pause for a tour or do one at the end of your cycle. To continue with the cycling route, after turning onto Railroad St, go immediately right onto Quigleys Line Rd. Take this around and out to the Bell Island lighthouse, following the small signposts for the Keeper's Café. The lighthouse, which is one of this route's highlights, has had several incarnations, the most recent dating to 2004, and the chairs in front are prime for gazing out over the water and trying to spot whales.

07 Retrace your steps back along the lighthouse access road for about 1.3km to Quigleys Line Rd, where you go left and then, after about 300m, left again onto East End Rd. Follow this to the junction with Main St, where you again turn left and continue downhill to the ferry dock.

Take a break

Many of Bell Island's eateries come with views. KEEPER'S CAFÉ at the lighthouse has an outdoor sea-facing deck. On the island's southwestern edge, the cosy ROSE CASTLE CAFE has seating indoors or on the outdoor terrace. With luck, at both places, you may spot minke and other whales, especially around July and August. At DICKS' FISH & CHIPS, a local favorite near the ferry terminal, enjoy fish and chips while waiting for the boat.

Bell Island ferry at Portugal Cove

Bell Island Ferry

Daily ferry services connect Portugal Cove with Bell Island from early morning until late evening, but expect cancellations due to weather and breakdowns. The sail takes about 20 minutes. Buy your ticket ($4) at the small office near the top of the hill leading down to the Portugal Cove ferry dock and park in the lot near the boarding area. There is no additional charge for bicycles. The ferry also takes vehicles ($10), but expect a queue, especially on weekends. When departing Bell Island, look back to the island's southeastern edge to see the rock formation resembling huge boots.

Also Try...

PAUL ANDREASSEN/ALAMY

Twillingate – Winery & Beach

DURATION	DIFFICULTY	DISTANCE
1hr	Moderate	12.6km

Twillingate's network of hiking routes *(rockcut trails.ca)* and burgeoning cycling scene mean you can explore entirely on your own steam. Cycling is on-road, but traffic is generally light. For this out-and-back route, rent a hybrid bike at the Artisan Market (which also has picnic sandwiches) or an e-bike at Isles E-Bike Rentals, cross Shoal Tickle Bridge and follow Main St to Great Auk Winery for a tour. Continue along Main St to its terminus at the second parking area (to the right, shortly after the first, on the left), from where it's 500m further on an unpaved trail to French Beach. Retrace your steps to Twillingate and finish with visits to the Wooden Boat Builders Museum and other sites *(twillquest.com)* or a meal at Georgie's.

T'Railway from St John's to Bowring Park

DURATION	DIFFICULTY	DISTANCE
1hr	Easy	8km

This out-and-back route gives you an introduction to Newfoundland's 883km T'Railway. Rent a bike in St John's at Pedego E-Bikes or Freeride Mountain Sports, get a sandwich to o at Rocket Bakery and head southwest along Water St to the trailhead behind the Railway Coastal Museum (pictured above). Cross the wooden bridge, continue along the Waterford River, with its nature signposts, then ride up a small hill (at 0.6km), across Blackhead Rd and onto Southside Rd before merging again onto the riverside path. Follow this past woodlands and quiet neighborhoods to Bowring Park, where you can picnic. Lock your bike near the tennis courts, cross the stone bridge and walk along the scenic South Brook Trail for about 1.5km (including up some stairs) to Eagle Bridge. Retrace your steps to St John's.

KYLE TAM/ALAMY

Western Brook Pond

DURATION	DIFFICULTY	DISTANCE
30min	Easy	5.6km

Western Newfoundland's cycling hub is Cycle Solutions in Corner Brook. Arrange your bike rental with them – they also rent car racks to get your bike to the trailhead and sometimes offer shuttle service. Start this out-and-back route with a drive along Rte 430 to the Western Brook Pond parking area, from where it is a flat, 2.7km cycle along a multi-use trail to Western Brook Pond, part of Gros Morne National Park. Tour the fjord by boat (pictured above) before cycling back. Advanced cyclists: try the approximately 83km loop beginning in Norris Point (about 35km south of Western Brook Pond), cross to Woody Point on the Bonne Bay Water Shuttle, then cycle on relatively lightly traveled Rtes 431 and 430 via Wiltondale back to Norris Point.

St John's to Cape Spear

DURATION	DIFFICULTY	DISTANCE
1½hrs	Hard	14.8km

For this challenging one-way route, it is the destination – Cape Spear, Canada's most easterly point – that makes the ride special. Rent a bike in St John's at Freeride Mountain Sports, then make your way via the Railway Coastal Museum to Blackhead Rd, where the very hilly ride begins. There is no shoulder; early morning and late afternoon generally have less traffic. The first 4km climbs almost continuously, at grades of 9 percent or more in points. As you approach Cape Spear, the road, flanked by stands of pine, becomes increasingly scenic. Once at the Cape, allow time to visit the historic lighthouse (Newfoundland's oldest) and museum, see the WWII defensive battery, hike and take in the views. There is also a seasonal cafe.

BEST BIKE RIDES: CANADA   141

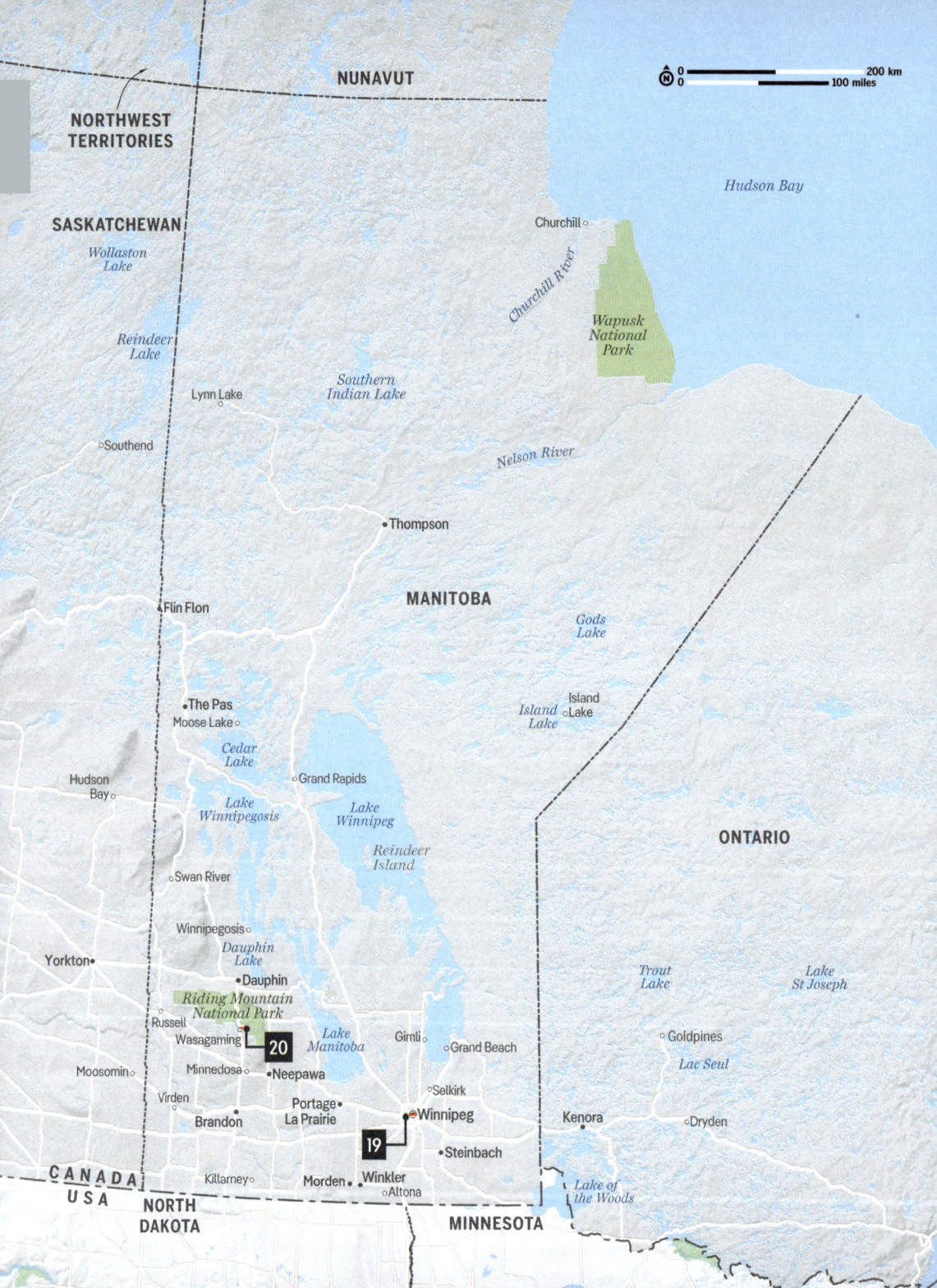

Clear Lake (p150)

Manitoba

19 Winnipeg

Trace Winnipeg's two rivers on an out-and-back linking St Boniface, the Forks and Assiniboine Park while learning about the French Canadian, Métis and Indigenous heritage that shapes the city and waterways. At the park, visit polar bears at the zoo, wander through the English Gardens and experience Canada's largest indoor waterfall before returning along the rivers. **p146**

20 Lakeshore Trail

Pack a towel and swimsuit on this out-and-back ride following Clear Lake's shoreline. From Wasagaming's main beach, ride to the Deep Bay beach area for a jump off the dock. Continue on to the Wishing Well, a shaded picnic spot with flower gardens. Return to town where ice cream and cinnamon buns await. **p150**

Explore

Manitoba

Manitoba sits at Canada's geographic center: a patchwork of prairie, boreal forest, Precambrian shield and tundra. Winnipeg, the main urban hub, offers trails linking its two rivers, while beyond the city, routes weave through small towns, provincial parks and cottage country. Lakes punctuate the landscape, shaping rural rides, and wildlife is a constant companion – moose, elk, deer and, far to the north, polar bears. From flat prairie lanes to winding forest trails and lakeside paths, Manitoba's rides offer a mix of terrain, scenery and adventure, giving even short outings a taste of the province's diverse cycling country.

Winnipeg

Winnipeg is the province's major city and the base for exploring nearby trails at Bird's Hill Provincial Park, Pinawa and Seven Sisters. The city's cycling network includes riverside paths, quiet streets and dedicated lanes. Amenities are plentiful with bike shops, cafes and markets where you can stock up. Make sure to allow extra time to explore the city. The Assiniboine Zoo is home to polar bears, the Leaf botanical garden features Canada's tallest indoor waterfall, and the Canadian Museum for Human Rights offers moving exhibits. Notably, Qaumajuq at the Winnipeg Art Gallery houses the world's largest public collection of contemporary Inuit art. The Forks, at the confluence of the Red and Assiniboine Rivers, is a must-visit for foodies. The area serves as the city's cultural hub, featuring public art, riverside green space and a food market. Top options include spelt bread from Tall Grass Prairie Bread Co, sushi made to order at Fusion, or Fergie's Fish 'n Chips with Manitoba-grown russet Burbank potatoes and Lake Winnipeg pickerel.

Wasagaming

Wasagaming is the resort townsite within Riding Mountain National Park and a natural starting point for cycling in the area. Only three hours northwest of Winnipeg, it's easily accessible by car. Bike rentals are available at several shops. Riders can explore paved and gravel routes along the lakefront, forested singletrack within the park, or venture north to the Northgate Trails and south toward Minnedosa's Squirrel Hills. The townsite offers a range of amenities, including

WHEN TO GO

Winters are long and cold, with short daylight hours and heavy snow, though fat biking on groomed trails is becoming increasingly popular. Still, most cyclists will want to avoid the deep freeze. Spring can be wet and muddy but summer is prime riding season, with warm weather and sunsets lingering past 9:30pm in June. Autumn is another excellent time, bringing crisp days and vibrant foliage.

restaurants, a bakery, a movie theater, sports courts and boat rentals. Accommodations range from campgrounds and lodges to resorts and nearby microcabins at Northgate. With its combination of access, facilities and scenic surroundings, Wasagaming is ideal to tie together several short loops or longer exploratory cycling adventures.

Dauphin

Dauphin lies less than an hour north of Wasagaming in Riding Mountain National Park and minutes from the Northgate Trails, making it a convenient base for exploring western and central Manitoba trails. The town offers essential services, including grocery stores, restaurants and accommodations from motels to small hotels. Though cycling infrastructure is limited, Dauphin provides insight into prairie and parkland life, early pioneer settlements and rail history at the Fort Dauphin Museum and the Dauphin Rail Museum & CNR Station. Cafe Trocadero and The Bloom 'n Bean serve up caffeine fixes, while Corrina's is the place for pierogies, a Polish dumpling popular throughout the province.

WHERE TO STAY

Winnipeg has the widest hotel selection, from big-name chains to boutique stays close to the Forks and downtown attractions. Small towns typically have motels, while lake country is dotted with cabins and cottages, from rustic hideaways to full-service resorts. Across the province, camping is a summer favorite, with communities and parks providing sites for tents and RVs with amenities like showers, outdoor kitchens and general stores. Glamping options, including canvas tents, yurts, tipis and domes, are becoming more common and easily booked online or through Airbnb. Many accommodations are located near lakes and parks, making it easy to plan riding routes.

TRANSPORT

Manitoba is easiest to navigate by vehicle, as public transport between towns is limited and communities are spread apart. Winnipeg is the main gateway, with flights from across Canada and beyond. VIA Rail serves northern Manitoba while regional flights connect remote areas. In larger centers, buses and taxis provide transportation.

WHAT'S ON

Festival du Voyageur
(heho.ca) Nine-day winter festival in February celebrating French-Canadian heritage with music, food and snow sculptures.

Winnipeg Folk Festival
(winnipegfolkfestival.ca) Outdoor music festival featuring local and international artists in Birds Hill Provincial Park in July.

Folklorama
(folklorama.ca) Multicultural festival in August with pavilions showcasing food, music and dance from around the world.

Icelandic Festival of Manitoba
(icelandicfestival.com) Gimli-based celebration of Icelandic culture held in August with a viking village, mock battle and local cuisine.

Resources

Travel Manitoba *(travelmanitoba.com)* Province-wide resource for trip planning, maps and events.

Tourism Winnipeg *(tourismwinnipeg.com)* Local information and guides for city events and attractions.

Riding Mountain National Park *(pc.gc.ca/en/pn-np/mb/riding)* Resource for the national park including maps, trail updates, permits and camping.

19

Winnipeg

DURATION	DIFFICULTY	DISTANCE	START/END
3hrs	Easy	32km	Woodcock Cycle Works

TERRAIN	Paved & gravel paths, roadway

Esplanade Riel suspension footbridge

Spreading across the prairie under wide open skies, Winnipeg is a city of culture, history and festivals, anchored at the meeting point of the Red and Assiniboine Rivers. Cycling is a growing part of city life, with riverside trails, dedicated bike lanes and quiet residential streets making it easy to explore on two wheels. Cafes, markets, galleries and public art punctuate this out-and-back route. French Canadian and Métis heritage in St Boniface and Indigenous history at the Forks share the city's past, while landmarks like the Canadian Museum for Human Rights highlight Winnipeg's resilience, creativity and sense of possibility.

Bike Hire

Woodcock Cycle Works (woodcockcycle.com) rents e-bikes, and mountain, fat and road bikes. Staff are knowledgeable and online booking is simple. The best all-round choice for this route.

Starting Point

Start at Woodcock Cycle Works and ride west toward the nearby Red River. Connect with the river trail system here, the gateway north through St Boniface and onward to Winnipeg's downtown.

01 St Mary's Rd, part of Trans-Canada Highway 1, is far too busy to cycle along, so avoid it. Instead, turn right from Woodcock Cycle Works onto Fifth Ave, then left at the stop sign onto Des Meurons St. Continue until Caton St, then turn left again. This quieter residential street crosses St Mary's and becomes Lyndale Dr, where you'll join one of Winnipeg's seasonal bike routes. Here, traffic is slowed to 30km/h, with sections closed to through-vehicles, creating a relaxed start.

BEST BIKE RIDES: CANADA

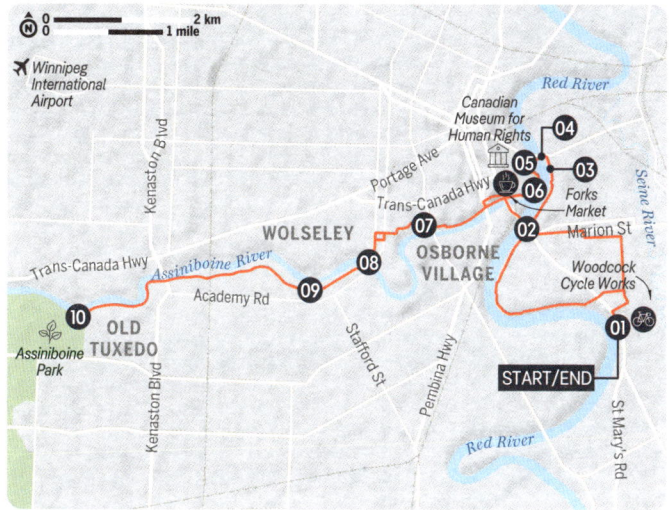

Elevation (m)

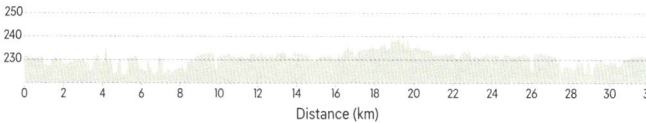

Canadian Museum for Human Rights

The Canadian Museum for Human Rights is an unforgettable experience, both architecturally and emotionally. Its striking exterior, with its angled glass overlapping like wings of a dove, signals hope and peace. Inside, the design guides visitors from darkness to light, reflecting humanity's journey toward justice. As you ascend 100m, spaces grow brighter, culminating at the top platform with city views. Exhibits share stories of struggle and triumph, reminding visitors of the ongoing fight for human rights. The combination of bold architecture and powerful storytelling makes this museum deeply moving, leaving you inspired and hopeful for the future.

02 A mix of gravel and paved riverside trail parallels Lyndale Dr, dipping down beside the Red River where benches dot the grassy embankment. Follow the pathway until you reach Walmer St. You'll join another traffic-free section where barricades limit cars. Stick to the road alongside Lyndale Drive Park North. Just after the Winnipeg Rowing Club building on your left, connect back to the river path as it ducks beneath Norwood Bridge.

03 Riding along the east bank, you'll enjoy views of the Canadian Museum for Human Rights and the Esplanade Riel suspension footbridge, framed by the river. Pause for photos at Belvédère Saint-Boniface, a small riverside deck, and watch Winnipeg Waterways' yellow riverboats zip past. Further along, listen for the bells of St Boniface Cathedral as you explore its cemetery and the final resting place of Louis Riel, leader of the Métis People and founder of Manitoba. The cathedral's dramatic stone facade features a hollow rose window open to the sky since a 1968 fire. A modern church now sits within the ruins, creating a striking contrast between past and present.

04 Cross over the Esplanade Riel, a cable-stayed bridge named after Riel. Its 57m pylon rises like a sail above the Red River, connecting St Boniface to downtown and the Forks, a historic meeting place where the Red and Assiniboine Rivers converge. For over 6000 years, Indigenous Peoples gathered here. Later it became a hub for fur traders, settlers and railways. Today it is Winnipeg's cultural center, filled with markets, green space and museums.

05 Follow the path curving right toward Festival Park, where the giant 'Winnipeg' sign provides a perfect photo backdrop with the Canadian Museum for Human Rights behind it. Nearby, the CN Stage hosts summer concerts, while Ai Weiwei's *Forever Bicycles* installation, an archway of over 1200 welded frames, celebrates cycling's place in global culture.

06 On the upper trail, pause at the Orientation Circle and the *Path of Time* sculpture, which celebrates the procession of prairie history. Nearby, you'll find the Children's Museum, playground and Odena Celebration Circle. For a quicker route, descend toward the water level along the River Walk, a wide gravel trail passing the Forks National Historic Amphitheatre. Continue under the Forks bridge to the Historic Port, then follow the path up the riverfront plaza to the Forks Market.

07 Leaving the Forks, follow the tree-lined River Walk trail west, next to the Assiniboine River. You'll pass under the train bridge and Midtown Bridge. Under the Osborne St Bridge, the path rises to meet city streets. The best route climbs to Granite Way, where a dedicated two-way bike lane goes past the Beer Can. This mix of riverside trail to urban bike lanes showcases Winnipeg's seamless cycling infrastructure.

08 Follow the bike path as it turns left onto Balmoral St and curves left into Young St. At the stop sign onto Westminster Ave, the bike path splits to either side of the road. Continue across Maryland St, and take the path south over Maryland Bridge where you join Wellington Cres, one of Winnipeg's loveliest cycling avenues.

09 This section of Wellington is closed to through traffic, making it safe for all riders and popular with road cyclists. Leafy yards and grand homes flank the street, while a central greenway provides a safe space for pedestrians. Across from Wellington Park, the riverside path resumes under St James Bridge, where shaded forest follows the bends in the river.

10 The path delivers you directly into Assiniboine Park. Here is the ride's formal turnaround point, but don't skip exploring. Pedal to the English Gardens, visit the Leaf, stop at the zoo, or continue to the Leo Mol Sculpture Garden before returning through the Forks to Woodcock Cycle Works.

☕ Take a break

The Forks is Winnipeg's must-stop mid-ride break. Lock your bike and refuel inside the FORKS MARKET, where food stalls serve everything from sushi to fish and chips, alongside bakeries, breweries and local artisan shops. The open-seat hall makes it easy to sample and share. Outside, a covered plaza with a canopy, high-top tables and Adirondack chairs line the riverfront, providing a welcoming spot to sit, gather and watch people go by along this lively public space.

Assiniboine Park

Assiniboine Park

A full day can easily be spent at Assiniboine Park. Start at the zoo's Sea Ice Passage tunnel to watch polar bears swim overhead, then discover animals from Asia alongside interactive conservation exhibits. Cycle to the Leaf botanical garden to experience the four biomes, six themed gardens, koi pond, butterfly garden and Canada's tallest indoor waterfall. Continue through the English Garden and Leo Mol Sculpture Garden, let kids play at the playground and family center, or hop on the historic steam train. Outdoor summer performances by the Royal Winnipeg Ballet at the Lyric Theatre add culture to the greenery.

20

Lakeshore Trail

DURATION	DIFFICULTY	DISTANCE	START/END
1hr	Easy	12.2km	Riding Mountain NP Visitor Centre

TERRAIN	Flat multi-use trail, paved & crusher dust

Beach, Wasagaming

Riding Mountain National Park is a popular four-season destination in Manitoba, drawing families, campers and cottagers to its forests, rolling hills and the sparkling waters of Clear Lake. The townsite of Wasagaming is the park's central point, with restaurants, shops and a beach that fills with visitors on sunny days. The Lakeshore Trail is the park's signature out-and-back ride. It is an easy family-friendly route that follows the shoreline linking a swimming dock, picnic spots and viewpoints before arriving at the shaded rest stop and gardens of the Wishing Well.

Bike Hire

Clear Lake E-Bike Rentals provides Norco mountain bikes and e-bikes from the bike shed next to the Tempo Gas Station at the intersection of Wasagaming Dr and Buffalo Dr.

Starting Point

The paved, tree-lined trail to Clear Lake picks up around the back of Riding Mountain National Park Visitor Centre, heading north toward the main beach.

01 Pick up a park map from Riding Mountain National Park Visitor Centre and turn west down Heritage Lane to reach the start of the trail. Here, a wooden structure with an embedded sign points the way down the paved path to the main beach. A bike rack with an attached air pump makes for a convenient tune-up spot before setting off.

150   BEST BIKE RIDES: CANADA

Elevation (m)

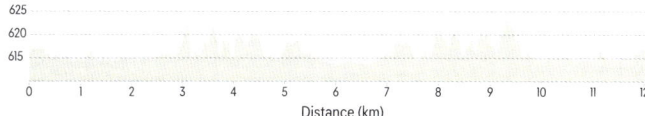

Distance (km)

Clear Lake

True to its name, the water at Clear Lake is so transparent you can spot fish and the sandy bottom from the shore. It's fed by a natural spring and is oligotrophic, which means the lake's clarity is a result of minimal sediment runoff and low nutrient levels, which prevent algae blooms and murky water. Formed during the last glacial period 10,000 years ago, these factors create the remarkably clean and clear waters seen today. The lake supports a variety of wildlife including birds and 14 fish species. Its calm, shallow bays make it an ideal spot for swimming and paddling.

02 Ride past tree-lined picnic tables and outdoor barbecues. From here, you'll come to tennis courts, mini-golf and public washrooms ahead on your left. Take a right through the day-use area arriving at the main beach, the park's busiest attraction. The trail skirts the grassy back edge of the beach, offering views of sand, sunbathers and the Clearwater Dock and Clear Lake Marina. Here you can rent pedal boats, paddleboards and kayaks. It's best to stay off the boardwalk close to the water as it's intended for pedestrians, but there are plenty of beach access points to park your bike and dip your toes in the lake.

03 At the east end of the beach, the trail curves into a quieter tree-lined stretch along the shoreline. Public docks are popular with swimmers and loungers and on your right, private cottages with manicured backyards line the route.

04 At High Point View, a yellow fence runs perpendicular to the trail, across from a covered sitting area. The paved path dips down to the left and widens into a hard-packed gravel trail edged with riprap. These basketball-sized rocks provide protection against waves and winter ice damage. On the right, a steep tree-covered embankment with the occasional staircase connects cottages to the docks.

05 Clear Lake lives up to its name and it's easy to spot minnows and the sandy bottom as you ride along the shore. The gravel trail ends near a collection of canoes and kayaks pulled in safely under the protection of the trees. This is a popular photo spot. A forested singletrack along the water offers a shortcut to the beach. However, you'll want to take the gently climbing paved path to the right to the Deep Bay parking area.

06 At Deep Bay, the beach access makes this a perfect stop to cool off before pedaling on. Facilities are basic, with an outhouse and waste and recycling bins in the parking lot. A wooden staircase and path lead down to a popular swimming hole, where a dock extends out into a startlingly deep drop-off. Brave beachgoers leap from the end while others lounge on the sandy beach or paddle past in the water.

07 Back on the trail heading east, the surface returns to smooth pavement and the ride flows easily through the forest. Glimpses of the lake appear between stands of spruce, pine and aspen. Watch for a viewpoint turnoff. This leads you to a pair of signature red Adirondack chairs and a picnic table, a quiet place to pause for a snack and enjoy the view.

08 A subtle downhill grade makes this section a joy, requiring only light pedaling. The air smells of pine and lake water, and if the wind is calm, Clear Lake stretches out mirror-like on your left. The trail ends in a small parking area where you'll turn left onto Wishing Well Road. This is a quiet spur where the golf course borders one side and the lake hugs the other, with two docks for boaters to launch from. It's a short jaunt to the ride's end point. While traffic is light, watch for cars turning off the highway.

09 The ride's turnaround point at the Wishing Well is one of the park's most charming picnic spots. Underneath the boughs of evergreens are shaded tables, a bike rack, wood animal carvings and another pair of red chairs overlooking the lake. Several short bridges cross the creek and are surrounded by a manicured flower garden. The namesake well still stands – toss in a coin, which goes to support Riding Mountain Historical Society's Pinewood Museum. If you planned ahead, this is the perfect spot to unwrap a maple-dipped cinnamon bun from the Whitehouse Bakery before heading back to Wasagaming.

Take a break

There are no food stops along the trail, so plan to pick up something in town before you go. Line up early at WHITEHOUSE BAKERY for their popular cinnamon buns. They come in three flavors: maple, cream cheese and original. No one will judge you if you order all three and staff will even wrap them up so you can carry them in your backpack. After the ride, ice-cream lovers will appreciate VELVET DIP or the BOARDWALK, and CHOCOLATE FOX for gelato.

Black bear, Riding Mountain National Park

Beware of Black Bears

Black bears are common in the park, and scat can be seen along the trails. Bears are typically shy and move off quickly, but can be unpredictable. While biking, carry bear spray in a holster for quick access and make noise. Call out or ring a bike bell – especially around corners – to avoid surprising wildlife. If you encounter a bear, slow down or stop and let it move away. If a bear shows aggression, back away slowly, make yourself look bigger and be ready to use your bear spray. Most encounters end once the bear feels unthreatened.

Also Try...

ASHLYN GEORGE

Pinawa to Seven Sisters

DURATION	DIFFICULTY	DISTANCE
3hrs	Easy	31.2km

This town-to-town ride connects Pinawa and Seven Sisters, taking in the spillway along the way. Starting on the Ironwood Trail in Pinawa, the route follows the Winnipeg River, where benches and interpretive signs dot the route. The trail enters a shaded forest along a rolling gravel path. It shifts onto a grassier section connecting to an old gravel road, part of the Trans Canada Trail. Watch for black bears. Pause at the Seven Sisters Generating Station (pictured above), where you can bike across the top and peer over the edge of the spillway to see the exposed Precambrian rock below. Stop in Seven Sisters for a bite at the motel before returning the same way. Bike rentals are available at the Pinawa Motel.

Lakeview Trail

DURATION	DIFFICULTY	DISTANCE
30min	Easy	7km

While the beach draws the crowds, the Lakeview Trail offers families an easy way to explore around Birds Hill and Kingfisher Lakes. This well-signed paved path in Birds Hill Provincial Park traces the two lakes and starts from several points, including the campground, riding stable and both ends of the beach. The route winds through mixed forest before opening into a meadow with benches and picnic tables. Side spurs lead to volleyball courts, a playground and sandy beaches, perfect for a swim or snack. A 2km inner trail hugs Birds Hill Lake, while a shortcut between the lakes makes for a quicker outing. Bee2gether Bikes *(bee2getherbikes.com)* rents a variety of unique rides from tandems and cruisers to sidecars and tricycles.

ASHLYN GEORGE

Squirrel Hills Trail Park

DURATION	DIFFICULTY	DISTANCE
45mins	Moderate	5.3km

Located just outside Minnedosa, Squirrel Hills Trail Park (pictured above) offers 8km of singletrack (for mountain bikes) through forest and along the Little Saskatchewan River Valley. The blue route begins with a slow climb before winding through curves and shaded sections, manageable for most riders. A highlight is a side jaunt to a well-cared-for warm-up cabin with matching orange outhouse. A short green trail connects the loop back to the trailhead, which features a timber-frame pavilion, skills area, maps and parking. Separate double-wide cross-country ski trails run through the park. The trails are groomed in winter for skiing and fat biking. After riding, drive into town for a treat at Dari Isle Drive-In or swim at Lake Minnedosa.

Northgate Trails

DURATION	DIFFICULTY	DISTANCE
1-2hrs	Moderate	26km

North of Riding Mountain National Park and just south of Dauphin, Northgate Trails show Manitoba's Parkland has more flow, features and scenery than you might expect. This 26km network of trails winds through creek valleys, forest and open fields, blending smooth, approachable routes with singletrack that curves along boardwalks and crosses narrow bridges, including a few wet creek crossings. In shaded stretches, ferns and mossy spruce give the trail an almost rainforest vibe. Five all-season microcabins sit among the trees at the trail head, each with wi-fi and a deck with bike stands. Whether racing through or pausing to notice art sculptures and birdhouses tucked among the trees, Northgate highlights the trails, the surrounding forest and the local community's involvement.

Prince Albert National Park (p166)

Saskatchewan

21 Meewasin Valley Trail

Trails along Saskatoon's riverbank cover more than 105km, blending paved and gravel paths with city streets, parks and riverside views. Highlights include bridge crossings, public art and pelicans fishing at the Weir. An easy half-day loop passes cafes, playgrounds and museums with optional singletrack for cyclists seeking a more adventurous ride. **p160**

22 Prince Albert National Park

From Waskesiu townsite, a 14km multitrail loop winds along the lakeshore and onto shaded forest tracks. Riders may encounter elk, deer and abundant birdlife, with grassy, rolling singletrack adding flow. Benches, beaches and forest breaks offer chances to pause while local bakeries and ice-cream shops await in town for post-ride refueling. **p166**

Explore

Saskatchewan

In southern Saskatchewan, summer fields of bright yellow canola and golden wheat stretch across the countryside, highlighting the province's thriving agricultural sector and making a lovely backdrop during a ride. But Saskatchewan isn't all flat prairie. Rolling valleys, coulees and boreal forest create a surprising variety of landscapes for cycling and exploration, with chances to spot wildlife such as deer, elk and beavers along the way. Trails thread city parks, river valleys and provincial and national parks, offering both urban rides and wilderness adventures as cycling infrastructure continues to grow and improve.

Saskatoon

Saskatoon is the province's northern gateway for the Meewasin Valley Trails, Dakota Dunes Trails and Prince Albert National Park. The South Saskatchewan River bisects the city, lined with bridges, public art and riverside parks. A downtown highlight is the Remai Modern, with its cantilevered design inspired by the prairie landscape and the world's most complete collection of Picasso linocuts. Saskatoon's dining scene excels in locally sourced cuisine, with farm-to-fork restaurants like Odla, Primal and Pique Cafe as standout spots.

Regina

Regina serves as a southern base for Wascana Park, Wakamow Valley Trails and Buffalo Pound Provincial Park Trails. Worthwhile cultural stops include the Royal Saskatchewan Museum, offering exhibits on the province's natural history; the MacKenzie Art Gallery, with rotating contemporary and Indigenous art exhibitions; and the RCMP Heritage Centre, showcasing the history and legacy of Canada's iconic police force. Regina's core neighborhoods offer casual and fine dining, from sourdough donuts at the Everyday Kitchen to homemade sandwiches at Italian Star Deli and afternoon high tea at the Burrow.

Moose Jaw

Located 70km west of Regina and 30km south of the mountain-bike trails at Buffalo Pound Provincial Park, Moose Jaw features the Wakamow Valley Trails. Downtown reflects the city's bootlegging past, with guided Tunnels of Moose Jaw tours exploring underground

WHEN TO GO

Winters in Saskatchewan are long and cold with short daylight hours, making outdoor riding challenging. Summers, by contrast, shine with more than 2300 hours of sunshine per year. May to September is prime riding season, with trees leafing out by late May and wildflowers in June. July brings heat, mosquitoes and the bright yellow blooms of canola fields. August offers berries while September delivers cooler temperatures and brilliant autumn colors.

passages once used by rum runners during Prohibition, blending history with local lore. Temple Gardens Mineral Spa is popular for its indoor and outdoor geothermal pools, a helpful stop for post-ride recovery. Dining ranges from casual cafes like Deja Vu Cafe, serving wings and milkshakes, to atmospheric spots such as the Yvette Moore Gallery or the patio at Rosie's on River Street. Boh's Cycle & Sporting Goods rents bikes for town rides or trips to nearby Buffalo Pound.

Waskesiu

Waskesiu, the townsite of Prince Albert National Park, fronts a sandy beach on Waskesiu Lake and is a gateway for camping, boating and trail exploration. Set in the boreal forest, it has a lively resort-town vibe with art galleries, a heritage museum, a theater and an outdoor store. Order tacos from Hecho en Waskesiu, coffee at Evrgreen or a famous cinnamon bun from the Waskesiu Trading Post. Many visitors stay in the campgrounds and Parks Canada rents rustic cabin-like oTENTiks, or you can upgrade to one of the many accommodations that rents fully equipped cabins.

WHERE TO STAY

Hotels are plentiful in Saskatoon and Regina, but the countryside offers more memorable stays. Saskatchewan's glamping scene is growing, with options like tipi cabins, yurts, tiny cabins and even converted grain bins – an ode to the province's farming-based economy.
Campgrounds are widespread throughout small communities as well as regional, provincial and national parks. They're well used in summer, with many visitors pulling campers and setting up for longer stays or pitching tents, often beside lakes, beaches or trail networks. Most sites offer shower facilities and power, while some are rustic, making it easy to match your budget and style of adventure.

TRANSPORT

It's DIY travel in Saskatchewan. The best option is to rent a vehicle in Saskatoon or Regina, both with international airports and national connections. Distances between towns and trailheads are long, so plan accordingly. Public transport between communities is virtually nonexistent, though city buses and taxis operate within the major cities.

WHAT'S ON

First Nations University of Canada Powwow
(fnunivpowwow.ca) April; a multiday ceremony celebrating First Nations culture with traditional song, dance and regalia.

Saskatchewan Roughriders
(riderville.com) Regina's CFL football team packs Mosaic Stadium with enthusiastic green-and-white fans from May to October.

Saskatchewan Jazz Festival
(saskjazz.com) Ten days of jazz, funk, blues and indie performances on Saskatoon's riverbank stage in July.

Nutrien Fireworks Festival
(nutrienfireworksfestival.ca) A September weekend of choreographed pyrotechnics paired with music, food trucks and family activities along the Meewasin Valley Trail.

Resources

Tourism Saskatchewan *(tourismsaskatchewan.com)* Comprehensive province-wide resource for trip planning, maps and events.

Tourism Saskatoon *(discover saskatoon.com)* Local tips, guides and event listings for the city and area trails.

Parks Canada *(parks.canada.ca/pn-np/sk/princealbert)* Details on Prince Albert National Park, including camping, permits and trail info.

21

SASKATCHEWAN

Meewasin Valley Trail

DURATION	DIFFICULTY	DISTANCE	START/END
1½-2hrs	Easy	17.8km	Life Outside Gear Exchange

TERRAIN	Flat multi-use riverside trail, mix of paved & crusher dust

Dancers, River Landing (p165)

Saskatoon's riverbank is the city's defining feature, and there's no better way to experience it than on two wheels. The Meewasin Valley Trails extend for more than 105km along both sides of the South Saskatchewan River, winding past bridges, parks, cafes and galleries while always keeping the water within view. The name Meewasin comes from the Cree word *miýwâsin*, meaning 'it is beautiful.' It's a fitting description for this route that blends urban life with river scenery. This easy loop highlights the best of both worlds, making it an accessible half-day ride with plenty of opportunities to pause and explore.

Bike Hire

Bike rental options in Saskatoon are limited. Life Outside Gear Exchange (lifeoutsidegx.com) is a used-gear shop offering mountain bikes, electric and non-electric cruisers and double-wide bike trailers to pull young children.

Starting Point

Begin at Life Outside Gear Exchange on Clarence Ave and 12th St E. From here it's a short ride through residential streets before you connect with the riverside trail.

01 From Life Outside Gear Exchange, ride west along 12th St E, turning right at the first intersection onto Albert Ave. This route avoids heavier traffic on 12th. One block later, turn left on 13th St, following its curve across University Dr. Two blocks further, cross Saskatchewan Cres E to reach the paved trail and head north. The transition from city streets to the Meewasin Valley Trail is immediate as you leave traffic behind to roll under shaded trees, catching first glimpses of the South Saskatchewan River.

BEST BIKE RIDES: CANADA

Delta Bessborough Hotel

Often called the 'Castle on the River,' the Delta Bessborough Hotel was built by the Canadian National Railway and opened in 1935 as part of a chain of grand railway hotels stretching across Canada. Designed in the Châteauesque style, its turrets, steeply pitched roofs and stone walls were intended to evoke a French castle. Over the decades, the hotel has welcomed royalty, politicians and celebrities, serving as a social hub. Even if you don't stay overnight, its dramatic waterfront setting makes it impossible to miss, and its architecture anchors Saskatoon's skyline, establishing its place in the city's cultural life.

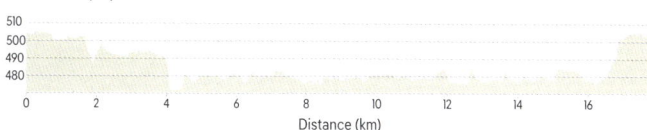

02 Ahead, a pull-off with benches and interpretive panels introduces Saskatoon as the City of Bridges. With six crossings in the downtown core alone, bridges have shaped the city's growth and remain key landmarks. From this vantage point, you'll spot the castle-like Delta Bessborough Hotel dominating the downtown skyline. It's a perfect spot to take in the views.

03 As the paved path continues north, you'll reach University Bridge. A large Meewasin Valley map marks Cosmopolitan Park, making it a good orientation stop. Rather than heading across the bridge into downtown, take the path left down the switchbacks and beneath the bridge's steel span. The trail climbs slightly under a canopy of trees across two metal bridge walkways. The shared path is busy with walkers, runners and other cyclists, so make sure to stay on the right around corners.

04 The river curves gently here, framing the white dome of the Shakespeare on the Saskatchewan tent across the river next to where the Prairie Lily riverboat docks for summer cruises. Benches and viewpoints line the way, providing spots to rest. Keep to the leftmost path as you pass along the edge of the University of Saskatchewan campus and Jim Pattison Children's Hospital on your right.

05 A tight hairpin turn brings you into a marshy corner with reeds and cattails. If you're lucky, you may glimpse beavers at work – gnawed tree stumps reveal their presence. A keystone species, beavers help

☕ Take a break

Downtown Saskatoon tempts with tasty stops and lively sights just off 21st St E. Grab ice cream at BUS STOP REFRESHMENTS, a bright red double-decker London bus, or settle on the east-facing patio at Cathedral Social Hall. Wander down 2nd Ave S for craft beer, pubs and casual bites or head to 3rd Ave S for hand-pulled noodles at NUMBER 1 NOODLE HOUSE or Brooklyn-style pizza at THIRTEEN PIES PIZZA. Along the way, take in the colorful murals that brighten the streets.

shape this riverside ecosystem as they create habitat for other types of animals like birds, fish, insects and amphibians.

06 From here, a side path leads to the Diefenbaker Canada Centre, a museum showcasing Canadian politics and celebrating the Right Honorable John G Diefenbaker, the 13th prime minister of Canada. It's a worthwhile detour for history buffs. Otherwise, remain on the main trail where benches along the curve provide river outlooks.

07 A short distance ahead on the right, a grassy field hides a quirky sculpture garden on the University of Saskatchewan campus. About two dozen concrete, wood and metal urban art pieces stand scattered across the lawn. Watch out for gopher holes if you detour through.

08 Back on the trail, you'll soon reach the Weir, a low dam completed in 1940 as a Depression-era project to raise water levels for boating and city intakes. After Gardiner Dam assumed that role in the 1960s, the Weir became a city landmark and popular pelican-watching spot. At this point, the signature experience is to push your bike up the ramped stairway and walk it across the CPR Bridge's narrow wooden deck. If you prefer to stay in the saddle, continue 1.6km north to ride across Circle Drive Bridge instead and return on the other side.

09 Now on the west side of the river, ride south to the end of the Weir parking lot. Take a short jaunt to the left on a wooden boardwalk down to the Weir to watch pelicans up close. From spring through autumn, these giant white birds congregate here to fish in the turbulent water. Rejoin the main paved trail paralleling Spadina Cres E, a smooth, wide stretch where elm branches arch overhead, forming a leafy ceiling that turns this part of the trail into a natural green corridor.

10 Soon you'll roll past the Children's Discovery Museum and Kinsmen Park, a family-friendly area with a Ferris wheel, miniature replica freight train on a track and playground. Beyond the parking lot, gender-neutral washrooms and water fountains sit near the Shakespeare on the Saskatchewan Festival site, where colorful banners and a white-tented amphitheater hint at the city's lively arts scene.

Canadian Pacific Railway Bridge

Canadian Pacific Railway Bridge

The Canadian Pacific Railway Bridge is Saskatoon's most distinctive river crossing. Suspended 19.5m above the water, planks creak underfoot and pigeons scatter from the trestles on the narrow wooden pedestrian walkway as you cross beside the active rail line. Views stretch north toward Circle Drive Bridge and south to the downtown skyline. If a train rumbles past, the combination of sound, movement and whoosh of air delivers a visceral, unforgettable adrenaline rush that makes this crossing a one-of-a-kind experience.

SASKATCHEWAN 21 MEEWASIN VALLEY TRAIL

The Remai Modern

The Remai Modern is Saskatoon's contemporary art museum, distinguished by its bold cantilevered design that echoes the region's iconic grain elevators. Its collection spans over 8000 works, including the world's largest collection of Picasso linocuts. Rotating exhibitions showcase local, prairie and international artists, with a strong focus on Indigenous creators and contemporary voices. Visitors are greeted by Nick Cave's *Spinner Forest* in the entry hall – strands of thousands of colorful wind spinners cascading from ceiling to staircase. The ground-floor restaurant, Hearth, serves locally inspired dishes while the 2nd floor and rooftop terrace offer striking views of the river.

Remai Modern

11 Continue under University Bridge and up to Spadina Cres E and 24th Street E. Take the left pathway past a wooden gazebo, dipping down alongside a grassy embankment lined with benches toward a fountain feature, perfectly framing the Bessborough Hotel. The section of the Kiwanis Memorial Promenade behind the hotel recently underwent a $5.5 million enhancement, including replacement of the asphalt trail, an updated riverside promenade and two new viewpoint nodes. It's part of the Meewasin Valley Authority's ongoing effort to improve downtown trail experiences while preserving river views and public amenities.

12 Continuing south, ride under the Broadway Bridge and the steel-arched Traffic Bridge to reach River Landing, Saskatoon's riverfront hub. On summer evenings, locals gather at the amphitheater for salsa dancing or at the Sugar Shack for ice-cream treats. A children's spray pad features an interactive model of the Saskatchewan River Basin, playfully exploring its geography and hydrology. At street level, you'll find a French bakery and cafe and several restaurant patios, all perfect spots to relax and soak in the atmosphere.

13 From River Landing, the trail passes beneath Idylwyld Bridge, where buskers' music often fills the air and a mural brightens the underpass. On the water, paddleboarders and rowing teams are a common sight. To the right, Riversdale Park features an outdoor gym and basketball courts, creating a community atmosphere. The trail into Victoria Park remains paved and smooth, bordered by grassy areas and public art, including the Chinese Zhongshan Ting Pavilion and a 27ft-tall Indigenous stainless-steel arch featuring a wind chime.

14 Follow the trail to the right, west of the Saskatoon Canoe Club. Passing the water treatment plant, it parallels Spadina Cres W before joining the Southwest Trail Link. Benches and a large turnaround circle mark the start of this double-wide 1.3km section. It's flanked by trees and shrubs, and the trail's smooth wide surface makes this corridor a joy to cruise along.

15 Named for Saskatoon's legendary hockey star, the Gordie Howe Bridge features a dedicated walkway beneath the roadway. Trains rumble across the nearby Grand Trunk Bridge. Once across, turn north (left) and ascend the path along Diefenbaker Park. The trail shifts from pavement to crusher dust as it winds through a riverside section. On the river, birds gather on sandbars and islands midstream.

16 Ahead, Gabriel Dumont Park has a playground, picnic tables and public washrooms. A wooden bridge links back to street level at Saskatchewan Cres W. Ride carefully along this 650m stretch of road lined with prestigious homes. At the stop sign, turn left and rejoin the Meewasin Valley Trail, passing beneath Idylwyld Bridge and into Rotary Park. This is a popular spot for picnics and yoga, with open lawns. From here, you'll also find excellent vantage points to photograph the city skyline across the river.

17 Under Victoria Bridge and just past Broadway Bridge, a steep hairpin climb to the right leads up to Cosmopolitan Park and Broadway Ave. You may need to hop off and push your bike up this short section to reach street level. Broadway is busy with cafes, bars and shops, making it worth a stop. When you're ready to finish the ride, take the river path north and turn right onto 13th St E until the right turn at Albert Ave and a final left on 12th St E, bringing you back to Life Outside Gear Exchange.

TOP TIP:

Tougher Trails

Adventurous cyclists can explore the lower Meewasin Valley Trails, where dirt paths hug the riverbank more closely. Steeper gradients and winding tree-lined singletrack provide a rewarding challenge for confident riders.

22

Prince Albert National Park

Best for
WILDLIFE

Waskesiu Trading Company (p168)

DURATION	DIFFICULTY	DISTANCE	START/END
1-1½hrs	Moderate	14km	Prince Albert NP visitor center

TERRAIN	Paved path, grassy forest track

Prince Albert National Park sits at the southern edge of Canada's boreal forest, where aspen parkland meets conifer woods. This transition zone creates a rich habitat for wildlife – elk, deer and bears are often seen alongside smaller mammals and birds. Waskesiu, the park's townsite, fronts a broad sandy beach and serves as the launching point for camping, boating and trail exploration. From here, a biking loop combines sections of the Red Deer Blue and Yellow routes and the Fisher Trail, following the lakeshore, winding through forest and returning to town. It offers a perfect introduction to the park's mix of wilderness and resort amenities.

Bike Hire
Grey Owl Center next to the visitor center has rented bikes since 1998. Its fleet includes matching blue Konas with wide tires for local trails plus e-bikes for easier cruising.

Starting Point
The trail begins at the Prince Albert National Park Visitor Centre in Waskesiu. From the parking lot, cross Lakeview Dr to the marked path next to the main beach.

01 The Red Deer Yellow route sets off along a smooth paved path beside Waskesiu's main beach. It's a gentle warm-up, passing newly upgraded public washrooms, picnic spots and lake views right from the first kilometer. Benches appear regularly, offering excuses to pause and watch the waves. The tree-dotted route skirts along the lake, tracing the shoreline east. You'll pass a ball diamond, disc golf course, community hall and more public parking on the right.

Waskesiu Lake

For many holidaying families, Waskesiu's sandy beach is the park's star attraction. Stretching the length of the townsite, it fronts Waskesiu Lake, which reaches 19m at its deepest yet stays surprisingly warm and clear for a northern lake. Kids gravitate to the playground set right on the sand, while the long breakwater extending into the water makes for a leisurely stroll. Updated washroom and shower facilities double as mini-galleries, displaying wildlife photography by local artist Jason Bantle of All in the Wild. Benches line the lakeshore path, providing a spot to linger for one of the lake's fiery sunsets.

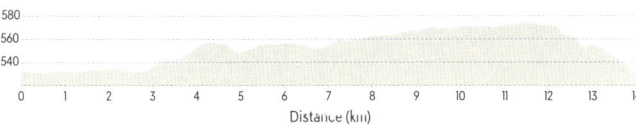

02 The busy townsite trail soon runs alongside a wide grassy strip that separates lakeside cabins and rental cottages from the water. In the forest, raspberry bushes and fireweed edge the trail beneath the shade of jack pines. Pulling away from the lakeshore, the trail curves right to meet a paved connector road on the Red Deer Blue route. A trail map helps you re-orient. This is Old Waskesiu Dr, which runs past Beaver Glen beach and campground with an outhouse on the left and parking lot on the right.

03 Passing the Kapasiwin Bungalows, the trail climbs to meet Kingsmere Rd where a miniature stop sign marks your crossing. You'll dip back into the forest briefly before coming to a second road crossing. On the other side, a large trail map confirms you're re-entering the Red Deer Blue trail system.

04 From here, the trail officially gives way to a forest track – grassy in the center, with shallow dirt and gravel wheel ruts guiding your tires in sections. The canopy closes overhead as spruce, aspen and willow replace the lakeshore views. This section rolls with an overall increase in elevation across a few short climbs and descents that make for a fast-flowing ride.

05 Another road crossing loops you back over Kingsmere Rd and toward the back side of Beaver Glen Campground. You'll connect to the quiet campground road for a short stint. Here, the scent of pine needles mixes with wood smoke from campsites. A diamond-shaped yellow road sign directs traffic to the right, but you'll want to ride straight, off the road and slip back onto the forest trail.

06 Red Deer Blue meets Yellow again and you'll cross Kingsmere Rd at Ajawaan Rd to reach the start of a gravel road. Turn right onto the signed trail leading into the community's fuel-break – a managed stretch of land designed to reduce wildfire risk. The trail here is broad and airy, lined with tall grass and edged by mixed forest. It runs roughly parallel to the highway but is surprisingly peaceful. A fence and berm on the left hint at nearby Parks Canada's facilities.

07 At the signed intersection, turn left onto the Fisher Trail, the highlight of the ride. It begins as a gravel singletrack sprinkled with bright red bunchberries, then narrows to mossy spruce forest. Roots make the trail the most technical so far but give way in sections to a soft carpet of needles and smoother ground. At the back end of the loop, the trail passes through a boggy patch and runs alongside a small lake fringed with purple fireweed. Look for squirrels and deer, and keep an eye on the trail for bear scat or elk prints pressed into the dirt – signs of the park's resident herd. The last half of Fisher is fast and flowy, with wide curves and gentle descents that make it the most exhilarating and rewarding stretch of the day.

08 Turn left as the Fisher Trail reconnects with Red Deer Yellow. From here, the track is an old grassy road as your path continues out to the trail's small parking lot. There's a large information board and toolkit here including a tire pump. Crossing Kingsmere Rd one last time, it's an easy wind-down along forested Red Deer Yellow and a last chance to notice details like purple wildflowers edging the path and the rustle of poplar leaves overhead. As you reach the mini-golf and sports courts on the left, you'll come out to the intersection of Lakeview Dr and Waskesiu Dr. A left turn onto the road and a quick right take you back into the visitor center parking lot and the bike rental, where bakeries and ice-cream shops are not far away.

☕ Take a break

Once you leave Waskesiu's townsite, there's nowhere to buy food or water on the trail, so stock up before you ride. The WASKESIU TRADING COMPANY bakery is a local legend, turning out up to 800 cinnamon buns a day in summer. Post-ride, enjoy tacos at HECHO EN WASKESIU or join the queue for a cone at BIG OLAF SUNDAES or the SCOOP ICE CREAM PARLOR. Surprisingly for a small resort town, you'll also find Mexican, Asian and Italian dining options.

Elk, Prince Albert National Park

Elk Crossing

Waskesiu takes its name from the Cree word *wâwâskêsiw*, meaning 'elk' or 'red deer,' and the townsite has its own resident herd to prove it. It's not unusual to see elk ambling through campgrounds, grazing ditches or blocking trails near the golf course. In fall, males bugle loudly and may clash antlers during rut, so give them space. Parks Canada recommends at least 100m between you and larger wildlife like elk, bears or bison. Carry bear spray on trails and bring a telephoto lens for photos – it's far safer than testing how strong an elk really is.

Also Try...

ASHLYN GEORGE/LONELY PLANET

Wascana Lake Loop

DURATION	DIFFICULTY	DISTANCE
1hr	Easy	10.5km

Circle Regina's manmade Wascana Lake, the centerpiece of one of Canada's largest urban parks, on this easy loop ride. The flat paved trail starts at the foot of the gardens in front of the Saskatchewan Legislative Building (pictured above) and crosses the historic Albert St Memorial Bridge. Benches and viewpoints such as the Wascana Observation Deck invite stops, while Sky Cafe inside the Science Center is ideal for coffee; Bar Willow, overlooking the lake, offers a patio worth lingering on. The loop west of Broad St shows its urban character with gathering spaces and groomed grounds, while east of it the landscape softens into marsh and naturalized shoreline where pelicans, ducks, geese and the occasional painted turtle can be spotted.

Wakamow Valley Trails

DURATION	DIFFICULTY	DISTANCE
2½-3hrs	Moderate	26km

The Wakamow Valley Trails weave through Moose Jaw's river valley, offering a mix of paved paths, grass lanes and flowy singletrack. Starting downtown, murals and heritage buildings hint at the city's character before this out-and-back route follows a boardwalk along the river. Benches and pavilions provide spots to rest, and side loops connect to playgrounds, parks and picnic areas. The trail climbs up the valley, paralleling a farmer's field, to several viewpoints overlooking the river and city. A highlight includes crossing a suspension bridge before dipping into a singletrack ecological zone that encompasses a marsh, meadow and woodland. Bikes, including e-bikes, can be rented at Boh's Cycle and Sporting Goods, making it easy to explore these multi-use trails.

ASHLYN GEORGE/LONELY PLANET

Dakota Dunes Trail

DURATION	DIFFICULTY	DISTANCE
30mins	Easy	6.1km

Pedal through rolling sand hills and prairie grassland on this quick e-bike escape (pictured above), set on Whitecap Dakota First Nation lands. Dakota Dunes Resort is the starting point for this 6km loop near the South Saskatchewan River valley. E-bikes rented from the resort make the gentle climbs effortless. The wide gravel trail circles the property and skirts Dakota Dunes Golf Links, Saskatchewan's top-ranked public course. Short but varied, the ride winds through the mixed-grass prairie landscape and rolling dunes under big-sky views with chances to spot deer, foxes and coyotes. A visit to the resort afterward offers insight into Whitecap Dakota traditions and history, making this a meaningful ride that blends outdoor adventure with a cultural connection to the land.

Buffalo Pound Provincial Park

DURATION	DIFFICULTY	DISTANCE
30mins	Moderate	5km

Twist through a coulee of the Qu'Appelle Valley and race down flowing descents on Buffalo Pound Provincial Park's 30km of mountain-bike trails. Start at the Lower Chalet parking lot, which has camping, toilets and bike service tools. Individual trails are short but link via connectors, letting you craft a choose-your-own-adventure ride. Beaver Loop is an easy introduction, while adding Weeping Fee creates an intermediate 5km loop of more technical singletrack. Expect tight turns, roots, rocks, short climbs and fast descents. Pause at viewpoints to admire the glacier-carved valley and keep an eye out for deer and coyotes. Nearby rentals at Squirrely Putt & Play get you riding, while the Trailhead Cafe is your stop to refuel.

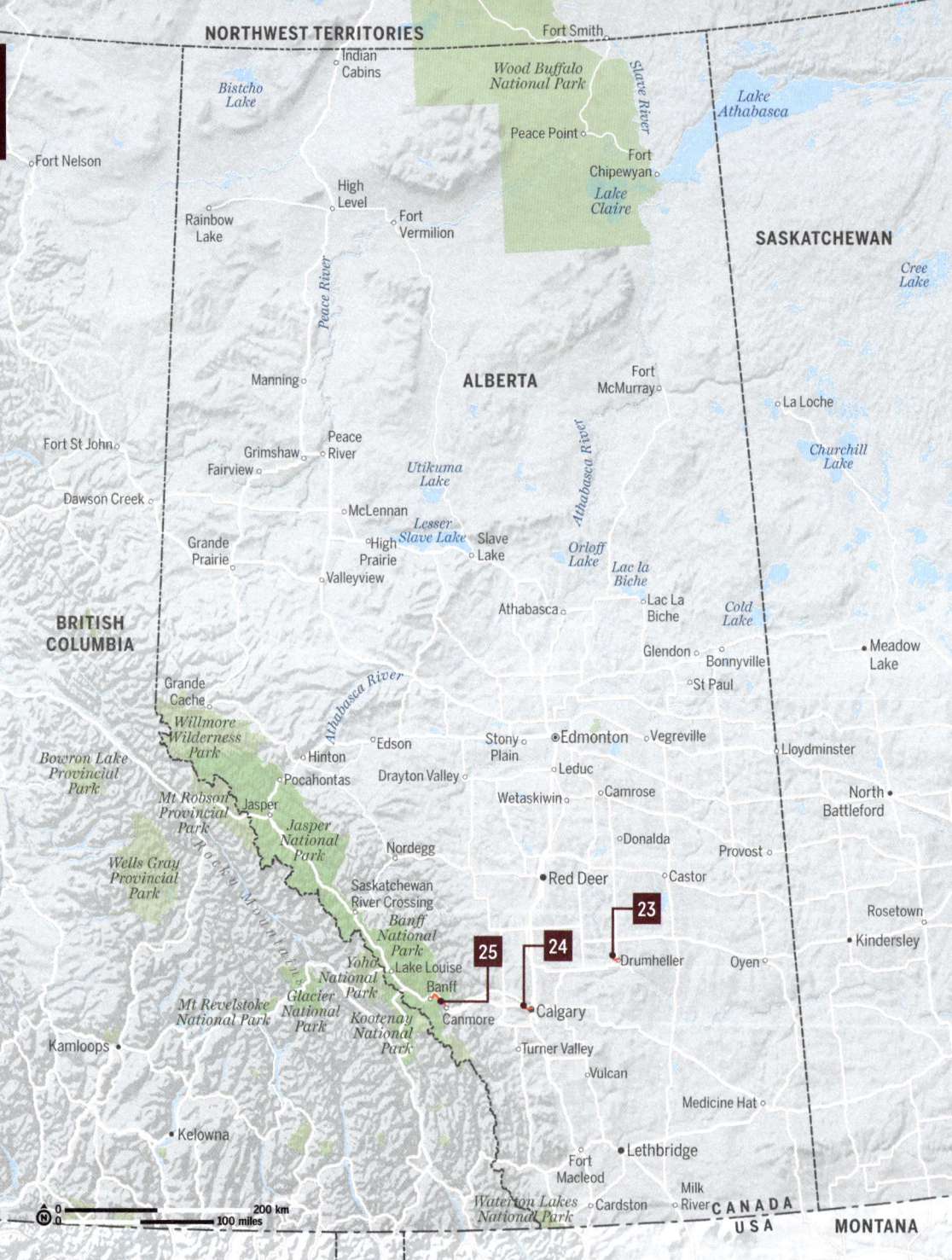

Bow River Pathway (p180)

Alberta

23 **Drumheller Dinosaurs**
Delve into dinosaur country on this easy ride from the Badlands hub of Drumheller to the renowned Royal Tyrrell Museum, taking in landscapes of weathered columns and colorful canyons along the way. **p176**

24 **Calgary's Bow River Pathway**
Historic sites, skyline views, urban parks, and food and drink are the highlights of this flat, family-friendly cycling route beginning and ending at Calgary's iconic Peace Bridge. **p180**

25 **Rocky Mountain Legacy Trail**
This much-loved, traffic-free trail takes you from Canmore to Banff with stunning views of the Three Sisters and Cascade Mountain en route, and plenty of options to shorten or lengthen your ride. **p184**

Explore
Alberta

Alberta – Canada's fourth-largest province – is where the glacial lakes, pine forests and steep slopes of the Canadian Rockies cascade down to meet the prairies. The province's largest city, Calgary, is renowned as home of one of North America's most extensive urban biking networks. East of here are plains brilliant yellow with summer fields of canola, and beyond these, the hoodoo-studded Badlands where dinosaurs once roamed, and where finding fossils amid the wind-sculpted rocks is still a regular occurrence. Especially in southern Alberta, cycling routes are abundant, bike-rental shops are (almost) everywhere, the terrain is varied and the scenic backdrops are unbeatable.

Calgary

This is Alberta's main international gateway, and it is likely that you will have at least a night here at the beginning or end of your travels. Use it to the full, exploring on the city's extensive urban bike pathway system, strolling in its parks and soaking in the diverse and lively cultural scene. The most accessible part of the bike pathway for visitors spreads out along the Bow River east and west of Peace Bridge, with bike-rental shops, restaurants and cafes nearby. There are also hotels in this area, although most are upmarket. For better pricing, try the HI Calgary hostel (just east of the center and near the river) or hotels in Northeast, which lacks downtown's appeal but is convenient to the airport and an easy Uber ride from the center.

Drumheller

Drumheller is small but, as the hub of the Badlands, it is very traveler-oriented. Only a 90-minute drive northeast of Calgary, the town is easy to visit as a day trip from the city. However, to really delve into local history and visit nearby dinosaur sites, stay for at least one night. Several mostly midrange hotels and a campground cater to those wanting to linger. Don't miss stopping at Horseshoe Canyon en route to or from Calgary. Drumheller's sole bike-rental shop also runs a cafe, and there are other eateries in town and along the bike trail.

Canmore

A 90-minute drive west of Calgary, Canmore sits in the Bow River Valley surrounded by mountains. It is less crowded and less expensive than nearby

WHEN TO GO

The best time for cycling is from late April into September, with the season peaking in July and August. Mid-September brings autumn splendor to Alberta's larch and aspen trees. From October to April, many areas are covered with snow. Some bike shops, including Kananaskis Outfitters in Kananaskis Village and Snowtips-Bactrax in Banff, rent fat bikes for winter riding. The Banff & Lake Louis tourism website *(banfflake louise.com)* has trail suggestions.

Banff and makes an ideal base for exploring Banff National Park and surroundings, with camping, a good selection of reasonably priced accommodations and restaurants, well-stocked supermarkets, a laundromat, bike-rental shops and cycling paths. Bike-friendly Roam Transit buses link Canmore with Banff, and Banff with Lake Louise, Johnston Canyon and other local attractions. Canmore's Three Sisters Taxi service (tel 403-493 9900) offers bike transfers for riders wanting to do routes in areas not serviced by Roam Transit.

Banff

Banff is a 25-minute drive northwest of Canmore via the Trans-Canada Highway. It's another popular hub for exploring this part of the Rockies, although overcrowding can be considerable during peak summer season and prices are high. Compensating for this is a lively cafe, pub and eatery scene, numerous bike-rental shops, bike trails, a range of accommodations, including hostels and nearby camping, and a supermarket.

TRANSPORT

Calgary International Airport receives flights from all over Canada and internationally. You can also fly into Edmonton International Airport (300km north). Renting a vehicle is the most feasible way to get around the province, although once you are in hub towns, you can easily get around by Uber or taxi (Calgary), or on foot or by bike (Canmore, Banff and Drumheller).

WHERE TO STAY

Many mountain areas, including Canmore, Banff, Lake Louise and Kananaskis, have hostels and camping areas, and these will be the cheapest and most bike-friendly places to stay. Calgary also has a hostel, and Drumheller has camping. All accommodations fill up during the summer peak season, so book well in advance, although dorm beds are often available on short notice. If booking a standard hotel with your bicycle ask about its bike policies, as some places will not allow bikes in the rooms. A few hotels, including Juniper hotel in Banff, lend or rent bicycles to guests.

 **WHAT'S ON**

Tour de Bowness

(tourdebowness.com) Get inspired at Alberta's premier amateur cycling event, held in early August in and around Calgary and also including a street festival.

Gran Fondo Badlands

(granfondobadlands.ca) Watch or consider participating in this multidistance event held in early July in the Badlands terrain around Drumheller.

Alberta Bike Show

(abbikeshow.com) A hub for all things bike. It is held in late March in Calgary's Stampede Park.

Resources

Travel Alberta *(travelalberta.com)* Helpful cycling pages.

Alberta Bicycling Association *(albertabicycle.ab.ca)* Provincial cycling group.

Cycle Alberta *(cyclealberta.ca)* Cycling routes.

Alberta 66 Mountain Biking *(alberta66mtb.com)* For mountain-bike afficionados.

Bike Calgary *(bikecalgary.org)* Route maps.

Gravel Experience *(thegravelexperience.com)* Alberta gravel rides.

Canmore + Area Mountain Bike Association *(camba.ca)* Access Canmore area's mountain-bike scene.

BEST BIKE RIDES: CANADA   175

23

Drumheller Dinosaurs

Best for
HISTORY

'World's biggest dinosaur,' Drumheller

DURATION	DIFFICULTY	DISTANCE	START/END
1½hrs	Easy	16.8km	Badlands Community Facility

TERRAIN | Mostly flat, paved paths, several short hills

Drumheller is synonymous with dinosaurs and – whether you think you are interested in paleontology or not – the wealth of bones and other fossil remains that have been found in the area is sure to impress. Surrounding town are Canada's Badlands, known for their colorful canyons and hoodoos – weathered, chimney-like rock formations sculpted over the millennia by wind, water and erosion. The setting is even more remarkable considering that the entire area was once covered by a shallow inland sea. Thanks to Drumheller's mostly flat and fat bike–friendly trails, the town makes an ideal year-round destination for exploring on two wheels in this in-and-out route.

Bike Hire
Bikes & Bites, inside the Badlands Community Facility, rents e-bikes for teens and adults and standard-gear bikes for older children. They'll also pack a picnic for you to enjoy en route.

Starting Point
The Badlands Community Facility at 80 Veterans Way in Drumheller is a 1½-hour drive northeast of Calgary. Pay for parking using the Hotspot QR code posted in the lot.

01 From the starting point in the Badlands Community Facility parking lot, go left around to the back of the building to get on the bike path. Cycle west on this, past the aquatics center, and continue for about 400m to the small traffic bridge. As you go, watch for a glimpse of the 'world's largest dinosaur' rising over the buildings to your left. The dinosaur is currently slated for closure in late 2029, so if you want to visit (or climb up to his mouth), now is the time. Back on the bike: you will need to cross the traffic bridge on foot, staying

Royal Tyrrell Museum

The Royal Tyrrell Museum is considered to be one of the best paleontological museums in the world and is a Drumheller highlight. Inside – where it is easy to pass two hours or more – is an extensive collection of dinosaur fossils and skeletal reproductions, plus interactive displays and stations where you can speak with staff about their work with fossils. Among the highlights are a toothless, 21m-long ichthyosaur skeleton – the world's largest known marine reptile – plus the 'Black Beauty' Tyrannosaurus rex exhibit and displays highlighting Alberta's time spent partially covered by a shallow inland sea.

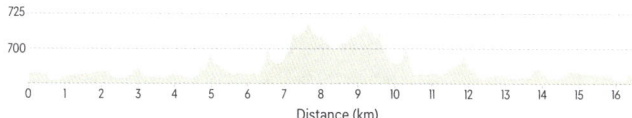

on the left-hand pedestrian walkway. Immediately at the end of the bridge, there is a small, paved pathway to your left leading downhill to the river. Follow this down and then go right onto Poplar St and into a quiet residential area. Follow sparsely traveled Poplar St around as it bends right at the River Grove Campground. Continue on Poplar St, crossing Larch Ave and Grove Ave, before taking the third left onto Poplar Crescent. Follow this for about 160m.

02 As Poplar Crescent bends left, leave the tarmac and head slightly right onto a short, narrow, gravel feeder track taking you to a bike path leading over a bridge. Continue following this path, which runs alongside (but divided from) Rte 838 (N Dinosaur Trail Road) for about 1.5km, past the Homestead Antique Museum. The museum makes an interesting stop on your return ride, especially if you are cycling with children.

03 At about the 3km mark and just after crossing Health Center Dr, take the signposted left-hand turn at the large Morris the Hike-a-Saurus billboard. This takes you away from the main road and toward the river.

04 You will now find yourself cycling on the edge of a quiet residential street and alongside the river. At about the 1.5km mark, the path goes underneath an old railway bridge and into Midland Provincial Park. It is worth pausing here and taking the short detour up onto the bridge to admire the river views. Back down on the path, continue into the heart of the ride, as the now-attractive route winds through sweet-smelling woodland greenery and over a small wooden bridge, with the river still accompanying you to your left. Continue following the path as it curves right into Midland Park's McMullen Island Day Use Area.

BEST BIKE RIDES: CANADA

05 At about the 6km mark, the woodland thins out. Go left at the fork here, through a set of wooden stiles marked by a small Morris the Hike-a-Saurus sign. (The right fork takes you to some picnic tables and toilets.) The path continues 0.7km from the small Morris sign, through an increasingly dry and barren landscape, to Rte 838, where there is a crossing signal. Once on the other side of the road, the path – which has been mostly flat up until now – becomes hilly as it winds its way gradually upward through Midland Provincial Park's starkly beautiful Badlands terrain, with impressive rock formations, small canyons and fine views in all directions.

06 At about the 7.6km mark, you will reach the first of two short but very steep hills. Younger children especially and less confident cyclists will likely be more comfortable hopping off the bike for both the ascents and the equally steep descents. Near the top of the second hill, ignore the right-hand path marked 'cyclists dismount,' going instead to the left, where the path takes you down a short, steep slope and then onto some more gentle ups and downs as it curves through the Badlands landscape to the Royal Tyrrell Museum of Paleontology.

07 The museum has racks to lock your bike, plus a cafeteria and restrooms. After visiting and walking through the surrounding landscape on the signposted 1.4km Badlands Interpretive Trail, follow the same cycling route back to Drumheller, finishing up at the Badlands Community Facility. Especially if you are doing this ride in the afternoon, allow time to photograph the Badlands scenery, which is at its most richly colored in the setting sun. The viewpoints from the tops of the two steep hills are ideal for panoramic shots.

Badlands

☕ Take a break

BIKES & BITES has hearty sandwiches (from $11) and picnic baskets for pre-order, with vegetarian, vegan and gluten-free options available. There are picnic tables at the McMullen Island Day Use area, shortly before the bike trail crosses the highway. Royal Tyrrell Museum also has a cafe with indoor and outdoor seating. To stretch your legs before cycling back to town, there are walking trails through the Badlands scenery of Midland Provincial Park, starting from the museum.

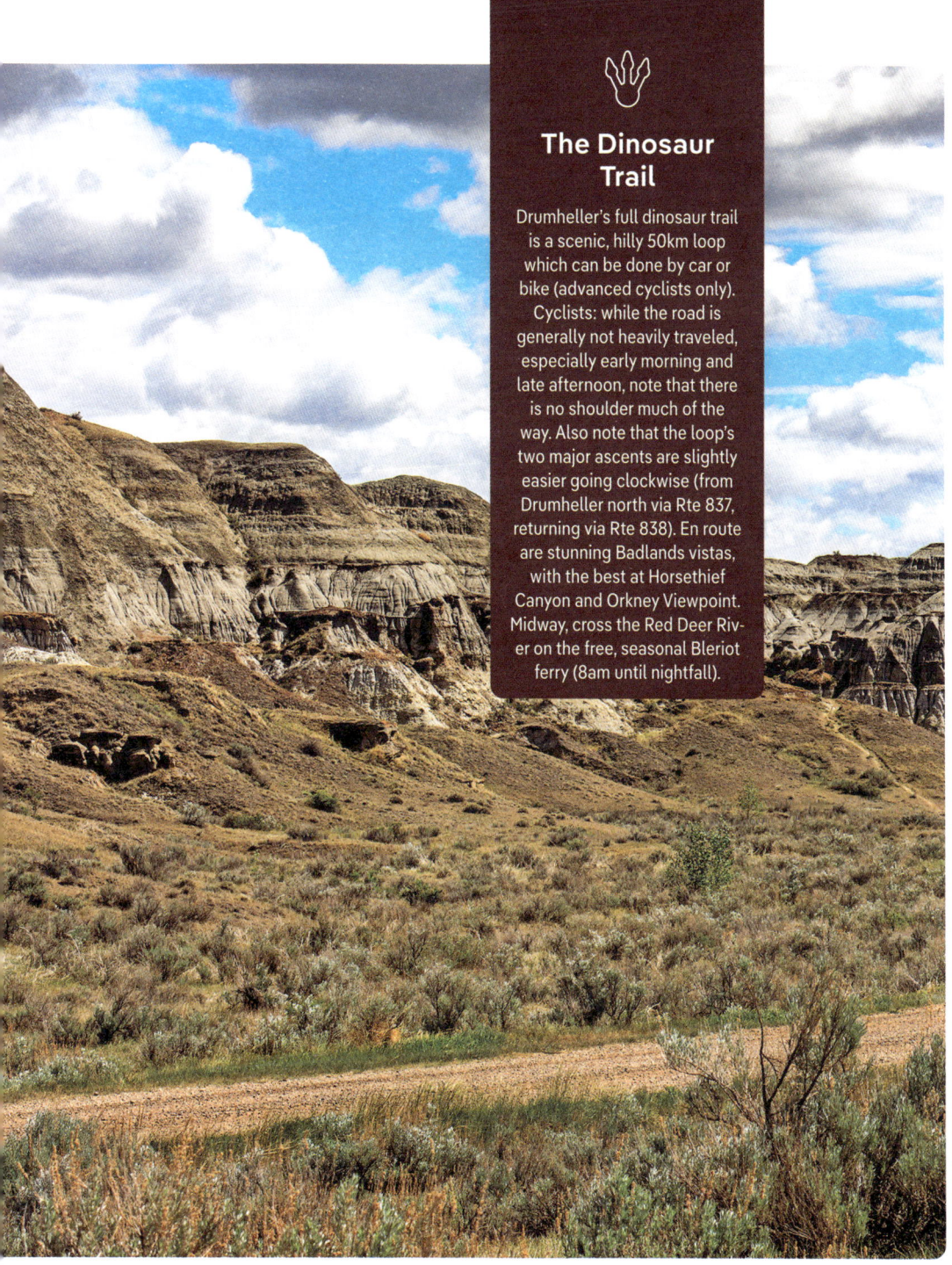

The Dinosaur Trail

Drumheller's full dinosaur trail is a scenic, hilly 50km loop which can be done by car or bike (advanced cyclists only). Cyclists: while the road is generally not heavily traveled, especially early morning and late afternoon, note that there is no shoulder much of the way. Also note that the loop's two major ascents are slightly easier going clockwise (from Drumheller north via Rte 837, returning via Rte 838). En route are stunning Badlands vistas, with the best at Horsethief Canyon and Orkney Viewpoint. Midway, cross the Red Deer River on the free, seasonal Bleriot ferry (8am until nightfall).

24

Calgary's Bow River Pathway

Best for
FOOD

Peace Bridge

DURATION	DIFFICULTY	DISTANCE	START/END
1½hrs	Easy	19km	Peace Bridge (south side)

TERRAIN	Flat, paved, multi-use trail

What better way to get acquainted with downtown Calgary than on the flat, family-friendly Bow River Pathway, beginning and ending at the city's iconic Peace Bridge. With its mix of urban parkland, local landmarks and historic sites, this ride has something for everyone. Take in the Calgary skyline, get a feel for the city's multicultural vibe at Eau Claire Park and Prince's Island, enjoy a meal at one of several cafes en route or detour to the Calgary Zoo. For more experienced cyclists, there's also the chance to extend the ride along the Elbow River to Glenmore dam and reservoir.

Bike Hire

Joe's Garage Bicycle Rental & Repair *(joes-garage.ca)* and Bow Cycle East Village E-Bikes *(bowcycle.com)* have rentals directly on the route. Ridley's Cycle *(ridleys.com)*, on the opposite side of the river, also has e-bikes.

Starting Point

From the riverside bike-rental shops, it's an easy cycle to the Peace Bridge start. Parking downtown is challenging; it's better to take an Uber to the rental shop.

01 From the south end of Peace Bridge, head west along the marked Bow River cycle path. This is the southernmost of the two riverside paths – the one closest to the water is for pedestrians, while the upper one is a shared trail, including for bikes. The 126m-long Peace Bridge, which has no supports in the river, was designed by Spanish architect Santiago Calatrava Valls. Its red-and-white color scheme was chosen in honor of both Canada's and

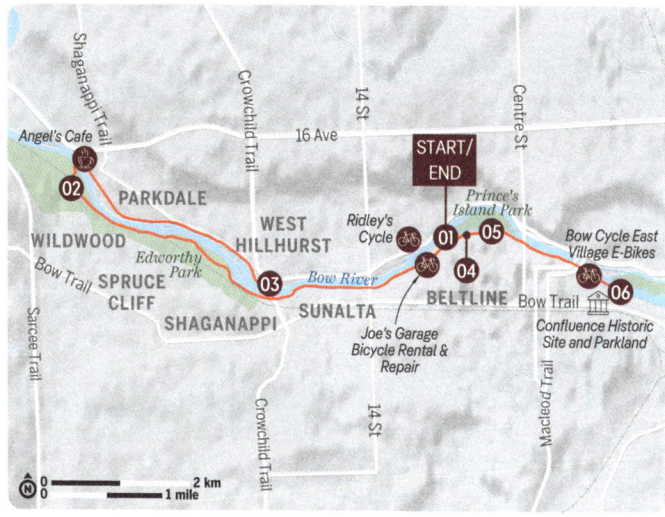

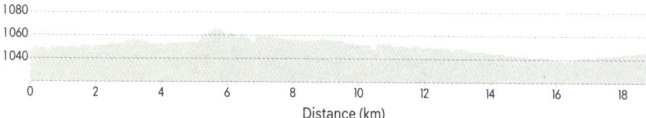

Glenmore Reservoir Ride

From Confluence Historic Site, follow the Elbow River path through Enmax Park – pausing to take in the park's Cenovus Legacy Trail, which tells Calgary's story from a First Nations perspective. The trail is tricky to follow, especially at the outset; watch for blue detour signs painted on the pavement and also check maps.calgary.ca/pathwaysandbikeways.

Continue along and near the river, taking in skyline views, and then through quiet, upmarket neighborhoods around Riverdale Ave SW and across the Sandy Beach pedestrian bridge to Glenmore Dam and Reservoir, which you can cycle around before retracing your steps (about 25km, including circling the reservoir).

Calgary's flags, while its sleek, tubular design emphasises accessibility, aesthetics and minimal environmental impact. Just after the bridge is Peace Park, commemorating fallen soldiers from various wars. Continue past the park, along the river and under the 10th St Bridge, which has dual pedestrian and vehicle sections. Throughout, the cycling is flat and easy. At about the 3.5km mark, the path enters a woodsy section of Edworthy Park near the Douglas Fir walking trail. While the walking trail is currently closed, the shady surroundings provide a respite from the sun, with scampering chipmunks and birdsong as a backdrop.

02 Continue on – Edworthy Park's popular picnic spots are ahead. At about the 6.6km marks the route turns right and takes you over the river on a pedestrian bridge. On the other side are washrooms and Angel's Cafe, making this a perfect spot for a break.

03 Once refreshed, follow the trail – with the river now to your right – for about 3.5km to the pleasant Crowchild Trail pedestrian bridge (which is tucked under the main highway bridge). There is currently construction along the Bow River's north side. Once it is completed, you will be able to stay on the north side of the river. For now, cross over the bridge back to the river's south side (which in any case tends to be quieter than the north side), retracing your steps back toward the Peace Bridge. If you choose to end the ride here, you will have done a 13.5km loop.

04 If you're still up for cycling, there is so much more to see. Continue east, past the Peace Bridge and through Eau Claire Park, where there is always something happening, especially during summer.

05 To your left is Prince's Island, which hosts July's Calgary Folk Music Festival and is worth a detour at any time of year to enjoy its walking paths and nature trail. Three bridges connect the island with the river's south bank, with the first just east of Peace Bridge and the main one 450m further east. The island is also home to the popular River Cafe, in case you'd like another break. Back on the mainland side of the river, continue along the now-wide path, going under several underpasses. To your left, watch for the domes of St Vladimir's Ukrainian Orthodox church on the far side of the river. Calgary Riverwalk signposts along this stretch regularly mark the distance.

06 At about the 16km point you will reach Confluence Historic Site and Parkland (formerly known as Fort Calgary) at the spot where the Bow and the Elbow Rivers meet. This was initially territory of the First Nations, including the Métis and the Blackfoot, and the displays are full of First Nation history. The site gained notoriety in the late 19th century as a hub of illegal whiskey trading. In 1875, Fort Calgary was built here to stem the trade and promote ties with the First Nations until it was razed in the early 20th century. Several buildings have meanwhile been reconstructed and the site now hosts an ongoing series of exhibits and events.

From Confluence, you can turn around and retrace your steps back to Peace Bridge or your bike-rental shop. Alternatively, it is just a short (750m) detour to Apprentice Cafe & Creamery. Intermediate and advanced riders who want to continue cycling can get on the Elbow River Pathway here and follow it to Glenmore Reservoir (p181) and back again. If you are cycling with kids, the best detour from Confluence is to the Calgary Zoo on nearby St George's Island, where there are racks to lock up your bike, washrooms and eateries.

☕ Take a break

The riverside ANGEL'S CAFE, directly on the bike path at the western end of the route, makes a perfect stop for a drink, a piece of cake or a sandwich, and has bike racks out front. The APPRENTICE CAFE & CREAMERY, in Calgary's Ramsay neighbourhood, is just a short detour from the main route (and just off the Elbow River pathway), but worth it for the delicious, chef-crafted foccacia breakfast sandwiches, hot drinks and house-made ice cream.

Confluence Historic Site

Museum Hopping En Route

Just west of Confluence Historical Site, turn off the riverside path by 4th St SW. About 500m up is Studio Bell, home to Canada's National Music Centre. Inside are five floors of instruments (some of which you can play), displays, recording studios, Canada's Country Music Hall of Fame and TONTO (The Original New Timbral Orchestra) – the largest synthesizer of its type in the world. Cyclists doing the Glenmore Reservoir detour (p181) can also call in at Heritage Park, a large living museum including a First Nations section and a collection of antique cars. Both places have bike racks.

25

Best for

FOOD

Rocky Mountain Legacy Trail

Legacy Trail, Canmore

DURATION	DIFFICULTY	DISTANCE	START/END
2hrs	Moderate	23km one way	Canmore/Banff

TERRAIN	Paved multi-use trail gently ascending; one short, steep hill

Cycling this classic route is a fine introduction to Canada's Rocky Mountain scenery and makes a perfect outdoor day. There are rest stops en route, eateries at both ends and full-on views of the Cascade Mountain as you approach Banff. Although carrying bear spray is recommended, this is one of the few Banff area trails that is primarily behind wildlife fencing, making it a good choice for riders of all ages and abilities. You can do the route in either direction, turn around at any point, cycle both ways or take the bike-friendly Roam Transit bus back to your starting point.

Bike Hire

Shops at both ends offer bike and e-bike rentals, including GearUp Sports and Rundle Bike Shop in Canmore and Banff Cycle+Sport, Black Diamond Bike Rentals and Snowtips-Bactrax in Banff.

Starting Point

In Canmore, park at the free Legacy Trail parking lot (where there are also washrooms) opposite the Legacy Trail bus stop. In Banff, park free at Banff train station or Cascade Ponds.

01 From any of Canmore's bike-rental shops, it is an easy cycle to the start of the trail using the bike path along the left-hand side of Bow Valley Trail road. Once at the trailhead (at the Legacy Trail bus stop, opposite the Legacy Trail free parking area), set off on your adventure. The trail throughout is in excellent condition and heavily used by cyclists, inline skaters and others. If you are planning to picnic en route, bring snacks or lunch with you as there are no shops.

BEST BIKE RIDES: CANADA

Roam Transit

Roam Transit buses *(roam transit.com)* link Banff with Canmore (Route 3, $6 one way), Lake Louise, Johnston Canyon and other local attractions. All buses are equipped with exterior racks, each taking three bikes for no charge; some buses also have interior bike space, making one-way cycling routes easy. While you can board in theory with a bike at any stop, during peak season when bike space is at a premium, it is best to board at Roam's Banff High School Transit Hub, where all routes start. At all stops, you will need to load the bike yourself. See the website for details.

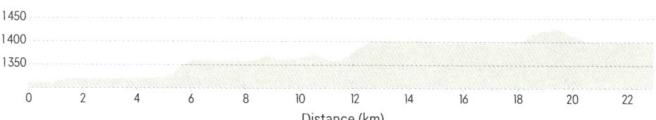

02 At the outset – with the trail closely paralleling the highway to the right and the train tracks and the Bow River to the left – the main highlight is just being outdoors and taking in the beauty of it all on a bike. Look back over your left shoulder for views of Canmore's famous Three Sisters peaks – Little Sister, Middle Sister and Big Sister (although these are actually best seen cycling back from Banff toward Canmore). Ahead to your left is Mt Rundle and, to the right, the main peak dominating the view is Mt Lady MacDonald.

03 At about the 3km mark, the road bends slightly left into a more peaceful, wooded stretch away from the highway. Just beyond this, pass a welcome sign marking the eastern entry of Banff National Park. Then – as you approach the 5km mark – you will reach a short but steep ascent (which is matched by a short but steep descent at around the 10km mark). Apart from this, the ascent toward Banff is so gradual that you might not even realize you are climbing.

04 At about 9.1km – between the ascent and descent noted in the previous step – the trail passes the woodsy Valleyview Picnic Area, which makes a nice spot for a picnic or just to pause, sit in the big red chairs and enjoy the views of the peaks across the valley. This is also the last spot with toilet facilities until the Cascade Ponds detour or Banff town.

05 After leaving Valleyview, don't forget to look up from your handlebars now and then and take in the

BEST BIKE RIDES: CANADA **185**

vistas. As you approach Banff, Cascade Mountain, with its stratified rock layers and clearly demarcated tree line, fills the view. One particularly nice part of the trail comes while approaching the 16km mark, with Cascade Creek flowing through its rocky bed immediately next to you. At 16.7km, there is a signposted path leading under the highway to Cascade Ponds. Even if you don't want to stop at the ponds for a picnic, it is worth taking this very short (500m) detour just for the views. Back on the main trail, cross over a wildlife mat immediately after the detour turnoff.

06 Approaching the 20km mark, the trail enters the outskirts of Banff town, taking you on Banff Ave – which is usually not too busy at this point – past Hotel Canoe to your left (where there is a Roam bus stop) and into the heart of Banff. To bypass some of central Banff's peak-season congestion, turn right on Marmot Cres and then take the first left onto Cougar St. Follow this 0.6km to Squirrel St, where you go left and then right onto Elk St, around the traffic circle in front of the train station onto Railway Ave and then right onto Mt Norquay Rd.

07 Cross Mt Norquay Rd to get on the bike path, which takes you 0.6km to the start of Vermilion Lakes Dr. This marks the end of this route and the start of the Vermilion Lakes to Johnston Canyon ride (p189). Within a radius of about 200m are a riverside multi-use trail, eateries, bike-rental shops and more. When entering Banff, if you would rather instead head straight to the valet bike parking, follow Banff Ave all the way in for about 2km to Wolf St. The Banff Visitor Centre and bike parking area will be across Wolf St to your left. In addition to the valet parking, there are many bike racks in town. Enjoy sampling Banff's eateries before cycling further or returning to Canmore by bike or with the Roam bus.

☕ Take a break

During summer high season (June to August), there is free bike valet parking next to Banff Visitor Centre – ideal if you want to wander around Banff town. The choices for a meal are almost limitless. BEAR STREET TAVERN serves signature pizza while WILD FLOUR has lighter bites, including vegetarian options. In Canmore, try ROCKY MOUNTAIN FLATBREAD, with pasta, pizza, soup and salad, or SUMMIT CAFE, with soup, salad and picnic lunches to go.

Vermilion Lakes

Extend Your Ride

To extend your ride from Banff: do the Vermilion Lakes to Johnston Canyon route (p189), or just cycle the first 4km of it along the sparsely traveled lakes road, with views of Mt Rundle en route. From Canmore, advanced riders can follow the mostly wide doubletrack of Goat Creek Trail (no e-bikes) from near Canmore Nordic Centre toward Fairmont Banff Springs hotel and then return via the Legacy Trail (45km total). Note that if you park your vehicle in Banff town, you'll need to buy a parks permit. This isn't required if entering Banff on your bike.

Also Try...

RAMON CLIFF/SHUTTERSTOCK

Banff to Sundance Canyon

DURATION	DIFFICULTY	DISTANCE
1hr	Easy	12km

For an enjoyable half-day-plus excursion with kids, rent bikes in Banff town – many outfitters have kids bikes, including Black Diamond, which is close to the riverside multi-use trail where the out-and-back ride starts. Follow this to the first (Nancy Pauw) bridge, cross over, then cycle east along the river toward the second (Bow River) bridge, where you can pick up the flat and easy bike path that leads past horse stables and the Banff Recreational Grounds to Cave and Basin National Historic Site. After visiting and taking in the historical displays and interactive exhibits, continue for 3km along the Bow River to Sundance Canyon, where you can lock the bikes, picnic and hike before following the same route back to town.

Lake Louise by Bike

DURATION	DIFFICULTY	DISTANCE
1½hrs	Moderate	10.2km

To beat traffic for Lake Louise, hire a mountain bike (e-bikes are not allowed on trails) from Wilson Mountain Sports and hop on the signposted path at the edge of Samson Mall parking lot. Follow the path around the traffic circle and across the Bow River bridge, and then look for a rough, shadeless gravel track going steeply up the hillside via two switchbacks, with the highway below you to your left. After about 400m of this, the trail (pictured above) levels out, taking you through shady forest to the Lake Louise parking area. About 1.5km from the start is a fork with wooden bridges; bear left. (The right fork, via Louise Creek, is for hikers only.) Return via the same route.

CHAIWAT SORNTIRUX/SHUTTERSTOCK

Kananaskis Ribbon Creek Trail Loop

DURATION	DIFFICULTY	DISTANCE
1½hrs	Moderate	8.6km

Experience wild Kananaskis (pictured above) minutes from Kananaskis Village. Buy a day pass *($15, alberta.ca)*, rent a mountain bike at Kananaskis Outfitters and follow signs to Terrace North and to Link. Don't miss the viewpoint at 1.8km. At 2.8km, stay right (straight). At 3.5km, cross the bridge and turn right; the creek will now be to your right. At 4.4km, go right at the fork, then negotiate a series of wooden bridges back and forth over the creek. Walk these – many have rough joinders and one ends abruptly in stairs. At Ribbon Creek Day Use Area (6km) there are washrooms and a final bridge that takes you back via Terrace to Kananaskis Village. Kananaskis is bear country: cycle in groups, check *albertaparks.ca* advisories and follow local advice.

Vermilion Lakes to Johnston Canyon

DURATION	DIFFICULTY	DISTANCE
2hrs	Hard	24km

This beautiful route is best done in May, June or September, when vehicle traffic on the Bow Valley Parkway (1A) is restricted. Follow Vermilion Lakes Dr past the lakes to a traffic-free bike trail. This will take you alongside the Trans-Canada Highway and through two wildlife gates. After passing through the stiles at the end of the bike path, go under the two highway overpasses, watching for vehicles entering from the right-side access ramp, and then through the parkway welcome arch. From here, the road winds gently upward for 17km through pine forests and past fine mountain backdrops to Johnston Canyon, where there are bike racks, washrooms and canyon hikes. Cycle back or take the Roam bus.

BEST BIKE RIDES: CANADA

Kelowna (p193)

British Columbia

26 **Myra Canyon**
This section of the historic Kettle Valley Rail Trail features restored trestles, tunnels and dramatic canyon views along an accessible pathway. **p194**

27 **Penticton to Little Tunnel**
Vineyard views and Okanagan Lake provide the backdrop for this scenic stretch through the Naramata Bench wineries, offering easy access to tasting rooms along the way. **p198**

28 **NorthStar Rails to Trails**
Panoramic lookouts and crossing an authentic railroad trestle are among the highlights of this fun ride linking Cranbrook and Kimberley. **p202**

29 **Vancouver Seawall**
Vancouver's most iconic path traces the coastline showcasing ocean, mountain and city views, and connecting attractions like Stanley Park, English Bay and Granville Island. **p206**

Explore
British Columbia

From the Rocky Mountain peaks to the Pacific, British Columbia is one of Canada's most picturesque provinces. Lush rainforests, sun-soaked vineyards, glaciers, lakes and wildlife sightings are among the highlights of this all-season playground. Vancouver and Victoria are ideal for those craving the energy of a buzzing city with nature on its doorstep, while the Okanagan lures wine lovers to spots like Kelowna and Penticton to visit award-winning wineries. If it's adventure you're after, head to the Kootenay Rockies or take the Sea-to-Sky Highway north from Vancouver to Squamish and Whistler. Many cycling routes are mostly car-free with bike hires nearby, making it easy to explore Canada's westernmost province on two wheels.

Vancouver

Vibrant Vancouver has a world-class culinary scene, diverse culture, eclectic neighborhoods and, of course, stunning scenery thanks to its enviable perch on the Pacific with the surrounding Coast Mountains. Find nature right in the city in Stanley Park and along its famous seawall, or go a bit further to spots like Grouse Mountain and Cypress Mountain for skiing, hiking and mountain-bike adventures. Back in the city, do some high-end shopping on Robson St and explore areas like the West End, Yaletown, Gastown and Granville Island.

Victoria

With a lively waterfront and flower-filled streetscapes that look like something straight out of London, BC's capital city impresses at every turn. Duck into Fan Tan Alley, North America's narrowest commercial street at less than a meter wide, which leads to specialty boutiques and eateries in the heart of Canada's oldest Chinatown. Grab a matcha, browse the shops along Government St, and admire the elegant exterior of the iconic Fairmont Empress hotel, then stop in for its famous afternoon high tea. Victoria is one of BC's best biking cities; cycling is an easy way to get around and there's even a free bike valet beside Victoria City Hall. Those up for more of a ride will want to hop on the 55km Galloping Goose Regional Trail connecting downtown to the community of Sooke, which links up with other popular path systems along the way.

WHEN TO GO

Spring, summer and autumn are all wonderful seasons for cycling in British Columbia, with less extreme weather conditions than other provinces. Temperatures soar in July and August, so cyclists will want to time their rides for early morning or late in the day to beat the heat. Fall colors start to appear in September, and the Kootenays are transformed with golden larches in October.

Kelowna

This city in the sun-drenched Okanagan Valley is a favored vacation spot thanks to its beaches, farm-to-fork food scene, scenic trails and wineries. Hop on an e-bike through the Lime bike-share program to zip around the Okanagan Lake waterfront and explore the downtown scene. When it comes to wine touring, award-winning tasting rooms are a short drive away. Notable stops include French chateau-inspired Mission Hill Family Estate, and Summerhill Pyramid Winery, which ages its barrels in a four story–tall pyramid.

Invermere on the Lake

The community of Invermere in the Kootenay Rockies is primed for adventure. Winter means hitting the slopes up at Panorama Mountain Village and skating on Lake Windermere Whiteway, the world's longest skating trail with more than 30km of groomed ice. Warmer months bring activities like hiking, biking and teeing off at Greywolf Golf Course, which has spectacular mountain views from every hole. The lake is a hub of activity with speedboating and paddleboarders, and those looking to unwind can soak in natural thermal waters at nearby Radium Hot Springs and Fairmont Hot Springs.

TRANSPORT

Popular cycling trails in cities like Vancouver and Victoria can be reached by public transport including buses, trains and ferries. A vehicle is required to get to the trailheads for rural rides in the Kootenays and Okanagan regions, and it may be worth organizing a shuttle pickup through a local bike rental company for longer trails that aren't a loop.

WHERE TO STAY

Arriving without your own ride? Book into a hotel that offers free bike rentals for guests, like the wellness-focused Fairmont Waterfront steps from the Vancouver Seawall, and family-friendly Hotel Zed in Victoria, which is known for its playful, retro vibes (check out their vintage Airstream) and is located just blocks from the Galloping Goose Regional Trail. Cranbrook's Prestige Rocky Mountain Resort has complimentary cruisers, and allows guests to store bikes in their spacious rooms. In keeping with the area's railway heritage, the property has two glammed-out railcar designer suites fashioned from a restored 1921 first-class sleeping car so guests can spend the night in a real train.

 WHAT'S ON

Penticton Peach Festival
(peachfest.com) Peach Fest was started in 1947 to celebrate harvest season in the Okanagan, and the annual event has grown to five days of free entertainment including parades, live music and sports in a waterfront park in August.

Pacific National Exhibition
(pne.ca) The PNE is an end-of-summer (August and September) festival in Vancouver featuring big-name concerts, rides and cultural activities.

Interior Provincial Exhibition & Stampede
(armstrongipe.com) The five-day IPE fair in Armstrong in August celebrates farming and livestock with entertainment, rodeo events, vendors and family-friendly fun.

Resources

BC Rail Trails *(bcrailtrails.com)* BC's official website showcasing the province's extensive Rail Trails system is an excellent resource, rating each ride by difficulty while highlighting trail features like parking, restrooms and accessibility.

Mountain Biking BC *(mountainbikingbc.ca)* This site details mountain-bike trails and bike parks around the province, along with suggested multiday itineraries.

26

Myra Canyon

Best for

HISTORY

Trestle bridge, Kettle Valley Rail Trail

DURATION	DIFFICULTY	DISTANCE	START/END
2hr	Easy	24km	Myra Canyon Trail

TERRAIN	Packed gravel and wooden trestles

This easy out-and-back ride along one of the most iconic stretches of the Kettle Valley Rail (KVR) Trail near Kelowna features crossings over 18 wooden trestles and through two tunnels, giving riders a front-row seat to the engineering marvel. Completely restored after being badly damaged during a 2003 fire, the flat path is a family favorite thanks to its dramatic views of the surrounding canyon and lakes, and interpretive areas showcasing rock ovens and camps once used by railroad workers.

Bike Hire

Myra Canyon Bicycle Rental and Tours (myracanyonrental.com) offers guided and self-guided tours along Myra Canyon and the KVR; some have wine-tasting options and transfers from Kelowna or West Kelowna.

Starting Point

From Kelowna, follow McCulloch Rd past the golf course to the Myra Forest service road. There's a well-marked parking lot with restrooms at the start of the Myra Canyon Trail.

01 It doesn't take long before setting off from the trailhead for the first photo-worthy spot. Just before the 1km mark, admire views of the first trestle on this route, as well as the cities of Kelowna and West Kelowna spread out on the shores of Okanagan Lake below. While most of the retaining walls you'll see along the KVR were constructed from stone, this short stretch of the line was originally supported by a timber retaining wall that was destroyed in the 2003 fire. It has since been replaced by Gabion blocks faced with timber to recapture the historic value of the structure, and is best seen when crossing Trestle 18.

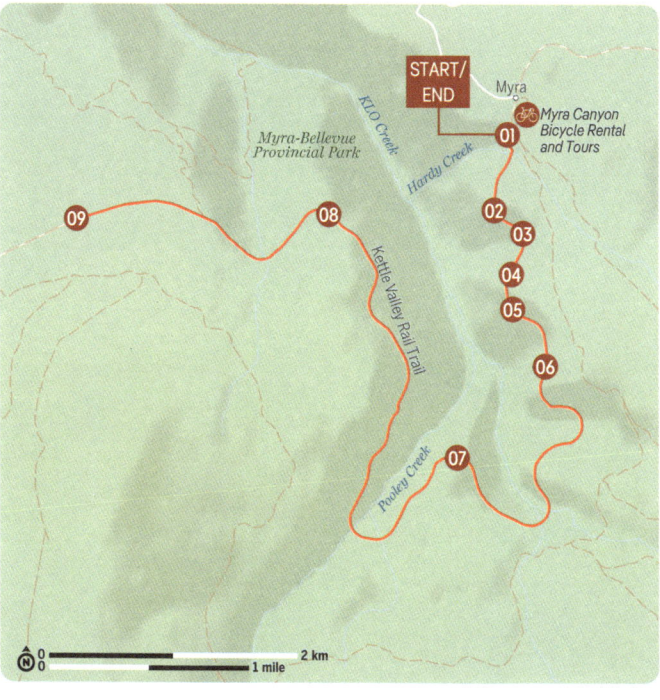

An Engineering Achievement

The Myra Canyon section of the KVR is celebrated as a national historic site of Canada, and an outstanding Canadian engineering achievement using conventional technologies in ingenious ways to construct the railway through challenging terrain where workers faced dangers posed by blasting and rock slides. This section of track was used for rail from its completion in 1914 until it was closed to train traffic in 1978, providing a vital all-Canadian link between the West Coast and the southern interior of BC. It was then developed for pedestrian use as part of the Trans Canada Trail, seriously damaged by fire in 2003 and rebuilt a few years later.

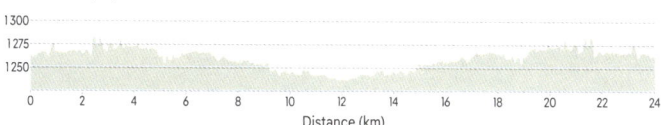

02 Continue through a narrow gorge that was originally designed to be a tunnel, but too much dynamite was used during blasting, which caused the roof to become unstable. Volcanic basalt overlies loose sediments in the bank above the open cavern, suggesting relatively recent volcanic activity.

03 The first trestle crossing is up next, and you'll see a plaque and a cross on the left. This sign is for Beverley Flores, an Indigenous woman who once lived in Kelowna. She passed away in 1999, and her wish was to have her ashes scattered here. A wooden cross was crafted in her memory by her nephews.

04 After crossing the trestle and getting back on the gravel path, look to the right to see impressive Trestle 6 across the valley and Pooley Creek flowing below. Trestle 6 was built from steel in 1931–32 to replace the original wooden structure, and this one is the longest (220m) and tallest (55m) in Myra Canyon. The peak in the distance is Little White Mountain, and with an elevation of 2170m it's the highest point in Myra-Bellevue Provincial Park. Experienced hikers tackle its out-and-back trail when weather allows during the summer months, as there are phenomenal panoramic views from the summit area, which is a huge exposed slab of rock.

05 The trail bends slightly to the left, where a series of six trestles await. Keep an eye on the dry stone walls built by Italian stonemasons without using mortar. These were sometimes used as retaining walls for the railbeds along the KVR, or to form the abutments for trestles. There are also telegraph poles on the edge of the bank on the right, once used to deliver messages from along the rail line.

06 Trestle 12 is the final one to cross in this section, and the other side marks the highest point on the KVR (1274m) and the entrance to the first tunnel. It's 114m long, and the pathway does a bit of a hairpin turn out the other side, navigating over Trestle 11, then back through a second tunnel and a quick succession of Trestles 10, 9 and 8. On the other end you'll see an old water tower which was used to help fuel the trains' steam engines, as well as the only restroom along the Myra Canyon Trail after leaving the parking lot.

07 The pathway does another sharp curve to the right toward the canyon, then loops back to the left as you ride over Trestle 7. The next tight loop to the right passes over Trestle 6, 5, 4 and 3, then straightens out as it nears Trestle 2. This section is where you'll see a rock oven that was used to bake bread for the railroad workers, and the path becomes more narrow and shaded by tall fir trees, causing the temperature to immediately drop a few degrees.

08 The final lookout point on this ride is at the 9km mark, called Valley View. Here, riders can see the Okanagan Valley, Okanagan Lake, Kalamalka Lake, Ellison Lake (nicknamed Duck Lake) and as far away as the runway for the Kelowna Airport. Trestle 1 is the final crossing, and it's an original thanks to the heroic efforts of firefighters who saved it from burning during the 2003 fire.

09 Ruth Station is the turnaround point for most riders. There's a small parking lot and a sign marking the entrance to the KVR Construction Camp, which visitors are welcome to walk through before cycling back along the same route to the Myra Canyon trailhead.

☕ Take a break

Accessing the Myra Canyon trailhead from Kelowna includes a 20-minute drive up a windy forest service road, and there are no services along the way or on the trail other than a couple of washrooms near the parking lot. Be sure to stock up on snacks and lots of water before heading up: the last chance to do this is at One Stop Convenience on KLO Rd at the McCulloch Rd turnoff.

Trestle bridge, Myra Canyon

Ruth Station

Ruth Station was named after one of the daughters of Andrew McCulloch, chief engineer on the KVR project. The KVR Construction Camp here was used from 1912 to 1914 to house maintenance workers, and is now a short interpretive trail. Visitors can see the remains of a section house where workers slept, a well fed by spring water, and rock ovens used to bake 2ft-long loaves of bread. Each man ate half a loaf per day, and worked a minimum of 10 hours a day except Sunday unless essential maintenance was required. They earned $2.75 per day, and paid $6 a week for room and board plus $1 per month for medical services.

27

Penticton to Little Tunnel

DURATION	DIFFICULTY	DISTANCE	START/END
2½hrs	Easy	32km	Penticton
TERRAIN		Packed gravel	

Elevation (m)

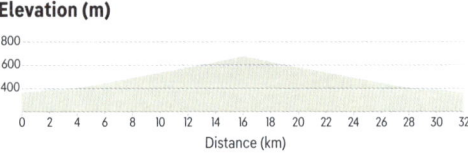

This section of the Kettle Valley Rail Trail is for wine lovers, with vineyard views and easy access to Naramata Bench tasting rooms. Starting in the lakefront city of Penticton, it doesn't take much effort to pedal along this flat, out-and-back route which leaves plenty of time to stop and sip at some of the 40-plus wineries along the way. Pedal past sun-soaked vines and over an authentic rail trestle as you head into Naramata's rolling hills. Finish with a quick spin through Little Tunnel before heading back to the city.

Bike Hire

Freedom Bike Shop *(free dombikeshop.store)* in Penticton offers bike rentals including full suspension mountain e-bikes suited for more challenging parts of the KVR. Epic Cycling *(epiccycling.ca)* also has rentals.

Starting Point

Follow Vancouver Ave in Penticton to Vancouver Place, and at the end of the street beside a driveway there's a sign on the right marking the beginning of the Kettle Valley Rail Trail.

01 Immediately after you head out of the neighborhood at the start of the trail, the dry bluffs and mountains framing Penticton come into view. It only takes a few minutes to reach the first winery along this stretch of the Naramata Bench, as Evolve Sparkling House is just steps off the path to the right overlooking Okanagan Lake Beach and rows of glistening white boats docked in the marina. Crowned as one of Canada's top sparkling producers, the family-owned winery focuses on

Best for

FOOD & DRINK

Building the KVR

Both the Adra Tunnel and Little Tunnel on the Kettle Valley Rail Trail were carved through solid rock – an amazing feat of engineering when construction for the rail bed along Chute Lake Pass was being planned in 1910. Hard-rock miners blasted out the rock cuts, and the rubble was cleared by laborers using picks and shovels. The labor force was primarily made up of immigrants from Italy, Scandinavia and central Europe, who constructed rock ovens along the trail to bake bread. Trail users can still see some of those today in Rock Ovens Regional Park, right along the pathway.

traditional-method sparkling and small-lot still wines. Their Splash + Dash tasting is ideal for cyclists, where three handpicked house favourites are sampled in 20 to 30 minutes so riders can enjoy a tasting and quickly get back on the trail. A multimillion-dollar estate awaits around the next bend, best known as the home of Alice the T-Rex. This 7m-tall, 7700kg stainless-steel dinosaur sculpture took two years to build, and was commissioned by an internet investor who grew up in the area. His intention was to have it on display in town, but when a suitable location couldn't be found, it was instead placed high on a hill on his vacation property for all to marvel at from the KVR.

02 The path continues to follow the lake past impressive homes, vineyards and the Lakeview Cemetery, then branches off to the right over a gulch. The McCulloch Trestle – named after the KVR's chief engineer – spans above it, and there are often 'love locks' fastened along the railings. This wooden railway bridge is one of the only sections where cyclists won't find themselves riding on packed gravel, and the Abandoned Rail Brewing Co just a bit further along the trail is a popular place to stop for a snack or a cold drink.

03 Approaching Poplar Grove Rd, there's a parking area on the left with a water fountain and a multi-tool for any needed bike repairs. Kids may want to tackle a few spins and jumps on the Penticton Pump Track before activating the pedestrian lights to cross Naramata Rd on the right; this is the only main road crossing on this trail. Coming into view shortly after, Hillside Winery & Bistro is considered one of the top wineries in the Naramata Bench and a good option for riders interested in an elevated dining experience during their day out. Their 'terroir-to-tasting' menu features locally grown ingredients on small plates for sharing, expertly paired with Hillside's own wines. The elevated outdoor patio has panoramic valley views, and children are welcome.

04 Continue another 6km along the KVR past the 'Welcome to Penticton' sign, a connector to the Adra Tunnel, which is a bypass for motor vehicles like ATVs and motorcycles not permitted to drive through the historic tunnel. This trailhead for the Arawana day use area also leads to some of the area's best hiking trails. The path is lined with thick forests of Ponderosa pine and Douglas fir that manage to thrive on these dry hillsides despite the semi-arid climate, and the clay silt soils underfoot are the remains of ancient Lake Penticton. The scree slopes, cliffs and rocky outcroppings along this section of the trail – also part of Penticton's Trans Canada Trail – are fragile habitats for wildlife like BC's official bird, the Steller's jay. Shortly after passing Arawana, the path takes a slight turn left toward the water and the landscape once again opens up to reveal dramatic views looking down at the shimmering lake, terraced green hillsides, wineries and communities of Naramata and Summerland.

05 Just before the 16km mark, Little Tunnel appears on the path ahead – 48m in length, it was blasted right through a mountain and is short enough that sunlight illuminates it the whole way through. This section is the only part that's paved on this stretch of the KVR. On the other side there's a restroom and picnic tables overlooking Naramata Village, making this a well-visited rest stop. Those interested in continuing a bit further north toward the Glenfir parking area will see a sign on the left denoting a heritage structure. You'll be able to catch a glimpse of a dry-stack wall that was constructed by Italian stonemasons in 1912, and has been used to support the railway grade ever since. To complete the route, turn back through the tunnel and return to Penticton the same way you came.

☕ Take a break

ABANDONED RAIL BREWING CO, a farm-based brewery, is located right along the KVR on the Naramata Bench, surrounded by vineyards and wineries about 3km from the start of the trail in Penticton. This family-friendly (and pet-friendly) spot serves pizzas, sandwiches, vegan and gluten-free salad bowls, sausage rolls, pretzels and snacks, as well as beer, wine, cider and non-alcoholic beverages like their famous Apple Slushie. There's indoor and outdoor seating on picnic benches, lawn games and a rack for storing bikes.

Vineyards, Naramata Bench

Naramata Bench Wineries

The Naramata Bench just outside Penticton is one of BC's top wine regions, with more than 40 producers within a 20-minute drive serving up award-winning varietals in tasting rooms with stunning vineyard, lake and mountain views. Grapes like Pinot Noir, Merlot, Syrah, Chardonnay and Pinot Grigio benefit from the long growing seasons and the area's distinct terroir. Many wineries are open year-round, and those looking to switch up their sips can enjoy craft beer, small-batch spirits and handcrafted ciders all located along one simple touring route. Notable stops include Hillside Winery, Evolve Cellars, La Petite Abeille and Bench 1775 Winery.

28

Best for
HISTORY

NorthStar Rails to Trails

DURATION	DIFFICULTY	DISTANCE	START/END
1½hrs	Easy	24km	Kimberley/Cranbrook

TERRAIN	Paved

Rocky Mountain Trench

Following a historical Canadian Pacific Railway route that once transported ore from mines to smelters, the NorthStar Rails to Trails links the small cities of Cranbrook and Kimberley in southeastern BC. The paved trail is within the Rocky Mountain Trench, a wide valley separating the Rocky Mountains from the Purcell range. In warmer months, wildflowers are framed by forests of Ponderosa pine and fields of native grasslands. Wildlife sightings like deer, elk and bears are frequent along the pathway, which is mostly void of any noise from nearby roadways as it gradually winds past clay cliffs (hoodoos) and over the St Mary's River.

Bike Hire

Bootleg Bike Co *(bootlegbikeco.com)* and Blackdog Cycle & Ski *(blackdogcycleandski.com)* provide rentals in downtown Kimberley. Northstar Bicycle Co *(northstarbicycle.ca)* has e-bikes, mountain bikes and fat bikes and is close to the Cranbrook trailhead.

Starting Point

In Kimberley, cross Rotary Dr at the Civic Centre, and the path starts behind the pedestrian sign. If you're doing the route out-and-back and starting in Cranbrook, head down Collinson Rd, turn right at the T-junction and go up the gravel track.

The Rocky Mountain Trench

The NorthStar Rails to Trails is within the Rocky Mountain Trench, a valley spanning from the Canada–US border to the BC–Yukon border, which is so large it's visible from space.

The trench is classified as a 'fire-maintained ecosystem,' meaning the grasslands require fire to regenerate. Fire burns periodically through the forest, opening the area and grasslands for better wildlife foraging and habitat while preventing overcrowding from too many trees. The trench is home to more than two dozen nationally endangered species, and is a critical migration corridor for wildlife like grizzly bears and bighorn sheep.

Elevation (m)

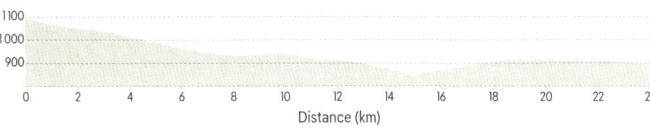

01 Departing from Kimberley, a trail map marks the start of this ride along a shaded, treed pathway on the way out of town. Riders soon pick up speed thanks to a slight decline and will barely need to pedal as they south toward the community of Marysville – named after the St Mary's River that flows through the narrow valley. Once a thriving town supported by rail and mining industries, it had a lively center including four hotels, livery stables, a newspaper called *The Tribune* and a town office. However, its economy began to slow in the early 1900s and it was subsequently ravaged by two floods and consistently threatened by fires, some caused by sparks from passing trains. Marysville was amalgamated into the city of Kimberley in 1968, and one of the main tourist attractions now is the 30m-tall Marysville Falls. Keep an eye out for deer grazing on the grassy hillsides as homes and mountain peaks come into view on the right.

02 Shortly after is one of the only road crossings on the trail, at Bootleg Gap Golf Course. A crosswalk marks the spot to cross Highway 95A, and on the other side there's a public restroom. The trail follows the curve of the road, then finally flattens out about 2km later.

03 Continuing parallel to the highway, a break in the trees reveals fantastic views on both sides of the path. On the left is the arid Wycliffe Prairie framed by buttes and the Hughes Range of the Canadian Rockies. One sign helpfully points out the different peaks including Teepee Mountain and Mt Fisher

BEST BIKE RIDES: CANADA   203

which both reach over 2800m high, while another shares details about the Rocky Mountain Trench and wildlife, flora and fauna found in the area.

04 Up next is one of the best views along the NorthStar Rails to Trails, overlooking St Mary's River. Veer off the pavement up a small slope on the right, and this lookout has sweeping views of the water, thick forests and Moyie Range. There are a couple of benches for those wanting to enjoy a quick break, and you can often see anglers trying to snag a catch in the river below.

05 Any car noise disappears as the trail branches away from the road, continuing toward the community of Wycliffe where homesteaders once sold potatoes and hay. Keep an eye out for the bald eagle perch on top of a utility pole on the right, as a narrow bridge appears ahead. This authentic rail trestle was once part of a Canadian Pacific (CP) railway route originally known as the North Star Branch, which transported ore to the smelters at Trail, BC. CP donated this rail right of way to help create the trail system. The trestle's surface was paved over and a high chain-link fence put in place on both sides as it stretches high across the river, making for some wonderful photo-ops.

06 After crossing the bridge, a gradual incline begins as riders head out of the valley and there are quick glimpses of the bone-dry hoodoos and mountains through the trees.

TOP TIP:
The Best Direction

We've presented this route as a one-way ride, and for cyclists doing it this way, Kimberley to Cranbrook is the best direction for less incline and better mountain views. But those doing the NorthStar as an out-and-back will want to start in Cranbrook for an easier return trip.

A picnic shelter is perched on a small hill on the left, providing shade and an ideal spot for a snack, with views of the Shadow Mountain Golf Course and the elevated McPhee Bridge in the distance. There's also a restroom, and bike stand for those interested in detouring for a quick hike down the steep walking trail that leads to the river.

07 A quick road crossing happens soon after at Wycliffe Park Rd, then the last stretch before reaching Cranbrook features another decline as the trail winds through semi-arid forests of tall firs and pines. Soak in the tranquility before arriving at a parking lot near Wildstone Golf Course, which marks the entrance of the Cranbrook trailhead. From here, riders can continue for another 15 minutes to get downtown.

Happy Hans Cuckoo Clock

Happy Hans Cuckoo Clock

The pride and joy of Kimberley is the Happy Hans Cuckoo Clock, which has bragging rights as the world's tallest freestanding cuckoo clock. Mr Happy Hans is 22ft high, and was built in the 1970s as a nod to the city's Bavarian theme, which was developed to attract visitors to the former mining town. Put a loonie in, and the beloved mascot pops out of the clock and starts yodelling – with a beer stein in hand, naturally. You can find him in the Platzl, a pedestrian-only street downtown lined with shops, restaurants and cafes.

29

Vancouver Seawall

DURATION	DIFFICULTY	DISTANCE	START/END
2hrs	Easy	34km	Vancouver Convention Centre
TERRAIN		Paved	

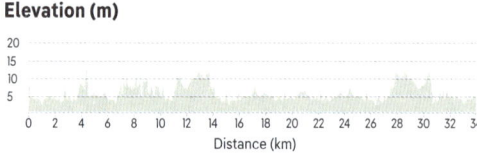

Elevation (m)

Vancouver boasts the world's longest uninterrupted urban coastal bike and walking path: the 28km Seaside Greenway, which includes the Stanley Park Seawall. Tracing the coastline just steps from the water in some spots, the car-free trail winds along beaches and through green spaces to link up with the happening districts of English Bay and Granville Island. There are lots of fun places to stop, and the flat, paved trail is ideal for all ages, making this a great day out for families. Soak up the scenery and city views during the out-and-back ride, which is the most efficient way to explore Vancouver's highlights.

Bike Hire

Cycle City *(cyclevancouver.com)* and Spokes Bicycle Rentals *(spokesbicyclerentals.com)* rent out all kinds of bikes including tandems, cruisers and accessories like kids trailers and child seats. The Mobi bike-share program has docking stations around the city.

Starting Point

Start at the Vancouver Convention Centre overlooking the waterfront along the seawall. While there are some parkades nearby, it's better to ride there or take public transit as this area is very busy with tourist traffic.

01 Hop on the saddle at the Vancouver Convention Centre downtown, which is a hub of activity thanks to the surrounding high-rise hotels, office towers, ferry and sea-plane terminals, restaurants and cruise port that hosts mega-ships. The pathway is divided by two clearly marked sections, with the inside path designated for cyclists while

Best for

COASTAL VIEWS

Stanley Park

the one closest to the water is for pedestrians. Of course this doesn't mean wide-eyed visitors are necessarily paying attention, so bike with caution as it's not uncommon for pedestrians to wander into the cycling path. Setting off along the seawall, the Cole Harbour Marina quickly comes into view where million-dollar condos overlook rows of gleaming yachts getting set to sail out to the Salish Sea.

02 At the end of this bay, the pathway curves to the right parallel to Stanley Park Dr, entering Stanley Park. Vancouver's first and largest urban park is a staggering 400-hectare natural West Coast rainforest with attractions including Canada's largest aquarium, 27km of scenic trails, Indigenous artwork, historic monuments, manicured gardens, a lagoon and beaches. Western red cedar, bigleaf maple and Douglas fir trees are among the tree varieties found here; some are more than 50m tall and centuries old with immense ecological and cultural value, and the park's 'monument trees' are protected by forest management. You'll see everyone (should be) heading in a counter-clockwise direction here, as it's a one-way path through the park.

03 As the coastline starts to loop back around the point, admire views looking back at the downtown skyline from Hallelujah Point and see the Nine O'Clock Gun, a 12-pound muzzle loader brought over from England in 1894 and used by mariners to set their chronometers and warn fishers of closings. The 1914 Brockton Point Lighthouse is up next, marked by a bright red stripe and tower, and visitors are welcome to walk under its supporting arches. At this point, the seawall heads northwest along the edge of the park, passing the nine totem poles at Brockton Point which are

BEST BIKE RIDES: CANADA   **207**

☕ Take a break

Grab a bite on the go at the Second Beach concession stand, which serves staples like hot dogs, burgers, fish and chips and sweet treats along with vegetarian options. The seasonal features list has seen the likes of fish tacos, steaming ramen soup and mini doughnuts, and many ingredients are sourced from local producers. Get your fruit fix at the Berry Mobile fruit stand, and keep an eye out for the Jim's Ice Cream vintage carts moving between the concession and Devonian Park.

BC's most visited tourist attraction. Other notable landmarks along this stretch are the *Girl in a Wetsuit* sculpture perched in the water, similar to Copenhagen's famous *Little Mermaid* statue, and the SS *Empress of Japan*, a replica of a ship's figurehead that looks like a dragon.

04 Approaching the Fox's Den children's spray park, cyclists reach a maze gate where they must dismount for a short time to walk through this pedestrian-only area, where there's also a small sandy beach on the right. After getting back on the bike and cycling for about 1km, the seawall passes under the imposing Lions Gate Bridge to reach the northern tip of Stanley Park. Spanning 1517m, the three-lane bridge, connects downtown Vancouver with the North Shore through Stanley Park, and is one of the city's most photographed landmarks and a National Historic Site of Canada. Construction was completed in 1938 and financed by Ireland's famous Guinness family. There is a separate pathway for cyclists and pedestrians who want to cross it to enjoy views of the first narrows of Burrard Inlet.

05 The pathway curves around to the left after passing the bridge and leads to Prospect Point, the highest point in the park. There's another small lighthouse looking out at the North Shore Mountains, and a steep rock face on the left. The path here is only 3km wide, so another maze gate prompts cyclists to dismount since it's shared with pedestrians. This section of trail can get very congested – especially on a sunny summer day – so take care around the bend.

06 The next kilometer feels like you're biking right along the water's edge, with a short stone ledge serving as the only barrier between the walking path and the rocky shoreline. Catch glimpses of Siwash Rock up ahead, a 32 million-year-old basaltic volcanic sea stack located just off the seawall that you'll eventually ride right beside while making a sharp left turn to continue south along the edge of Stanley Park and arrive at Third Beach. Dismount and push your bike through this busy hangout, which has a large sandy beach surrounded by towering trees, a snack stand and public restrooms. A sign on the left points out the entrance to the Teahouse, a beloved restaurant perched on Ferguson Point overlooking the ocean that's been around for nearly half a century and is a sought-after wedding venue.

Granville Island Public Market (p211)

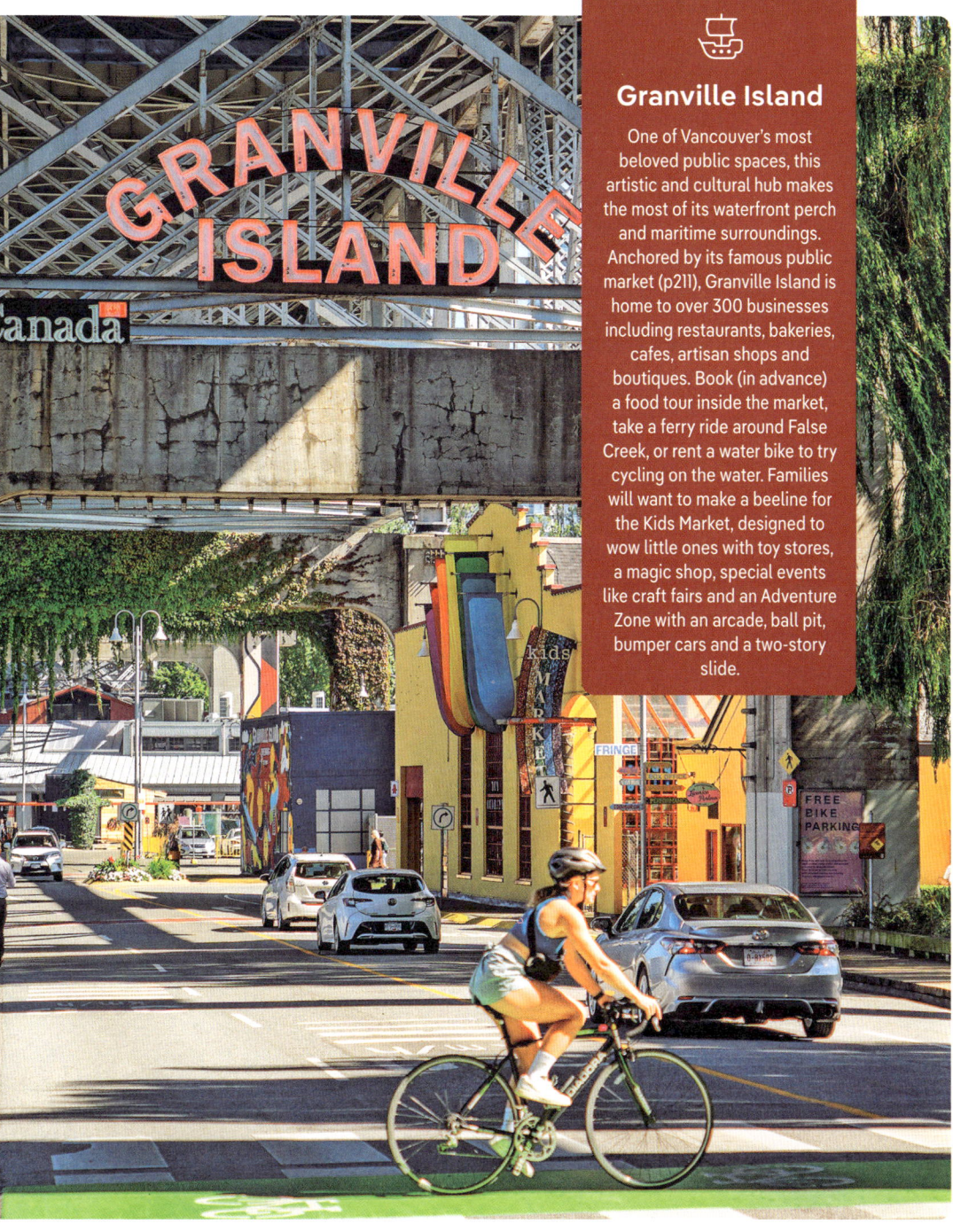

Granville Island

One of Vancouver's most beloved public spaces, this artistic and cultural hub makes the most of its waterfront perch and maritime surroundings. Anchored by its famous public market (p211), Granville Island is home to over 300 businesses including restaurants, bakeries, cafes, artisan shops and boutiques. Book (in advance) a food tour inside the market, take a ferry ride around False Creek, or rent a water bike to try cycling on the water. Families will want to make a beeline for the Kids Market, designed to wow little ones with toy stores, a magic shop, special events like craft fairs and an Adventure Zone with an arcade, ball pit, bumper cars and a two-story slide.

Gastown Steam Clock

The melodic toots of a steam whistle ring out in the Gastown district every 15 minutes, making this one of Vancouver's quirkiest landmarks. The Gastown Steam Clock has stood at the corner of Cambie and Water Sts since 1977, and was built to cover a steam grate and prevent people from sleeping on it during cold weather. The chiming of its five brass steam whistlers have attracted crowds of camera-toting tourists for decades – just don't tell them that while the pipes on top are steam fueled, the clock's mechanism is actually driven by electricity.

Gastown Steam Clock

07 Feel the sea air and breathe in the salty smell of the ocean while cycling another few minutes south, where high rises start to come into view over the trees as you approach a huge public outdoor pool, then Second Beach. Even busier than Third, this one is best for families thanks to the surrounding green spaces with playgrounds, picnic sites, restrooms and a large concession area with food trucks. There's a good chance you'll see a flock of Canada geese waddling beside the path. This is where you'll need to pay attention as the seawall starts to branch off in different directions: one is toward Granville Island, while the other cuts back through the park to downtown – you'll use this one on the way back. Be sure to keep the waterfront on your right: you'll know you're on the correct path if you pass the Ceperley Playground on your left as the trail curves right back toward the water, past the Stanley Park Lawn Bowling Club and out of the park to end up on Beach Ave.

08 A row of apartment buildings on the left marks the beginning of English Bay Beach, and the cycling path continues alongside it in dedicated bike lanes separated from traffic by concrete barriers. However, be aware that there are crosswalks through the lanes for pedestrians who have the right of way. Pass bars, cafes and Sunset Beach for the next 2km, then at the intersection of Beach Ave and Hornby St a sign notes the right-hand turn to go down a block to a roundabout where riders link up with the Seaside Bike Path. While passing under the Granville Street Bridge, catch a glimpse of the giant – and controversial – $4.8M chandelier decorated with 600 faux crystals hanging underneath it.

09 While Granville Island is just across the water, it takes another 7km of riding to get there since the trail circles around False Creek first. Fortunately, the pathway here is far less busy than the Stanley Park section. Pass a handful of marinas and BC Place stadium, then loop around at the futuristic-looking Science World and continue back toward Granville Island on the other side of the water. The final stretch through the False Creek community is a treat, where gigantic gardens line the pathway and well-kept homes are just steps from the pathway, giving it a bit of a European feel. You'll once again reach the Granville Street Bridge (the other side of it this time), and a crosswalk indicates where to dismount and walk across to reach the hub of activity at Granville Island.

TOP TIP:

Hop the Ferry

Save time on the return trip by hopping on an Aquabus ferry at Granville Island. The rainbow-coloured boats are bike-friendly, and route #1 quickly shuttles guests across the water near the Burrard Bridge to cut out the False Creek section on the ride back.

10 Once you've properly explored this happening spot and are ready to head back, take the same route through False Creek and English Bay toward downtown until you reach Stanley Park. As you near Second Beach, veer right at the playground toward Lost Lagoon. Once a tidal mud flat, it turned into freshwater when the Stanley Park causeway was built, and is now a sanctuary for many bird species. Continue past the lagoon, then turn right to exit the park and head back along the last section of the seawall to return to the convention center.

 **Take a break**

The indoor GRANVILLE ISLAND PUBLIC MARKET is a hub of activity, with fresh produce, coffee stands, baked treats and handicrafts from local artisans. Head to the food court which features international cuisine, or grab some fresh meats and cheese to make your own charcuterie board to nosh on in a nearby park. Don't miss the lobster rolls found at THE LOBSTER MAN, A LA MODE's sweet and savory pies, or the legendary Honey Dip doughnuts from mom-and-pop operation LEE'S DONUTS.

Also Try...

TAMARA ELLIOTT

KVR: Chute Lake to Adra Tunnel

DURATION	DIFFICULTY	DISTANCE
1hr	Moderate	25km

This out-and-back route along the Kettle Valley Rail starts at Chute Lake, which hosts a rustic lodge, campsites and glamping. The tree-lined trail is mostly flat, though there are tricky sandy stretches along the first section where an e-bike can be helpful. Okanagan Lake comes into view around the 7km mark, and riders soon pass through Rock Ovens Regional Park and by an old water tower once used to power the steam engines. The grand finale is riding through the 483m-long Adra Tunnel, which was constructed mostly by hand in the early 1900s and is now open to cyclists and pedestrians. An audio track mimicking a train whistle sets the scene, the motion-activated lights inside are solar powered, and there's even a chandelier.

Markin-MacPhail Westside Legacy Trail

DURATION	DIFFICULTY	DISTANCE
3hrs	Moderate	40km

This paved pathway runs parallel to Windermere Lake (pictured above) in the Columbia Valley, connecting the communities of Invermere and Fairmont with a few peekaboo views of the water en route.

The Westside Trail is separated from the quiet highway by a flower-filled median, curving away at points into wooded forests. Hoodoos, the serene Greywolf Pond, creek crossings and viewpoints overlooking the lake allow for plenty of spots to stop and catch your breath after tackling the rolling hills. The out-and-back trail features some leg-burning inclines, switchbacks and steep downhills in both directions, so it's best done on an e-bike for those who aren't up for a big workout. Bring sunscreen and bear spray, as most of the pathway has little shade and is frequented by wildlife.

CHRISTOPHER BABCOCK/SHUTTERSTOCK

Alta Lake Loop

DURATION	DIFFICULTY	DISTANCE
1hr	Easy	8km

This popular loop ride past several lakeside beaches is easily accessed from Whistler Village. Follow the paved Valley Trail past the Whistler Golf Course and Blueberry Park; it then loops back around Alta Lake. A highlight is Rainbow Park, where the pathway is lined with waist-high wildflowers and picnic spots, and its sandy beach has views across the water to Whistler and Blackbomb Mountain. Most of the ride is car-free, save for a quick stretch along a quiet residential road on the west side of the lake between Rainbow Park and Alta Lake Park.

Want to keep going? The Valley Trail also connects to nearby Alpha Lake, Nita Lake, Green Lake and the Sea to Sky Trail.

Saysutshun (Newcastle Island Marine) Park

DURATION	DIFFICULTY	DISTANCE
45min	Easy	5km

Take a spin around this car-free island (pictured above) popular with overnight campers, accessed by a 10-minute ferry ride from Nanaimo on Vancouver Island. Head along the waterfront Shoreline Trail, stopping at Kanaka Bay to search for sand dollars and feel barnacles and shells crunching underfoot at low tide. Cycle back along the Mallard Lake Trail to see the algae-covered lake, which cuts through the center of the island and completes the loop. There's also an option to add on the short Kanaka Bay Trail that winds through thick forests of oak, Douglas fir and arbutus trees.

Take care along the path, which is a mix of gravel and dirt: while it's a short distance and relatively flat, there are roots, loose stones and branches to contend with.

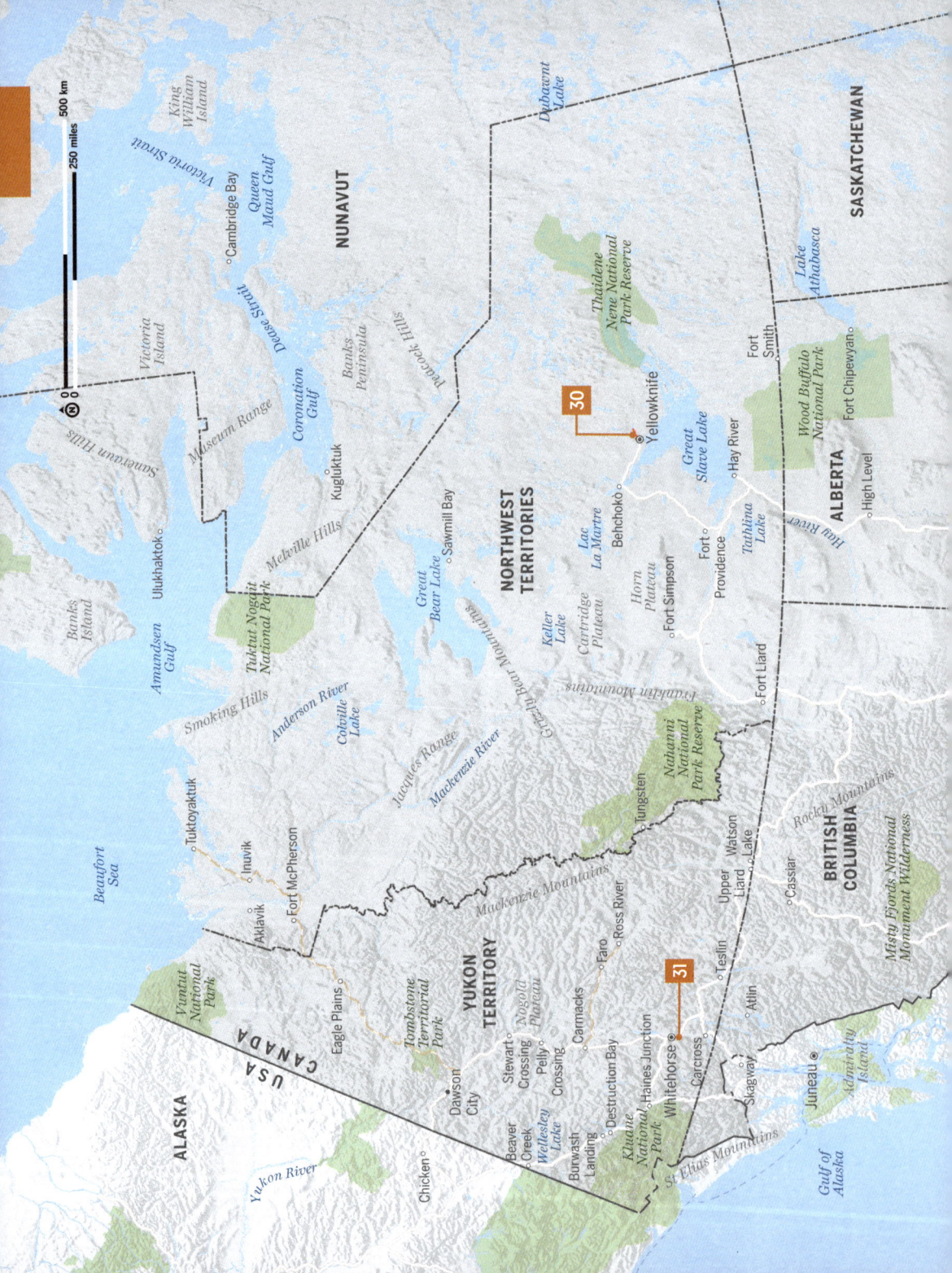

Yukon River (p222)

Yukon & the Northwest Territories

30 Yellowknife & the Ingraham Trail

Riding from Yellowknife's City Hall to the Ingraham Trail highlights how isolated the Northwest Territories' capital city can feel. It's less than 5km from downtown into the Taiga wilderness. Precambrian rock and lakes stretch in every direction from the smooth paved surface of the only scenic route in the region. **p218**

31 Whitehorse, Miles Canyon & Mt Sima

Pedaling from downtown Whitehorse to Miles Canyon, this short journey will take you from the city along a section of the Yukon River that shaped the territory's modern history. Discover how Miles Canyon and the Whitehorse Rapids struck fear into prospectors chasing the Klondike Gold Rush, spurred a sternwheeler and train hub, and grew what was once a small settlement into the territorial capital. **p222**

Explore
Yukon & the Northwest Territories

With nearly half of the 81,000 total residents living in the two capital cities, the Yukon and Northwest Territories can feel remarkably rural. Distances between small communities are vast, with roads cutting through endless boreal forest.

Stunning mountain peaks and rugged river valleys highlight the Yukon, while the Northwest Territories are a contrast between taiga and tundra.

Locals endure long winters and embrace fleeting summers with endless daylight. Tourism is booming and visitors share a resilience with their northern hosts. Few people end up in Canada's Yukon or Northwest Territories by chance.

Yellowknife, Northwest Territories

As the capital, Yellowknife is the largest city and service hub for the entire Northwest Territories. It's surrounded by boreal forest and Great Slave Lake, on the traditional lands of the Yellowknives Dene First Nation.

The city has grown into a vibrant community with a floating houseboat neighborhood, a historic Old Town and a cultural diversity that make it a gateway to the North. Bullock's Bistro is famous for its fish and chips made from local catch, while the Woodyard Brewhouse and Eatery is a local staple.

From mid-August to April, the city offers what could be the most reliable and accessible northern lights viewing. In May, June and July, daylight stretches into the night to draw people outside to hike, explore traditional canoe routes, and fish, often within walking distance of downtown.

Whitehorse, Yukon

Whitehorse became the transportation hub of the Klondike Gold Rush because it sat just downstream of a river-travel bottleneck caused by Miles Canyon and the Whitehorse Rapids. As the territorial capital and largest city, it is home to nearly 70 percent of Yukon's population. The city is located within the traditional territories of the Kwanlin Dün First Nation and the Ta'an Kwäch'än Council.

Surrounded by mountains, Whitehorse has earned its

WHEN TO GO

Most visitors travel to the Yukon or Northwest Territories during the short but intense summer. While the hub cities sit too far south to experience the midnight sun, it's never truly dark. For a chance to see the northern lights, plan to visit between mid-August and April, when the skies are dark.

reputation as the 'Wilderness City.' More than 850km of trails, including a section of the Trans Canada Trail, weave through the surrounding mountains. The Yukon River Quest canoe race and the Yukon Quest dogsled race are annual events that connect today's adventurers with the past.

Baked Cafe and Bakery and Dirty Northern sit on opposite sides of Main St; the scattered collection of food trucks across the city is also worth exploring.

Haines Junction

Haines Junction is a tourist hub at the entrance to Kluane National Park and Reserve, and roads connecting the Yukon and Alaska. The community lies within the traditional territories of the Champagne and Aishihik First Nations.

Although they're just out of sight, Canada's highest peak, Mt Logan, and the world's largest nonpolar ice field are nearby. The Da Kų Cultural Centre blends park information with exhibits about the local First Nation culture.

Village Bakery and Deli is famous for its baked goods, hearty meals, and trail-ready lunches, but it's the Mile 1016 Pub where you'll find the hardy character expected of an outpost at the crossroads of the Alaska Hwy and the Haines Hwy.

TRANSPORT

Vast distances and small populations make it easier to explore the territories on a road trip rather than by public transportation. Most flights arrive in Whitehorse or Yellowknife, where rental cars are available. Don't forget to refuel and pack food before leaving a community, as it can be several hours and hundreds of kilometers before the next services appear.

 WHAT'S ON

Old Town Ramble and Ride
An annual bike parade in Yellowknife in August kicks off a weekend of music and markets.

Yukon River Quest
(yukonriverquest.com) In June, international teams chase the midnight sun during this annual marathon-paddling race down the Yukon River from Whitehorse to Dawson City.

Kluane Mountain Bluegrass Festival
(yukonbluegrass.com) With more than 20 years of history, the only bluegrass festival in the territories continues to draw huge crowds to an otherwise quiet community in June.

 WHERE TO STAY

The Fred Henne Territorial Park campground is just 2km from downtown Yellowknife, and it highlights the city's remoteness. There isn't a road north from the campground until you reach the Arctic Ocean. Similarly, the city-owned Robert Service Campground in Whitehorse offers direct access to nature and downtown. During both the short summer season and peak northern lights months, accommodations can fill. Whether you choose a tent, an Airbnb or a hotel, space is often limited.

Resources

Up Here (uphere.ca) This magazine and blog inspires with outdoor, culture and lifestyle stories from across the territories.

Contagious Mountain Bike Club (cmbcyukon.ca) This mountain bike-focused resource details Whitehorse's seemingly endless singletrack trail networks.

What's Up Yukon (whatsupyukon.com) Event listings covering every corner of the Yukon.

30

Yellowknife & the Ingraham Trail

City Hall, Yellowknife

DURATION	DIFFICULTY	DISTANCE	START/END
6hrs	Hard	68km	Yellowknife City Hall

TERRAIN	Rolling hills, roads shared with vehicles

Choose your own adventure along this out-and-back ride, which can be as short or as ambitious as you like. Many cyclists aim for Prelude Lake Territorial Park, but anyone with extra energy will discover plenty further along. It doesn't take long to leave the city behind. The road quickly carries you out onto the rugged Canadian Shield landscape, highlighted by rough Precambrian rock, vast boreal forest and more lakes than you could possibly count. Dotted with territorial parks and lakeside cabins, the Ingraham Trail leads straight to the locals' favorite summer destinations.

Bike Hire

If visiting on a northern road trip, the paved route is suitable for nearly any bicycle you've brought. Overlander Sports *(over landersports.com)* rents hybrid e-bikes, making this longer journey easier.

Starting Point

Yellowknife's City Hall sits on Frame Lake and it's an easy launch point. Just steps away from downtown hotels, it's also only a few blocks from Overland Sports.

01

From City Hall, ride into Sombe K'e Civic Plaza, where the United in Celebration sculpture marks the beginning of your journey. Turn right to join the McMahon Frame Lake Trail. After a short distance, you'll pass the Ceremonial Circle, where the route turns left toward the Prince of Wales Northern Heritage Centre. Take a moment here, as the flags of all 33 NWT communities line the path. Save your energy and explore the heritage center when you return. Stay on the path and follow signs toward the Northwest Territories Legislature. Like Nunavut (and unlike the rest of Canada), the

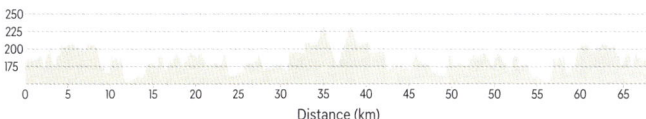

Yellowknives Dene First Nation

The Yellowknives Dene First Nations are descendants of the Tetsǫ́t'ıné, which translates to the 'copper people.' When fur traders arrived in the late 1700s, they met the Indigenous Peoples using yellow-colored copper tools. The association gave rise to the name Yellowknife.

Traditional Yellowknives Dene villages were all built at prime fishing places, where remains of cabin, graves and other historical artifacts remain. Today, most community members live on Great Slave Lake (Tindeè) in Yellowknife, Ndilǫ, and Dettah (Tʼèʔehdaà).

Every year, on June 21, the community gathers on the Yellowknife River (Wıı́lıı́deh) to celebrate National Indigenous Persons Day.

Northwest Territories has a unique consensus government. All 19 members of the legislature assembly are elected as independents, which forms a parliament led by a permanent minority.

02 From the legislature, the trail turns away from Frame Lake to meet 48th St. Cross carefully, then turn left. Although there is a bike path paralleling the road, stick to the wide, paved shoulder. The path soon diverts away toward Niven Lake. Continue along this road to the first intersection, where you turn left onto Hwy 3.

03 Hwy 3 begins with a short climb that offers a final view across Jackfish Lake toward downtown Yellowknife and the start of the route. Soon after, a right-hand turn marks the beginning of the Ingraham Trail. Although the rest of the ride shares the road with cars, traffic is light. The Ingraham Trail only leads to summer cabins and territorial parks before ending at Tibbott Lake.

04 Kilometer markers make navigation simple, but remember it's an out-and-back ride, so every kilometer out means another one back. At the 5km point, you'll pass Giant Mine. Discovered in 1935, the Giant Yellowknife Mine kicked off a post-WWII gold boom. The mine operated until 2004, but remediation efforts continue today.

05 Next, you'll cross the Yellowknife River, known as the Wıı́lıı́deh, which translates to the River of inconnu, among the Yellowknives Dene First Nation. Inconnu are a large whitefish that spawn in the river and live in Great Slave Lake. This river also marked the beginning of seasonal trails leading north to traditional caribou hunting grounds on the tundra to the north.

06 Near the 10km marker, the route passes an important intersection. The Ingraham Trail continues straight; however, the optional right-hand turn leads 11km to Dettah, a Yellowknives Dene First Nations community. During the summer, the community is 25km from Yellowknife, but in the winter the commute is shortened to just 5km when the Dettah Ice Road crosses Yellowknife Bay on Great Slave Lake.

07 Lakes and day-use areas appear every few kilometers, perfect for a rest stop or to stretch your legs off the bike. The 2.4km Cinnamon Island Viewpoint Trail begins at 10km, while Prosperous Lake Territorial Park is an excellent picnic stop at 16km. This is also a popular launch point for canoe trips and fishing, so conversations with other park users offer a glimpse into other unique adventure opportunities.

08 At 24km, Madeline Lake Territorial Park offers a window into the local cottage life. Several weekend cabins and the Aurora Lodge dot the northwest shore. More cabins appear on almost every lake, although most are accessible only by boat.

09 The largest developed park along the route, Prelude Lake Territorial Park, is a natural turning point. Turn left into the park and follow signs toward the day-use area and boat launch. Enjoy a refreshing 'North of 60' swim at the sandy beach area, have a lakeside picnic, and hike the short Panoramic Trail.

10 Prelude Lake Territorial Park marks the official turnaround point of the 68km out-and-back ride, but strong legs or an overnight plan invite you further along. The spectacular 17m-tall Cameron Falls are worth the one-hour hike, while Reid Lake Territorial Park offers lakeside camping near the end of the paved route.

Whenever you decide to turn back, the return is straightforward: retrace your path and use the kilometer markers to count down to Yellowknife. If you have the energy, spend an hour or two exploring the Prince of Wales Northern Heritage Centre before rolling back into downtown.

☕ Take a break

There are no services along the Ingraham Trail, so stock up before you leave Yellowknife. Locally owned favorites like Barren Ground Coffee, From Scratch Bakeshop, and Birchwood all make sandwiches and snacks perfect for this longer ride.

After your return, toast your Ingraham Trail adventure over fish and chips at Bullock's Bistro or a pint at NWT Brewing's Woodyard Brewhouse and Eatery. Both are staples for local guides, and a good place to overhear more local adventure tales.

Cameron Falls

Great Slave Lake

Great Slave Lake is the 10th-largest lake in the world. For centuries, the lake sustained Indigenous communities with fish and travel routes. In the 1930s, gold discoveries on the north side of the lake sparked the rush that founded Yellowknife here. Today, the lake is also home to an unusual neighborhood; a cluster of floating houseboats that embodies the independence of northern life. Great Slave Lake's name comes from the fact that the Cree First Nations People called the Dene First Nations People 'the Slavey' (or 'Awokanek' in Cree) and enslaved them. As many regional place names return to Indigenous names, pressure is mounting to rename it.

31

Whitehorse, Miles Canyon & Mt Sima

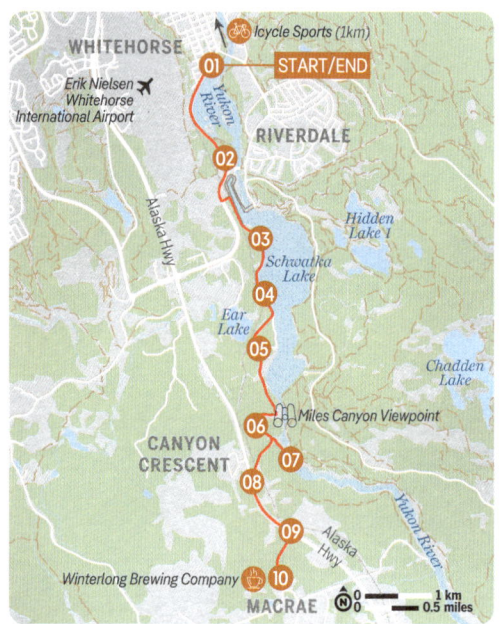

DURATION	DIFFICULTY	DISTANCE	START/END
3hrs	Moderate	20km	SS Klondike National Historic Site

TERRAIN	Rolling hills, roads shared with cars

Elevation (m)

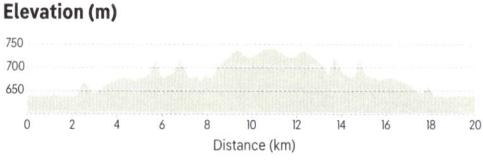

This out-and-back route leaves downtown Whitehorse, blending Klondike Gold Rush history with stunning landscapes along Schwatka Lake and the Yukon River. The basalt walls and roaring Yukon River in Mile Canyon shaped Whitehorse's past. The canyon caused a river-travel bottleneck that slowed gold prospectors on their journey north, creating a growing settlement and transportation hub that grew into the capital city. Be mindful of traffic along the ride, which uses a combination of bike lanes and quiet scenic roads. Because there are no services between Whitehorse and Mt Sima, consider bringing a picnic lunch to enjoy along the Yukon River.

Bike Hire
The paved route suits any bicycle. Bring your own or rent from nearby Icycle Sports *(icyclesports.com)*, which offers both gravel and city e-bikes perfect for the three-hour ride.

Starting Point
Begin at the SS Klondike National Historic Site, on the bank of the Yukon River. It's easy to reach from anywhere in Whitehorse, by bike, bus or car.

01 If you're exploring this route on a weekday, visit the SS Klondike National Historic Site before setting out. Once you're ready to ride, exit the parking lot and take the third exit from the roundabout onto the Robert Service Way bike lane. The road follows the

SS Klondike II

Before there were any roads in the territory, rivers were the only transportation. Sternwheelers hauled cargo along the Yukon River between Dawson City and Whitehorse from the 1860s until the early 1950s.

The original SS *Klondike* (1929–36) was the largest sternwheeler on the river, hauling nearly 50 percent more than its competitors. After it ran aground, the company salvaged what it could to build its identical replacement, the SS *Klondike II*.

Years after going out of service, the *SS Klondike II* was donated to Parks Canada and restored. It became a National Historic Site of Canada in 1967.

Yukon River toward the Whitehorse Dam.

02 After passing the Robert Service Campground, large Yukon Energy facilities will come into view. Immediately after passing these industrial buildings, follow traffic markings to turn left onto Miles Canyon Rd. Almost as soon as you make the left-hand turn, you'll come to a stop sign, where you turn right following signs for Lake Schwatka and Scenic Route.

03 The next 2km follows Schwatka Lake's calm shoreline, though it wasn't always so tranquil. The Whitehorse Dam tamed the once-feared Whitehorse Rapids that were a major navigational obstacle for prospectors rushing north for the Klondike Gold Rush. In that era, Whitehorse was just a small settlement downstream of the rapids, but when the White Pass and Yukon Railway arrived in 1901, it grew into the transportation hub that would eventually become the territorial capital.

04 Today, Schwatka Lake is popular for swimming and paddling, but it still serves as a busy hub for floatplanes. Not long after joining the lakeshore, you'll find floatplanes docked along the roadside. Both Alkan Air and Alpine Aviation have bases on the lake, along with several privately owned floatplane docks.

05 A series of climbs begins immediately after passing through the yellow gate that marks the entrance to the seasonal section of Miles Canyon Rd. Your effort will soon be rewarded with a panoramic view over Miles Canyon. Carefully cross to the viewpoint and take a moment to take it in: basalt walls cutting through vast spruce forest that stretches south toward Carcross between Golden Horn Mountain and Grey Mountain.

06 Watch for traffic as you exit the viewpoint parking area, and follow the road downhill. Signs for Miles Canyon will indicate a left turn, where the road continues descending toward the river's edge. Lock your bike at the parking lot and follow the short trail to the Robert Lowe Suspension Bridge. The fast-moving glacier-fed turquoise water contrasts spectacularly with the red-orange basalt cliffs. It's an impressive sight, yet it's harder to imagine what it looked like to the first prospectors. In their era, only boats given permission by the police could run the dangerous waters. Most opted to use a wooden tramway to portage around. When the Whitehorse Dam, which you passed earlier in the ride, was built, it raised water levels by 10 meters and slowed the river's passage through the canyon.

07 If you have the energy, explore the trails on the opposite side of Miles Canyon. A short walk along the rim offers different perspectives of the steep cliffs, but be careful not to get too close. There are no handrails or safety nets along the edge. If you have more time, a longer hike leads to Canyon City. When you are ready, remount your bike and follow the same road you descended earlier. At the first intersection, turn left and follow signs for the Alaska Hwy.

08 Turn left onto the highway and enjoy the rare opportunity to pedal a section of the historic Alaska Hwy. Built by the US military during WWII, the Alaska Hwy extended the Canadian highway system north from Dawson Creek, British Columbia, to Delta Junction, Alaska. This created the first continuous road connection between the United States' lower 48 and Alaska.

☕ Take a break

WINTERLONG BREWING COMPANY welcomes visitors of any age into its taphouse. It's a popular spot for locals, especially members of the active community who often relive their outdoor adventure over a pint. While the food menu is limited, food trucks often offer additional dining options, although their schedules vary.

If you'd rather pack a picnic to enjoy overlooking Miles Canyon, **BAKED CAFE AND BAKERY**, in downtown Whitehorse, has you covered with a selection of fresh sandwiches, sweet or savory croissants, and pastries.

09 Although the Alaska Hwy is a major highway, it's rarely busy and a wide, paved shoulder makes for an easy journey. Alternatively, an unmarked gravel path parallels the highway. Whichever route you choose, it's only a single kilometer until a right turn leads you onto the Mt Sima road. Follow it uphill for a short distance until you arrive at the Winterlong Brewing Company taphouse.

10 From here, simply retrace your path back to the SS Klondike National Historic Site in Whitehorse. The return trip will be quicker, too, because Whitehorse is located downriver and you've climbed more than 200m on the way here.

Canyon City

Extend your day on the Whitehorse, Miles Canyon, and Mt Sima ride with the 7km hike to Canyon City. The route starts after crossing the Miles Canyon suspension bridge and the trail goes upriver. The hike takes approximately two hours.

Although Canyon City is often linked to the Klondike Gold Rush, its history dates back much further. By the time the first settlers arrived, the Kwanlin Dün First Nation had been using the Canyon City site for thousands of years as an important seasonal salmon-fishing camp above the canyon. The Nation had also created the first portage trails around Miles Canyon and Whitehorse Rapids.

Miles Canyon

Also Try...

PECOLD/SHUTTERSTOCK

Carcross Mountain Biking

DURATION	DIFFICULTY	DISTANCE
4+hrs	All levels	from 6km

Located between Nares and Bennett Lakes, Carcross (pictured above) is home to the self-governing Carcross/Tagish First Nation. Their Singletrack to Success program, led by local youth, has transformed nearby Montana Mountain into one of the north's premier mountain-bike destinations.

Rent a bike at Icycle Sports Carcross *(icyclesports.com/carcross)* and head for the singletrack. Beginners can climb Lower Demi Kwáan before descending Sam McGee's Rd and AK DNR. Intermediates will find a rewarding loop climbing Moose and descending Beaver, Porcupine and Black Bear. Advanced riders can follow the same climb, and opt to descend Grizzly Bear or Black Bear, but most will want to tackle the legendary Mountain Hero Trail. This full-day route has earned the International Mountain Bicycling Association's coveted Epic status.

Whitehorse Millenium Trail

DURATION	DIFFICULTY	DISTANCE
1hr	Easy	8km

Rent a bike from Icycle Sports and set out on the Millennium Trail, a scenic loop that begins right at their door. The route follows the Yukon River through downtown Whitehorse. Enjoy a break at the Kwanlin Dün Cultural Centre, MacBride Museum of Yukon History, or Yukon Visitor Information Centre. When you reach the SS Klondike National Historic Site, the trail divides into a 5km loop, best ridden counterclockwise. When you cross the river, make the short detour to view the Whitehorse Rapids Fishway, the world's longest wooden fish ladder. From here, follow the river downstream and keep an eye out for kayakers playing in a series of standing waves along the river between the fishway and the SS Klondike.

JIRI KULISEK/SHUTTERSTOCK

Haines Junction to Pine Lake

DURATION	DIFFICULTY	DISTANCE
2hrs	Easy	12km

Haines Junction (pictured above) is the crossroads between Whitehorse, Fairbanks, and Haines, Alaska. The Kluane Range frames the town in an incredible setting. Buy a picnic lunch at Village Bakery, rent an e-bike from Raven's Rest Inn, and cycle the Great Trail to Pine Lake. This multi-use path is part of the Trans Canada Trail, which is the world's longest recreational trail network stretching across Canada. This ride is an easy out-and-back to the Pine Lake Day Use Area, where you can enjoy views of the Kluane Range and a northern swim. Don't be shy as you ride, because grizzly bears are common and Parks Canada recommends cycling in a group and making noise to avoid a surprise encounter.

Yellowknife to Dettah Ice Road

DURATION	DIFFICULTY	DISTANCE
4hrs	Moderate	12km

In winter, when northern lights displays are at their peak, there's a unique chance to ride a fat bike across the frozen surface of Great Slave Lake. Like other seasonal ice roads that connect remote communities, the Yellowknife–Dettah Ice Road opens from December to April. Rent a fat bike from Overlander Sports and ride down Franklin Ave to School Draw Ave. Turn right, follow the lakeshore, and look for the entrance to the winter ice road. From there, it's a 5km ride across the frozen lake to Dettah (p220), a Yellowknives Dene First Nation community with a cultural center for visitors to learn about the Nation. This is an out-and-back route, so turn around before the cold sets in.

Arriving

Canada is colossal, and there are thousands of ways to enter the country by land, air or sea. Despite recent tensions with the US, travelers arriving with proper documentation and appropriate belongings should pass through immigration with ease.

Traveling with a Bike

By far the easiest way to transport bikes into Canada is by motor vehicle. US–Canadian border crossings are generally low-stress, and you can freely transport your bicycle on a rack or in a car trunk without raising an eyebrow. Cross-country cyclists can pedal to the border and walk their bikes through with on-foot travelers.

If you're coming from further away, you can fly your bike into one of Canada's many airports by storing it in a standard bike box; expect to pay an 'oversize' fee, depending on the airline. A padded or hard-shell case is also generally permitted. At your destination, these boxes are usually placed on the side of the luggage carousel. If you have any trouble finding it, ask airport personnel to direct you to oversized luggage. A popular alternative is a folding bike; many airlines allow you to check smaller models, like Bromptons and Dahons, in regular luggage for no additional fee.

Airport to City Centre

	MONTREAL	TORONTO	VANCOUVER
TRAIN 	n/a	n/a	40 mins $10.90
BUS/SHUTTLE 	45 mins $11.25	45 mins $12.35	n/a
CAR 	25 mins	30 mins	30 mins

---

PASSPORTS & VISAS

Nearly all travelers require passports to enter Canada. Most US and EU citizens can enter without a visa, while nationals from Africa, Asia, Eastern Europe and Latin America are likely to require one.

WI-FI

Free wi-fi is available in many public spaces and large institutions across Canada, including several airports. When free service isn't available, you can expect password-protected wi-fi in almost any hotel or cafe.

MONEY

You'll find trustworthy ATMs in airports, service stations, retail centers and bricks-and-mortar banks. Cards are widely accepted across the country, and more and more merchants use digital wallet systems like Apple Pay and Google Pay.

TAXES ON GOODS

If you're staying in Canada for less than 24 hours, you can bring $200 of legal purchases back across the border tax-free. After 48 hours, this ceiling rises to $800.

Getting Around

A BIG COUNTRY

Canada is a nation of wide-open spaces, and a drive between two sizable cities could take days. There are lots of ways to get from Point A to Point B, and cyclists with time may find themselves hopping trains or flights to different parts of Canada. Bike touring is a common pursuit, and you can reach the most populated districts by road, but many travelers hunker down in a single place and explore its outskirts on two wheels.

DRIVING INFO

Drive on the right

110
Maximum freeway speed limit: 110km/h

16
Legal driving age in most provinces

Car

Driving is the most popular and flexible way to get around Canada, especially its countryside and small towns. Rental companies routinely allow cross-border travels from the US. EV stations are proliferating, with scattered options in the central provinces.

Train

Canada's intercity train system is VIA Rail *(viarail.ca)*, which runs across eight of Canada's 10 provinces. Folding bikes are allowed on board, space permitting, and VIA Rail is developing racks for bicycles, though bike-transport service is still patchy and confusing.

Bus

Canada does not have a national bus service but rather several private companies. FlixBus *(flixbus.ca)* has a global reach and services most major cities in the country's south. Most FlixBus vehicles accept bicycles, though service varies by route.

RV

RVs are extremely popular in Canada; more than 2 million households own some kind of campervan. You'll find a vast network of RV-friendly campgrounds and hookups. US travelers drive RVs across the border, and in-country rentals are easy to find.

CLOCKWISE FROM LEFT: EVGENY BAKHAREV/SHUTTERSTOCK, SOCKAGPHOTO/SHUTTERSTOCK

TRAVEL COSTS

Rental car
$85/day

VIA Rail one-way ride Montréal–Ottawa
$60

Level 2 EV charger
$1/hour

Gas
$1.70/liter

BEST BIKE RIDES: CANADA

Accommodations

STORING YOUR BIKE

Bringing your own bike can be a huge luxury, but where do you put it when you're not riding? Canadian cities are well stocked with bike racks, which are a boon during the daylight hours. Once you've finished riding, you'll want to avoid parking your bike on the street. If accommodations object to you keeping your bike in your quarters, ask about storage rooms, indoor garages or other secure options. Consider removing panniers and valuable equipment, such as headlights and affixable pumps, while your bike is unmonitored.

HOW MUCH FOR A NIGHT IN…

Tent site on private campground
$50

Hostel dorm bed
$40

Inn or auberge
$200

Hotels

For the sake of ease, new arrivals may appreciate a good old-fashioned hotel. Standard chains gather around suburban highways and near airports, making them a convenient option, especially for families. You can usually find amenities like indoor pools, fitness centers and free breakfasts, which can be welcome bookends to a long ride. Head into city centers for independent hotels.

Motels

Motels are cheap and straightforward, and you'll find them all across suburban and small-town Canada. When you're on a bike tour, motels are a handy option; sometimes all you want is a shower, AC and cable television. Motel owners often let you keep mud-spattered bikes and panniers in your room, as long as you don't make a mess.

Inns & Auberges

The most immersive lodging is the old-fashioned inn or B&B, and Canada excels in this genre. Inns often take the form of a large house with cozy rooms, and almost every sizable town has at least one. Stays can be pricey, but cyclists often get to meet owners and appreciate unique touches. The French equivalent is an auberge.

Hostels

Every major Canadian city has its hostels, and travelers can crash on dormitory bunk beds or sometimes score a private room. These are great options for youthful backpackers trying to save a buck, and you're likely to meet other sporty travelers as well. Canadian hostels are more likely to rent or loan out bicycles, but they may lack the space to store yours.

CAMPING

Camping is a favorite Canadian pastime, and the nation is home to thousands of private campgrounds. Quality varies, but there are plenty of options for tent-toting cycle-tourists, even in the remote prairies of Saskatchewan and the Yukon's boreal forests. You're wise to reserve a site ahead of time, especially in summer. Dispersed camping is permitted in Canada, depending on local laws.

Bikes

HOW MUCH FOR...

Standard bicycle hire
$50/day

City bike tour
$100

E-bike hire
$70/day

Bike Rental

Every major city in Canada has its bike-rental shops, which generally open in mid-spring. Many of these businesses double as ski shops during the winter, so diehard planners can inquire about bike rentals year-round. Prices vary widely; expect to rent bikes by the hour or day. Management may ask to scan or copy your photo ID to keep on file.

You will likely find a wide range of bicycles. Instead of a standard hybrid or mountain bike, you can often choose from gravel, performance and tandem bikes. The crème de la crème is the fat bike, which can roll over almost any surface and keeps cyclists moving all through winter, regardless of snow cover.

E-Bikes

E-bikes have exploded in popularity all over the world, and Canada has eagerly embraced the trend. For example, àVélo is a bike-share network in Québec City, and its fleet of 1800 units includes only e-bikes. A growing number of bike shops are renting out pedal-assist bikes and chargers, so recreational cycling in Canada is more accessible than ever. The motor's maximum output should be 500W or less, and the speed limit for e-bikes across Canada is 32km/h.

You can legally bring your own e-bike across the border, either by riding it or carrying it in a car. However, you are never permitted to take an e-bike battery in a passenger plane, regardless of airline or destination.

OTHER GEAR

Established shops should provide you with a helmet, and some will offer locks, repair kits and lights as well. If you're on the road and need to replace small odds and ends, such as Allen wrenches, inner tubes or tire levers, you're rarely far from a Walmart or other box store.

CLOCKWISE FROM LEFT: ANNE RICHARD/SHUTTERSTOCK, PASCAL HUOT/SHUTTERSTOCK

Health & Safe Travel

Weather

Always dress for weather. Canadian winters are legendary, and chilly temps persist in most parts of the country until June. Also keep an eye on the forecast: rain and wind can affect cyclists all year, leading to chills, colds and even hypothermia. Lightning strikes are always a possibility during electrical storms. Conversely, midsummer can get hot and bright; sunblock is your friend.

Wildfires

Wildfires have always been a danger in Canada, and climate change has gravely worsened the situation. Recent fires have led to severe travel restrictions and atmospheric disturbances across the continent. Keep up ro date on official advisories and avoid cycling during smoke-heavy days; you could be hundreds of miles from the fire and still feel its effects. Access Canada's Wildland Fire Information System at *cwfis.cfs.nrcan.gc.ca/home*.

Wildlife

Most wildlife in Canada is shy and benign. You're unlikely to encounter one of the four varieties of rattlesnake, and skunks and porcupines are mostly nocturnal. Bear and moose attacks are also rare. That said, all these species have powerful defenses, and cyclists should never provoke an animal. More common threats to riders are insect swarms and unleashed dogs.

Crime

Many visitors see Canada as a bastion of safety, defended by fearless Royal Canadian Mounted Police. But Canada does see a certain amount of crime, from widespread petty theft to occasional assault. For cyclists, this just means securing your bike with a strong lock, keeping tabs on your surroundings and staying vigilant around strangers on remote bike paths.

INSURANCE

In general, most comprehensive travel insurance will cover leisure cycling but not specialized cycling such as cycle touring or downhill mountain biking. Check the policy wording and make sure you purchase additional cover should you wish to include extensive cycling as part of your trip.

IN CASE OF EMERGENCY

If you have an issue with your bike, call your provider or head to the nearest cycle store for help. If you are injured or engaged in an accident, call the Canada-wide emergency number 911.

BIKE BREAKDOWN

Always ask for a contact number (a mobile number linked to a messaging service) from your bike-rental shop, if it's not already offered. The rental service will assist with persons and bike retrieval if the breakdown is due to a problem with the bike (and not as the result of an accident caused by you).

Responsible Travel

Climate Change & Travel

It's impossible to ignore the impact we have when traveling, and the importance of making changes where we can. Lonely Planet urges all travelers to engage with their travel carbon footprint. There are many carbon calculators online that allow travelers to estimate the carbon emissions generated by their journey; try r*esurgence.org/resources/carbon-calculator.html*. Many airlines and booking sites offer travelers the option of offsetting the impact of greenhouse gas emissions by contributing to climate-friendly initiatives around the world. We continue to offset the carbon footprint of all Lonely Planet staff travel, while recognizing this is a mitigation more than a solution.

Resources

Destination Canada
travel.destinationcanada.com
Multilingual advice and advisories.

Great Canadian Trails
greatcanadiantrails.com
A trove of self-guided cycling routes.

Cycling Canada
cyclingcanada.ca
Resource for sport cyclists.

EAT LOCAL

You'll find plenty of small and independently owned restaurants in Canada. Many businesses are owned by immigrants or First Nation entrepreneurs, and their menus often celebrate the nation's culinary diversity.

BUY LOCAL

Skip the mass-produced 'Manitoba is for Lovers' magnet. Canada is full of professional artists and crafters, as well as shops that specialize in local wares. Many enterprises advertise themselves as women-owned or LGBTIQ+-friendly.

WATER

Tap water is safe to drink across Canada. To cut down on plastic, consider bringing a reusable bottle. Bikepackers should avoid washing in freshwater ponds or streams and use only eco-friendly soaps and detergents.

Nuts & Bolts

GOOD TO KNOW

Time zones
6

Country code
+1

Emergency number
911

Population
41.3 million

Loonies & Toonies

The $1 Canadian coin is playfully known as a 'loonie' ('huard' in French), a reference to the peacefully floating loon embossed on its back. When the $2 coin was introduced in the mid-'90s, it only made sense to call it a 'toonie.' Both coins are well used across the country.

Tipping

Canada's tipping customs are nearly identical to those in the United States: It's 'optional' for waitstaff, taxi drivers and bellhops – among others – but you're expected to give 10-15% for standard service, and 20% is common for exceptional work. This practice often extends to cafes and counter-service restaurants.

ELECTRICITY 120V/60HZ

Type A
120V/60Hz

Type B
120V/60Hz

CURRENCY: DOLLAR $

Credit Cards

Most businesses accept credit and debit cards, and machines are generally outfitted with both swipers and chip scanners. The most widely accepted brands are Visa and Mastercard; American Express is hit or miss. Fraud detection technology has made it unnecessary to alert your credit card provider about travel, but take the usual precautions.

Weights & Measures

Canada uses the metric system across all provinces. US-based drivers usually have to adjust when crossing the border, as speed limits instantly switch from miles to kilometers per hour.

Opening Hours

Standard business hours are 9am to 5pm, and work weeks are a typical Monday to Friday, but these can vary considerably throughout the season, given the dramatic shifts in temperature and sunlight.

Smoking

Cyclists can breathe easy; Canada cracked down early on indoor smoking, banning most public tobacco use by 2004. Cigarettes and vaping are prohibited inside hotels, workplaces and most other enclosed environments.

HOW MUCH FOR A...

Cup of regular coffee
$2.50

Museum admission
$20

National Park day fee
$9

Bottle of water
$2.50

By Difficulty

EASY

Calgary's Bow River Pathway... 180
Drumheller Dinosaurs 176
Fredericton Two Rivers Ride 102
Gulf Shore Parkway (West)........... 114
Lachine Canal.. 64
Lakeshore Trail.................................. 150
Landscapes of Grand Pré 84
Lower Don River Loop..................... 38
Meewasin Valley................................160
Myra Canyon 194
NorthStar Rails to Trails 202
Ottawa's Waterways 26
Penticton to Little Tunnel.............198
Salt Marsh to Atlantic Trail............76
Vancouver Seawall 206
Winnipeg 146

MODERATE

Bay to Bay Trail.......................................80
Bonavista Peninsula Ride 132
Eastern Townships..............................50
Moncton's Riverfront Trail 98
Mont-Tremblant.................................... 54
Old Québec 58
Prince Albert National Park 166
Rocky Mountain Legacy Trail 184
St Peter's Bay to Lighthouse 118
Three Rivers Trail 122
Whitehorse, Miles Canyon
& Mt Sima...222

HARD

Bell Island Loop 136
Fundy Trail Parkway........................... 94
Niagara Trail... 32
Yellowknife & the
Ingraham Trail 218

BEST BIKE RIDES: CANADA   235

Index

A

Acadian Peninsula 109
Acadian Peninsula Veloroute 109
Acadians 85, 99
accommodations 17, 230, *see also individual regions*
Adra Tunnel 212
Alberta 173-89, **172**
   accommodations 175
   climate 174
   festivals & events 175
   resources 175
   transport 175
Alta Lake Loop 213
animals 12, 232, *see also individual species*
Annapolis Royal 89
Anne of Green Gables 115, 116
art galleries, *see* galleries & museums
art, public
   Fredericton 103
   Granby to Waterloo 51
   Kiweki Point 31
   Lower Don Valley 43
   Montréal 65, 66
   Québec City 60
   Saskatoon 162
   Vancouver 208
art routes 15
ATMs 228

B

Badlands 176-9
Banff 175-6, 186, 188
Banff to Sundance Canyon 188
Bay of Fundy 94-6
Bay to Bay Trail 80-3, **81**

Bike Rides 000
Map Pages 000

bears 12, 153, 169
Bell Island 136-9
Bell Island Loop 136-9, **137**
bike rental 231
birdwatching
   Cape Bonavista 133
   Salt Marsh 79
Bonavista 130, 132-5
Bonavista Peninsula Ride 132-5, **133**
books 19
   Anne of Green Gables 115, 116
British Columbia 191-213, **190**
   accommodations 193
   climate 192
   festivals & events 193
   resources 193
   transport 193
budget, *see* costs
Buffalo Pound Provincial Park 171
bus travel 229
business hours 234

C

Cabot Trail 88
Calgary 174, 180-3
Calgary's Bow River Pathway 180-3, **181**
Callander 44
camping 230
Canadian National Exhibition 17
Canadian Pacific Railway Bridge 163
Canmore 174-5, 184-5
Canyon City 225
Cape Bonavista 133, 135
Cape Breton Island 88
Cape John 89
Cape Spear 141
car travel 229
Carcross 226
Carcross Mountain Biking 226

Cavendish 116, 117
Charlottetown 112, 126-7
Château Frontenac 61
Citadelle 59
climate 16-17
   Alberta 174
   British Columbia 192
   Manitoba 144
   New Brunswick 92
   Newfoundland & Labrador 130
   Nova Scotia 74
   Ontario 24
   Prince Edward Island 112
   Québec 48
   Saskatchewan 158
   Yukon & the Northwest Territories 216
clothing 18
coastal rides 8
Cole Harbour 76-7
Collingwood 45
Confederation Trail 119, 126-7
Confluence Historic Site & Parkland 182
Corner Brook 131, 141
costs 234
   accommodations 230
   bike rental 231
   travel 229
Cranbrook 204
credit cards 234
crime 232
currency 234

D

Dakota Dunes 171
Dakota Dunes Trail 171
dangers 232
Dauphin 145
Dettah 220
Dingwell 119

dinosaurs 176-9
driving 229
Drumheller 174, 176-9
Drumheller Dinosaurs 176-9, **177**

E

Eastern Townships 50-3, **51**
e-bikes 231
electricity 234
elk 169
Elmira 126
emergencies 232
Estriade 71
events, see festivals & events
Evergreen Brick Works 39, 40, 41

F

family rides 7
Farnham 71
festivals & events 17, see also individual regions
films 18
First Nations, see Indigenous peoples
food routes 11
Forks, the 147-8
Fredericton 93, 102-7
Fredericton Two Rivers Ride 102-7, **103**
Fundy National Park 109
Fundy Trail Parkway 94-6, **95**

G

galleries & museums
   Beaverbrook Art Gallery 106, 107
   Canadian Museum for Human Rights 147
   Diefenbaker Canada Centre 162
   Fredericton Region Museum 103
   Heritage Park 183
   Maison Nivard-de-St-Dizier 69
   National Music Centre 183
   Remai Modern 164
   Royal Tyrrell Museum 177, 178
   Treitz House 99

Bike Rides 000
Map Pages 000

gardens, see parks & gardens
Gastown 210
gay travelers 42
Georgetown 124
Georgian Trail 45
Glenmore Reservoir Ride 181
Granby 49, 50-3
Grand-Pré National Historic Site 86
Granville Island 209, 211
Grebe's Nest 138
Gulf Shore Parkway (West) 114-17, **115**

H

Haines Junction 217, 227
Haines Junction to Pine Lake 227
Halifax 74
Harvest Moon Trailway 84
Harvest Moon Trailway 89
health 232
highlights 8-15
historic routes 14
hotels 230

I

ice skating 29
Île d'Orléans 70
Île d'Orléans 70
Indigenous peoples 40-3
   Bonavista 133
   Calgary 182
   St Peter's Bay 121
   Yellowknife 219
Ingraham Trail 219-20
insects 17
insurance 232
Invermere on the Lake 193

J

Johnston Canyon 189

K

Kananaskis 189
Kananaskis Ribbon Creek Trail Loop 189
Kate Pace Way 44

Kelowna 193, 194
Kentville 84
Kettle Valley Rail Trail 194-201, 212
Kimberley 202-3, 205
Kiwekì Point 30, 31
KVR: Chute Lake to Adra Tunnel 212

L

Labrador, see Newfoundland & Labrador
Lachine Canal 64-9, **65**
Lake Louise by Bike 188
lakes
   Alta Lake 213
   Clear Lake 151
   Dow's Lake 27
   Great Slave Lake 221
   Lac-Tremblant 56
   Lake Louise 188
   Lake Mercier 54
   Pine Lake 227
   Réservoir Chonière 51
   Schwatka Lake 224
   Wascana Lake 170
   Waskesiu Lake 167
Lakeshore Trail 150-3, **151**
Lakeview Trail 154
Landscapes of Grand Pré 84-7, **85**
language 19
Laurentian Mountains 70
Lawrencetown Beach 78
LGBTIQ+ travelers 42
Lindsey 45
Lower Don River Loop 38-43, **38**
Lower Don Valley 38-43
Lunenburg 74-5, 80-3

M

Macaza 70
Mahone Bay 82
Malagash Peninsula 89
Manitoba 143-55, **142**
   accommodations 145
   climate 144
   festivals & events 145
   resources 145
   transport 145

BEST BIKE RIDES: CANADA   **237**

markets
  Granville Island 211
  Moncton 100
  Montréal 69
  Winnipeg 148
Markin-MacPhail Westside Legacy Trail 212
media 18
Meewasin Valley Trail 160-5, **161**
metric system 234
Miles Canyon 224
Minnedosa 155
Mockbeggar Plantation 134
Moncton 92-3, 98-101
Moncton's Riverfront Trail 98-101, **99**
money 228
Mont Laurier 70
Montague 122-4
Montcalm 58-9
Montréal 16, 48, 64-9
Montréal International Jazz Festival 17
Mont-Tremblant 48-9, 54-7, **55**
Moose Jaw 158-9, 170
Morell 119-20
motels 230
Mount Stewart 126-7
movies 18
museums, *see* galleries & museums
music 19
Musquodoboit Railway 76-8
Myra Canyon 194-7, **195**

N

Naramata Bench 200, 201
Naramata Village 200
national parks, *see also* parks & gardens, provincial parks
  Fundy National Park 109
  Parc National de la Jacques-Cartier 71
  Prince Albert National Park 166-9
  Riding Mountain National Park 150-3
  Yamaska National Park 51
New Brunswick 91-109, **90**
  accommodations 93
  climate 92

Bike Rides 000
Map Pages 000

  festivals & events 93
  resources 93
  transport 93
New Minas 85
Newfoundland & Labrador 129-41, **128**
  accommodations 131
  climate 130
  festivals & events 131
  resources 131
  transport 131
Niagara Falls 32-7
Niagara-on-the-Lake 25, 32-3
Niagara Trail 32-7, **32**
North Rustico 114, 116
Northgate Trails 155
NorthStar Rails to Trails 202-5, **203**
Northumberland 89
Northumberland's Coastal Trail 89
Northwest Territories, *see* Yukon & the Northwest Territories
Nova Scotia 73-89, **72**
  accommodations 75
  climate 74
  festivals & events 75
  resources 75
  transport 75

O

Old Québec 58-63, **59**
Omemee Rail Trail 45
Ontario 23-45, **22**
  accommodations 25
  climate 24
  festivals & events 25
  resources 25
  transport 25
opening hours 234
Ottawa 24, 26-31
Ottawa's Waterways 26-31, **26**

P

parks & gardens, *see also* national parks, provincial parks
  Assiniboine Park 148, 149
  Bowring Park 140
  Cosmopolitan Park 161
  Edworthy Park 181
  Esplanade Park 59

  Festival Park 147-8
  Kinsmen Park 162, 165
  Madeline Lake Territorial Park 220
  Parc Caboose 52
  Parc Plage 56
  Place d'Armes 59-60
  Plains of Abraham 63
  Prelude Lake Territorial Park 220
  René Lévesque Park 66
  River Landing 165
  Rockwood Park 108
  Stanley Park 207
  Victoria Park 165
Parque National de la Jacques-Cartier 71
passports 228
Peace Bridge 180-1
Penticton 198-200
Penticton to Little Tunnel 198-201, **198**
Peterborough 45
Pictou 89
Pinawa 154
Pinawa to Seven Sisters 154
planning 18-19
podcasts 19
population 234
Prince Albert National Park 166-9, **167**
Prince Edward Island 111-27, **110**
  accommodations 113
  climate 112
  festivals & events 113
  resources 113
  transport 113
Prince's Island 182
provincial parks, *see also* national parks, parks & gardens
  Birds Hill Provincial Park 154
  Buffalo Pound Provincial Park 171
  Dungeon Provincial Park 133-4
  Midland Provincial Park 177-8
  Sugarloaf Provincial Park 108
P'tit Train du Nord 70
Pugwash 89

Q

Qu'Appelle Valley 171
Québec 47-71, **46**
  accommodations 49
  climate 48

festivals & events 49
resources 49
transport 49
Québec City 48, 58-63
Québec Summer Festival 17

R

rail trails
  Estriade 71
  Harvest Moon Trailway 89
  Kettle Valley Rail Trail 194-201, 212
  Musquodoboit Railway 76-8
  NorthStar Rails to Trails 202-5
  Peterborough to Lindsey 45
  Salt Marsh to Atlantic Trail 76-9
  T'Railway 140
Regina 158, 170
responsible travel 233
Rideau Canal 27-9
Riding Mountain National Park 150-3
road rules 229
Rockwood Park 108
Rocky Mountain 184-7
Rocky Mountain Legacy Trail 184-7, **185**
Rocky Mountain Trench 203
Rum Runners Trail 80-2
Rum Runners Trail 88
Ruth Station 197
RVs 229

S

safe travel 232
Salt Marsh to Atlantic Trail 76-9, **77**
Saskatchewan 157-71, **156**
  accommodations 159
  climate 158
  festivals & events 159
  resources 159
  transport 159
Saskatoon 158, 160-5
Saysutshun (Newcastle Island Marine) Park 213
scenic routes 6
Seven Sisters 154

Bike Rides 000
Map Pages 000

smoking 234
Squirrel Hills Trail Park 155
SS Klondike National Historic Site 222-3
St John's 130, 140
St John's to Cape Spear 141
St Martins 92
St Peter's Bay 118-21, 126
St Peter's Bay to Lighthouse 118-21, **119**
St-Jean-Sur-Richelieu 71
Sugarloaf Cycling Park 108
Summerside 113
Sundance Canyon 188

T

Tatamagouche 89
taxes 228
Three Rivers 122-5
Three Rivers Trail 122-5, **123**
tipping 234
Todmorden Mills Heritage Site 40
Toronto 24-5, 38-43
Toronto Islands 44
T'Railway from St John's to Bowring Park 140
train travel 229
travel seasons 16-17
travel to/from Canada 228
travel within Canada 229
TV 18
Twillingate 130, 140
Twillingate – Winery & Beach 140

V

Vague à Guy 69
Vancouver 192, 206-11
Vancouver Seawall 206-11, **206**
Verdun 68, 69
Vermilion Lakes to Johnston Canyon 189
Victoria 192
visas 228

W

Wakamow Valley 170
Wakamow Valley Trails 170
Wasagaming 144-5

Wascana Lake Loop 170
Waskesiu 159, 166-9
Waskesiu Lake 167
Waterloo 52
weather 16-17, 232
websites
  Alberta 175
  British Columbia 193
  Manitoba 145
  New Brunswick 93
  Newfoundland & Labrador 131
  Nova Scotia 75
  Ontario 25
  Prince Edward Island 113
  Québec 49
  responsible travel 233
  Saskatchewan 159
  Yukon & the Northwest Territories 217
Western Brook Pond 141
Whitehorse 216-17, 222-5, 226
Whitehorse, Miles Canyon & Mt Sima 222-5, **222**
Whitehorse Millenium Trail 226
wi-fi 228
wildfires 232
wildlife 12, 232, *see also individual species*
wine regions
  Naramata Bench 201
  Nova Scotia 86
Winnipeg 144, 146-9
Winnipeg 146-9, **147**
Wolfville 85-6
Wycliffe 204

Y

Yellowknife 216, 218-21, 227
Yellowknife & the Ingraham Trail 218-21, **219**
Yellowknife to Dettah Ice Road 227
Yellowknives Dene First Nation 219
Yukon & the Northwest Territories 215-27, **214**
  accommodations 217
  climate 216
  festivals & events 216
  resources 217
  transport 217

THE WRITERS

Robert Isenberg
Robert Isenberg is a writer and filmmaker based in Rhode Island. He produces the video series You Are Here. @youareheredocs

Jeff Bartlett
Jeff Bartlett is an adventure writer and photographer whose work blends cycling, travel, and landscapes into stories of connection. When he's not on assignment, he serves up community and caffeine as the owner of Cedar Stand Coffee Company on Vancouver Island.

Tamara Elliott
Tamara Elliott is a travel writer and photographer based in Calgary, AB who loves sharing unique experiences around the world, glamping spots and savvy travel tips. @globeguide

Mary Fitzpatrick
Mary is an Africa-based travel writer with Canadian roots who loves exploring by bike.

Ashlyn George
Ashlyn is a travel writer and photographer. Endlessly curious, she's explored all seven continents, chasing adventures on trails, rivers and roads. @thelostgirlsguide

Amy McPherson
Amy McPherson is a travel and cycling writer based in London, UK, writing travel features that advocate slow travel and co-authored *Best Bike Rides Italy*. When not at her laptop, she loves nothing more than to explore places less travelled on her bike.

Darcy Rhyno
Darcy is a travel writer and photographer and the author of two short-story collections, two novels for young readers and a memoir about the former Czechoslovakia. He's cycled in Japan, Europe and North America. darcyrhyno.com

BEHIND THE SCENES

This book was researched and written by Robert Isenberg, Jeff Bartlett, Tamara Elliott, Mary Fitzpatrick, Ashlyn George, Amy McPherson and Darcy Rhyno. It was produced by the following:

Production Editor Kate James

Destination Editor Alicia Johnson

Image Editor Clara Monitto

Cartographers Alison Lyall, Bohumil Ptáček

Cover Researcher Giada de Agostinis

Assisting Editors Holly Alexander, Imogen Bannister, Charlotte Orr, Maja Vatrić

Thanks Darren O'Connell

ACKNOWLEDGMENTS

Digital Model Elevation Data Contains public sector information licensed under the Open Government Licence v3.0 website http://www.nationalarchives.gov.uk/doc/open-government-licence/version/3/

Cover photograph Stanley Park, Vancouver, Anouchka/Getty Images